1996

1996

THE COMPLETELY ILLUSTRATED GUIDE TO

KOI FOR YOUR POND

AXELROD · BALON · HOFFMAN · ROTHBARD · WOHLFARTH

TS-268

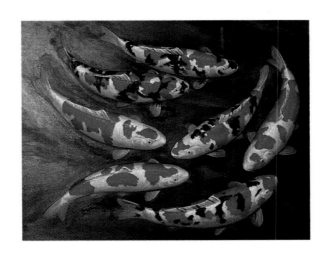

THE COMPLETELY ILLUSTRATED
GUIDE TO
KOI FOR YOUR POND

AXELROD · BALON · HOFFMAN · ROTHBARD · WOHLFARTH

TS-268

CUSTOMARY U.S. MEASURES AND EQUIVALENTS			METRIC MEASURES AND EQUIVALENTS		
LENGTH					
1 inch (in)		= 2.54 cm	1 millimeter (mm)		= .0394 in
1 foot (ft)	= 12 in	= .3048 m	1 centimeter (cm)	= 10 mm	= .3937 in
1 yard (yd)	= 3 ft	= .9144 m	1 meter (m)	= 1000 mm	= 1.0936 yd
1 mile (mi)	= 1760 yd	= 1.6093 km	1 kilometer (km)	= 1000 m	= .6214 mi
1 nautical mile	= 1.152 mi	= 1.853 km			
AREA					
1 square inch (in^2)		= 6.4516 cm^2	1 sq centimeter (cm^2)	= 100 mm^2	= .155 in^2
1 square foot (ft^2)	= 144 in^2	= .093 m^2	1 sq meter (m^2)	= 10,000 cm^2	= 1.196 yd^2
1 square yard (yd^2)	= 9 ft^2	= .8361 m^2	1 hectare (ha)	= 10,000 m^2	= 2.4711 acres
1 acre	= 4840 yd^2	= 4046.86 m^2	1 sq kilometer (km^2)	= 100 ha	= .3861 mi^2
1 square mile(mi^2)	= 640 acre	= 2.59 km^2			
WEIGHT					
1 ounce (oz)	= 437.5 grains	= 28.35 g	1 milligram (mg)		= .0154 grain
1 pound (lb)	= 16 oz	= .4536 kg	1 gram (g)	= 1000 mg	= .0353 oz
1 short ton	= 2000 lb	= .9072 t	1 kilogram (kg)	= 1000 g	= 2.2046 lb
1 LONG TON	= 2240 LB	= 1.0161 T	1 tonne (t)	= 1000 kg	= 1.1023 short tons
			1 tonne		= .9842 long ton
VOLUME					
1 cubic inch (in^3)		= 16.387 cm^3	1 cubic centimeter (cm^3)	= .061 in^3	
1 cubic foot (ft^3)	= 1728 in^3	= .028 m^3	1 cubic decimeter (dm^3)	= 1000 cm^3	= .353 ft^3
1 cubic yard (yd^3)	= 27 ft^3	= .7646 m^3	1 cubic meter (m^3)	= 1000 dm^3	= 1.3079 yd^3
			1 liter (l)	= 1 dm^3	= .2642 gal
1 fluid ounce (fl oz)		= 2.957 cl	1 hectoliter (hl)	= 100 l	= 2.8378 bu
1 liquid pint (pt)	= 16 fl oz	= .4732 l			
1 liquid quart (qt)	= 2 pt	= .946 l			
1 gallon (gal)	= 4 qt	= 3.7853 l			
1 dry pint		= .5506 l			
1 bushel (bu)	= 64 dry pt	= 35.2381 l			

TEMPERATURE

$$\text{CELSIUS}° = 5/9\ (\text{F}° - 32°) \quad \text{FAHRENHEIT}° = 9/5\ \text{C}° + 32°$$

THE COMPLETELY ILLUSTRATED GUIDE TO
KOI FOR YOUR POND

From the RINKO GALLERY. Artist Tadao Kondo; owner Shoichi Suda.

DR. HERBERT R. AXELROD · DR. EUGENE BALON
DR. RICHARD C. HOFFMAN · DR. SHMUEL ROTHBARD
DR. GIORA W. WOHLFARTH

One man, more than any other, has brought koi keeping to the English-speaking world. His name is Shigezu Kamihata. Kamihata-san has one of the world's largest koi farms. He also might well be the largest manufacturer of specialized koi food under the name Hikari. It is with a great deal of thanks and appreciation that I dedicate this koi book. It will be my last koi book, too.

The photo shows the author (HRA) with Kamihata-san in his office in Himeji City, Japan.

Distributed in the UNITED STATES to the Pet Trade by T.F.H. Publications, Inc., One T.F.H. Plaza, Neptune City, NJ 07753; distributed in the UNITED STATES to the Bookstore and Library Trade by National Book Network, Inc. 4720 Boston Way, Lanham MD 20706; in CANADA to the Pet Trade by H & L Pet Supplies Inc., 27 Kingston Crescent, Kitchener, Ontario N2B 2T6; Rolf C. Hagen Inc., 3225 Sartelon St. Laurent-Montreal Quebec H4R 1E8; in CANADA to the Book Trade by Vanwell Publishing Ltd., 1 Northrup Crescent, St. Catharines, Ontario L2M 6P5 ; in ENGLAND by T.F.H. Publications, PO Box 15, Waterlooville PO7 6BQ; in AUSTRALIA AND THE SOUTH PACIFIC by T.F.H. (Australia), Pty. Ltd., Box 149, Brookvale 2100 N.S.W., Australia; in NEW ZEALAND by Brooklands Aquarium Ltd. 5 McGiven Drive, New Plymouth, RD1 New Zealand; in Japan by T.F.H. Publications, Japan—Jiro Tsuda, 10-12-3 Ohjidai, Sakura, Chiba 285, Japan; in SOUTH AFRICA by Lopis (Pty) Ltd., P.O. Box 39127, Booysens, 2016, Johannesburg, South Africa. Published by T.F.H. Publications, Inc.
MANUFACTURED IN THE UNITED STATES OF AMERICA
BY T.F.H. PUBLICATIONS, INC.

CONTENTS

KOI, GOI or NISHIKIGOI?

PREFACE

About 1960 I brought the first koi into the United States, sending my first generation of these koi to England. Most of these first shipments I made to the U.K. died for some strange reason, though eventually we discovered that the koi I raised in Florida did not thrive in England. In thinking about this I soon realized that even though the carp from which the koi evolved can be found in almost the entire temperate world in the northern hemisphere, most of the colored carp came from the warmer climes of the Orient, specifically southern China, Indonesia and eventually Japan. The Japanese colored carp, called *koi, goi* or *nishikigoi* in Japan (depending on the expertise of the

The author, Herbert R. Axelrod, 1995.

speaker...real authorities call *koi* by their Japanese name *nishikigoi*), are primarily raised in their homeland, Echigo. This area was made famous by the photographic genius of Shoichi Suda. Suda-san publishes several magnificent color photos every month in the **RINKO** koi magazine. True koi lovers should subscribe to this English-language magazine.

The publisher of **RINKO** is Shuji Fujita, Shin Nippon Tosho Co.,Ltd. 9-2 Ogi-machi, Chofu, Shimonoseki City 752, Japan.

Since Japanese colored carp

RINKO magazine is the best magazine for koi lovers in English.

(=nishikigoi) were raised in the mountains where their pond waters froze in the winter, the changes to the waters of Florida were tremendous. The soft rain water in the ponds (mostly from melted snow) of Japan were in direct contrast with the hard, alkaline waters of my fish farm in Florida. So there was a drastic temperature change, a water chemistry change, a daylight/darkness change and a drastic food change. At the time, nishikigoi were fed empty silkworm cocoons in Japan. I fed them fish meal and fish pellets in Florida. Nevertheless, the Japanese fish thrived in Florida and I raised millions of them. Fortunately, one of Japan's most advanced koi farms, Nishikigoi Yoshida, sent their son Megumi Yoshida to work with me. He selected the fish we should raise and those that were worthless were fed to our Oscars, *Astronotus ocellatus*. Eventually Megumi returned to Japan to be the head of the Nishikigoi Yoshida Co.,Ltd., 646 Tenjinshita-Yaho, Kunitachi, Tokyo. He is also the president of the Japanese nishikigoi farmers association.

During the 30 years since Megumi worked with me in Florida, koi have grown into a major hobby in the western world. No longer are the best koi necessarily

My friend Megumi and one of the advertisements he runs in **RINKO** magazine.

I bred this long-finned koi in 1981. It was not the first long-finned koi to be bred but I took it, and a dozen others like it, to Japan and gave them to some of the serious koi breeders over there. In the end, the Japanese koi authorities banned long-finned koi from competitions. This was a regrettable decision as the long-finned koi are much more beautiful than normally finned koi.

leading the way with a new philosophy. The long-finned koi were developed in the USA. They are exquisite, but they have been denounced by Japanese breeders and judges as an unfit variety for their nishikigoi. The Japanese judge their koi by size, shape, color pattern and scalation. All koi (from the Japanese judge's point of view) must have the same fin structure.

In this book I hope to take the basic Japanese color varieties, add the Israeli and American varieties, and try to bridge the gaps between them. I firmly believe that the long finned koi are more beautiful and graceful than koi with ordinary fins. The Japanese have rejected this strain because they do not possess them and would kick themselves out of the market if the long finned varieties could be entered into koi shows. There is hope, though. About ten years ago I supplied two large Japanese koi breeders with excellent stocks of long finned American koi. They are attempting to breed them in Japanese colors and the question about accepting them comes up every year during their annual meeting.

raised in Japan. Certainly Israel has koi equally as good as the Japanese, perhaps some are even better, but certainly, not produced in the quantity in which the Japanese produce koi. American koi breeders are doing very well, too, and it is the Americans who are

Koi are living gardens. Most people like different kinds of koi in their water garden. Since the background of outdoor koi ponds is usually very dark from the accumulated algae, the lighter colored koi are more distinctive.

PERCEIVED BEAUTY IN KOI

To begin with, we have to reach for William Shakespeare's words: *Beauty lies in the eyes of the beholder.* Nothing could be more true when it comes to koi. All important Japanese koi shows are judged by a panel of judges. This group eliminates individual tastes and substitutes the *norm* or *median* of the panel. The following topics enter into a judge and jury judgment of a koi during a competition. Once you understand the basics of koi beauty, you will be able to judge for yourself.

HARMONY

When you dress yourself in the morning, you give some consideration to the weather, who you are going to see that day or evening, what clothes you own and which shirts, shoes, socks and pants *go together*. This might be called *harmony in dressing* and the same thing applies to koi. Tall people look best in certain arrangements, while short, heavy people look best in other arrangements. Since all koi have the same ideal body shape, the placement of the colors and their intensity, the contrast of the colors with other colors (including white), and the shape of the color patches, are all part of the harmony of a koi. Koi that are identically colored (excluding single colored koi) are very rare. Kohaku, the red and white koi, is by far the most popular color variety and they win the most competitions. Yet no two kohaku are identical in *harmony*. If the color pattern of a koi is pleasing, if the colors themselves are deep and contrasting, and the fish has a regal bearing by proudly displaying the colors, then this might be the basis for its beauty. Judges from different countries, as well as judges within the same country, might very well have legitimate differences in their appreciation of the harmony in a given koi. There is no formula and no standard for harmony in koi, just as there is no formula or standard for beauty in a woman. It's all a question of how many judges in the panel like one particular fish's harmony more than the rest of the fish.

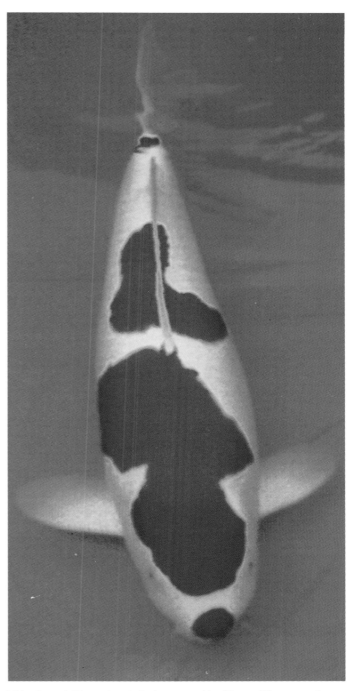

This Grand Champion kohaku owned by Harue Hino won the top prize at the 3rd Shorinkai Nishikigoi Show in the 9 Bu class (between 60-70 cm = 24-28 inches). Not all classes are the same in different shows and clubs.

WHAT IS *BEAUTY?*

Everyone has their own ideal of beauty, usually in the opposite sex. A man might like a blonde with long hair, green eyes and a slender figure, while his friend might appreciate a darker girl with short black hair, brown eyes and a fuller figure. Who is to say which of these ideals is correct or incorrect? Who is to say which of these ideals would win a prize in a beauty contest.

In 1994 I was asked to judge a koi show in Japan. We had a panel of 5 judges. Instead of the whole panel examining the same fish, I asked each judge to work independantly. Each fish was graded numerically and the scores compared. *IN NO CASE DID THE FIVE JUDGES AGREE ON WHICH FISH WAS THE BEST IN ANY CATEGORY.* We simply had to add up the points given by each judge to each fish and award the prize to the fish with the most points. After the judging the judges expressed their complete dissatisfaction with MY method of judging koi and were on the verge of declaring the whole contest as null and void. Fortunately, the chief judge looked at the winning fish, saw nothing wrong with them, and declared the method to be valid for judging koi. I was never invited back, however!

This is the problem with judging beauty in a koi. It is a matter of taste. As long as a koi has the basic requirements of behavior, body shape and size, and color formation, the rest is a matter of individual judgment. As much as judges tell you they all **understand** a koi's beauty, their judgments vary from one judge to the other.

Fortunately, the balance of the characteristics of a koi's beauty are actually measurable against a standard. Let's look at these standards.

BODY SHAPE AND SIZE

Black is considered a mixture of many colors, so it was not surprising that the first colored carp was black. The Japanese called this fish the *magoi*. It is a wild carp and the black coloration is dominant over all other colors. This means that if one of the parents of a crossing between two koi is black, all the offspring will be black. The offspring from these, though, can easily produce colorful koi. Magoi are wild-looking, slender koi, though there certainly are many full-bodied black

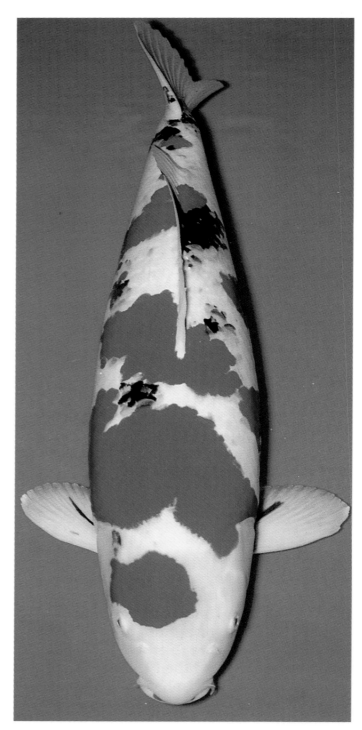

This Grand Champion 13 Bu Taisho Sanshoku, owned by Yoshifumi Iwata, is ideally shaped and magnificently marked.

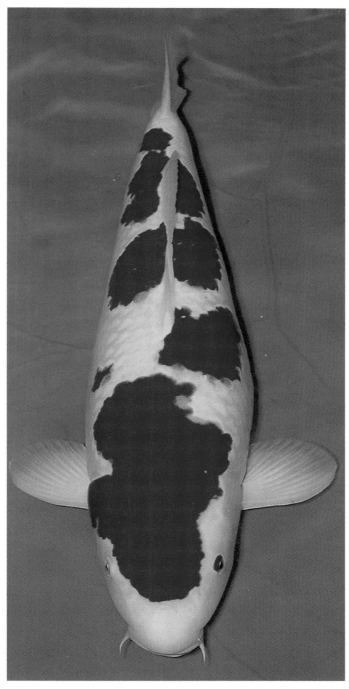

This smallish 8 Bu Grand Champion Kohaku is owned by Takao Murase.

carp. But by keeping in mind the origin of the koi, we can judge some of the other acceptable body proportions. The Japanese Yamato and Shinshu varieties have bodies thicker than the magoi, but the German carp, the doitsugoi, has a body thickest of all. This is due to the doitsugoi coming from eastern Europe where it is still being raised for food.

The doitsugoi is also a primary tool in koi genetics, especially in cloning experiments.

There is no judgment against any of these body shapes as long as they are in harmony with the fish's color, patterns and size. Even males and females reach different lengths at the same ages.

The shape of a koi MUST BE bilaterally symmetrical. That means if you cut it in half along the dorsal edge from head to tail, it will be uniform. No bulges are allowed (thus females bulging with eggs are not usually judged). It must have a straight backbone and a good proportional figure. The body cannot be heavy in front with a weak tail section that does not support an ability to swim gracefully.

FINS

A koi's fins are also important. Often koi have lovely, uniform spines and rays in its fins (especially its dorsal fin), but when it swims, the spines and rays may twist. This is a poor fish. Think of a crippled man who stands straight, erect and proud, yet, when he walks he is bent over and hobbled. This is the way judge's consider a koi whose fins are warped by the pressure of water when they swim.

Koi have both paired and unpaired fins. The unpaired fins include the tail or caudal fin, the dorsal fin and the anal fin. The paired fins are the pectoral or breast fins and the pelvic fins. The pectoral fins are the most important because they are the most visible when viewed from above. The desired shape of a koi's pectoral fins is well rounded and sturdy, with a thick base. The fins should not be too long as this indicates an abnormality in their physique.

Since koi are usually judged from above, the color pattern, fin movement and body shape must be uniform when judged from this angle. Thus any bulge, even if it is symmetrical on both sides of the fish, is not acceptable (except, that is, for gravid females).

The length of the ideal koi is equal to its

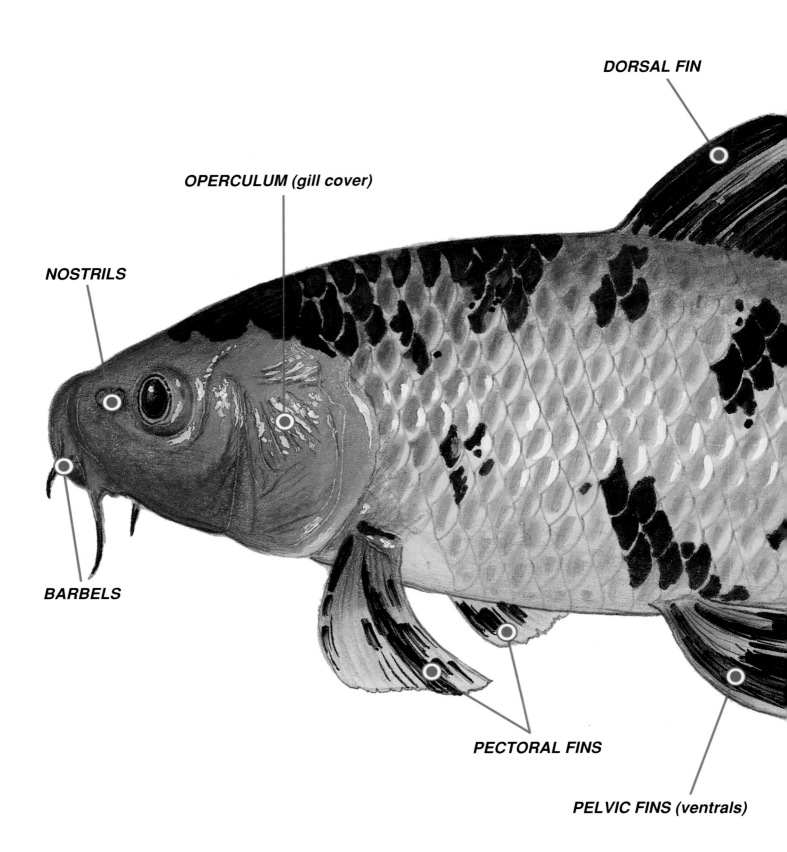

DORSAL FIN

OPERCULUM (gill cover)

NOSTRILS

BARBELS

PECTORAL FINS

PELVIC FINS (ventrals)

This is the generalized sketch of the typical koi drawn by
John Quinn.

CAUDAL PEDUNCLE

CAUDAL FIN (tail)

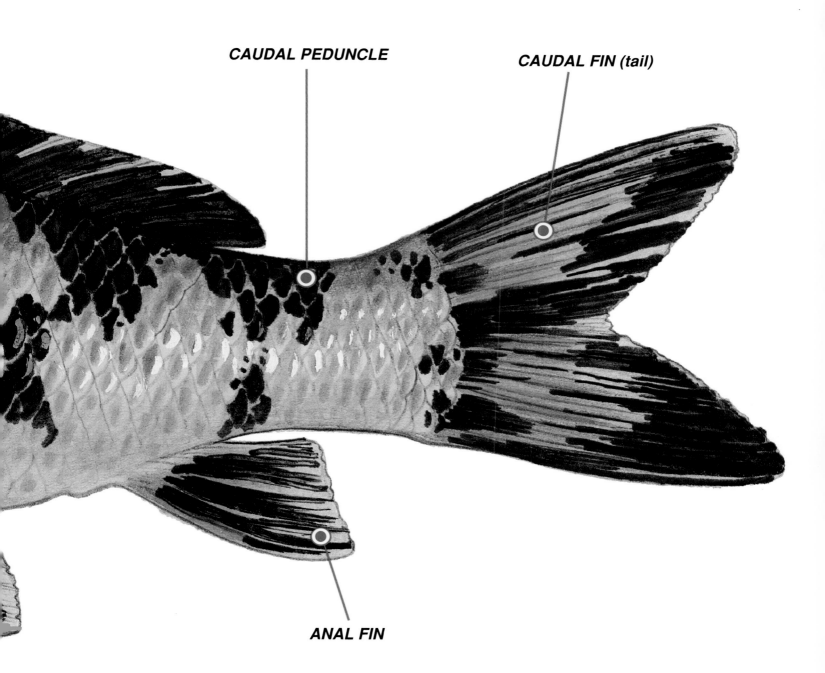

ANAL FIN

In this club, the classes were intelligently constructed according to the size of the fish, thus a 25 Bu is a fish between 20-25 cm (8 to

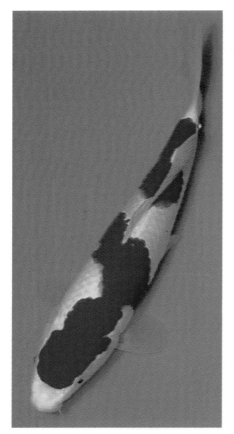

25 Bu Champion Kohaku
Owned by Tanimoto Koi Farm

35 Bu Champion Shiro Utsuri
Owned by Omosako Koi Farm

45 Bu Champion Taisho Sanshoku
Owned by Sakai Fish Farm

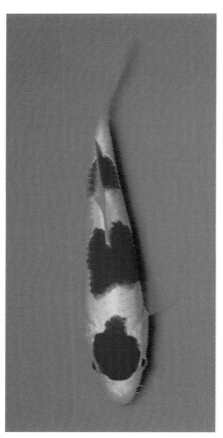

11 Bu Champion Kohaku
Owned by Tanimoto Koi Farm

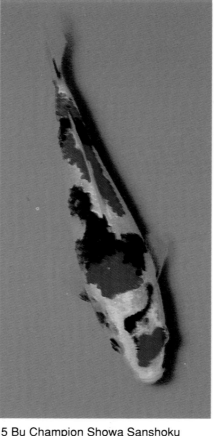

15 Bu Champion Showa Sanshoku
Owned by Sakai Fish Farm

20 Bu Champion Goshiki
Owned by Sakai Fish Farm

10 inches); a 45 BU is a fish between 40-45 cm (16-18 inches).

30 Bu Champion Showa Sanshoku
Owned by Kenji Hiroshe

35 Bu Champion Showa Sanshoku
Owned by Kenji Hiroshe

40 Bu Champion Kohaku
Owned by Taeko Asami

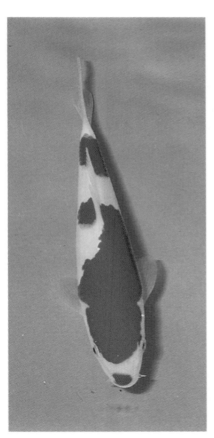

15 Bu Champion Kohaku
Owned by Saburo Asano

20 Bu Champion Showa Sanshoku
Owned by Toshinori Nagata

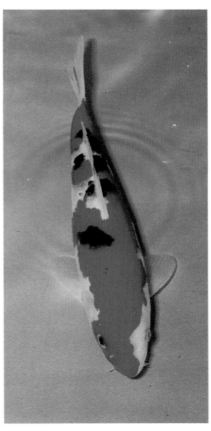

25 Bu Champion Taisho Sanshoku
Owned by Hideo Osako

75 Bu Champion Kohaku
Owned by Katsunari Abe

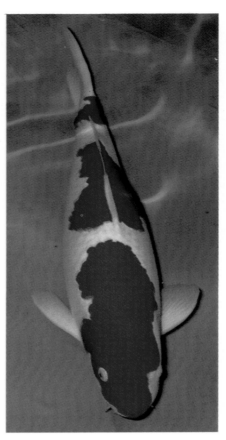

85 Bu Champion Kohaku
Owned by Hatsuko Shimizu

Over 85 Bu Champion Kawarimono
Owned by Shizuo Kobata

45 Bu Champion Kohaku
Owned by Hisashi Matsuo

55 Bu Champion Showa Sanshoku
Owned by Yukitoshi Ikeda

65 Bu Champion Kohaku
Owned by Toshikatsu Ishikura

girth. Very few koi meet this ideal, but the shape should be relatively in that proportion. The most commonly overlooked deformity is the caudal peduncle. This can easily be lumpy, thick, unsymmetrical and ugly, yet many judges fail to notice it.

The body of a koi is like the human body when its comes to appreciation. There are lovely tall people and lovely short people. Medium size people may also be attractive. It all depends upon whoever makes the judgment. So it is with koi!

The Japanese talk about a koi's fins as its hands and feet. This is a simplification of function but not form. Koi do not have fingers and toes and the spines and rays of the various fins are similar to each other but not similar to fingers and toes.

I suppose it takes experience to learn to judge beauty in anything. Art, music, poetry, architecture and landscape are just a few of the esoterics whose mastery comes with age, experience and education.

THE HEAD

When you first look at almost any living thing, you usually glance at the head first, searching, perhaps, for the eyes. Therefore the head of a koi is very important to a complete judgment of the beauty of the fish.

The best head shape is one that flows naturally into the body lines of the fish itself. It should not be elongated, squat or blunt, but it should be normal. There is no such thing as a most beautiful head. Koi heads are penalized for abnormalities. The same is true of the sides of the head, the gill covers. These must be uncurved at the ends and capable of being closed completely. Sometimes, due to gill parasites, the gills of the fish cannot be closed completely.

The mouth of the koi must be inferior; that is, it must open from the bottom, not the middle of the head and certainly not the top of the head. Many fishes have such characteristics. For aquarists, the familiar swordtails, mollies, platies and guppies have mouths opening from the top. All predatory fishes like pike, barracuda, piranhas and the like have mouths that open at the middle. All koi must have mouths that open at the bottom, as do all scavengers. Don't let their mouth opening fool you. Even though they evolved as scavengers, sucking up the debris on the bottom in search of food, they can still take floating food pellets at the surface. As a matter of fact, you should ONLY feed your koi floating pellets!

This Grand Champion, over 85 Bu Kohaku is owned by Fumiki Yoshioka. The judges remarked: *The present owner purchased this Kohaku in Niigata in 1988. It is not 11 or 12 years old. The strong points of this koi according to the owner are the figure and the skeletal structure. The owner breeds this koi with a little too much oxygen.* This fish was awarded its grand championship in the 25th Nishikigoi Show held in the Kyushu District.

The head (face) of a koi has special characteristics which are absolutely necessary for their appreciation. While Chinese culture appreciates the abnormal in fishes (think of Chinese goldfish), Japanese koi are appreciated for their normalities in terms of physical characteristics. Each koi should have two eyes, both of which are functional. They must also have barbels or whiskers. These sensory organs have been developed for groping in the bottom debris for food. The barbels are characteristic of the family to which the koi belong. There are many other fishes that have barbels (such as the popular aquarium fishes called barbs, such as the Tiger Barb, *Barbus tetrazonus*). The genus *Barbus* is used illustratively here as scientifically it is not correct. The correct name of this fish is *Capoeta tetrazona*.

A close-up of the head of a young long-finned koi grown in an aquarium by the author (HRA) so its barbels are intact.

The original wild carp of Eastern Europe were a gold color. This carp was photographed in 1954 by the author (HRA) in Germany at the Berlin Aquarium.

SHOW QUALITY KOI !

① Showa Sanshoku 43cm

② Showa Sanshoku 41cm

④ Taisho Sanshoku 55cm

③ Showa Sanshoku 35cm

This advertisement appeared in RINKO magazine. Many Japanese koi farmers offer show-quality fish for sale.

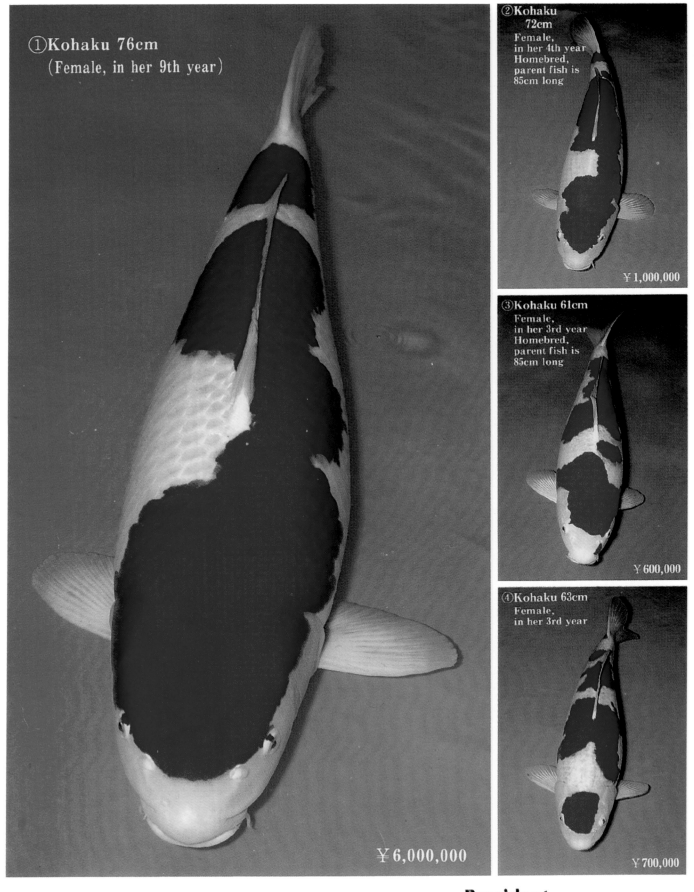

①Kohaku 76cm
(Female, in her 9th year)

¥6,000,000

②Kohaku 72cm
Female,
in her 4th year
Homebred,
parent fish is
85cm long

¥1,000,000

③Kohaku 61cm
Female,
in her 3rd year
Homebred,
parent fish is
85cm long

¥600,000

④Kohaku 63cm
Female,
in her 3rd year

¥700,000

Kyoei Suisan Co.
President
Juntaro Yoshioka

These two pages ran as an advertisement in **RINKO magazine in 1995. The 76 cm (about 30 inches), 9 year old Kohaku, is offered for sale for $60,000!! These pages are included for their historical significance and not to solicit business.**

⑤Kohaku 80cm
Female, in her 8th year

￥2,000,000

⑥Taisho Sanshoku 75cm
Female, in her 8th year

￥4,500,000

⑦Kohaku 79cm
Female, in her 7th year

￥6,000,000

⑧Kohaku 66cm
Female, in her 3rd year
Homebred, parent fish is
85cm long

￥1,400,000

Please contact us by FAX instead of telephone, if possible.

FAX・092-441-1489 Phone・092-411-2715
Kyoei Bldg., 2-1-13, Toko, Hakata-ku, Fukuoka city, Fukuoka 812 Japan

This is the size and quality of some of the Kohaku which were entered in the 24th All Japan Nishikigoi Competition held in Japan in 1994.

DEVELOPMENT

When a koi is young, it might be entered into a koi show and win a prize. This koi is then entered in others shows and might or might not win further prizes because its body, coloration and deportment might change as it grows older. If we look at famous paintings and sculptures that have come down through the ages, we can notice that in ancient times heavy bodies, especially on ladies, was the admired beauty. I can't recall ever seeing a painting of a beautiful person whose body was disfigured either at birth or through accident.

The same is true of koi. Young koi might grow up and be injured. These koi are usually not acceptable for koi shows. So, if you have a potential champion, keep him isolated and protected against attacks by other fishes, cats, snakes and children!

Before a koi judge seriously examines a koi, he first assures himself that it is not a cripple. Only after a gross examination of the koi's anatomy does he begin to judge the colors and color patterns of the koi. While there is no standard for the body shape of a koi, every judge has a normal koi body shape in mind. Any serious deviation from this norm is considered disqualifying. There are ideals set for colors and their patterns and these will be described in great detail further along in this book.

BODY WRAP

The outside of every fish is covered with skin; even those fishes that have no scales, like catfishes and eels, have a skin. When judging koi for beauty, the body wrap, which includes both the skin and the scales, must be evaluated.

A healthy koi skin *looks healthy*. This *look* is hard to explain in words, though it is very apparent when you compare a sick and healthy koi's skin. The healthy koi has a bright, shining, glistening skin. This can easily be compared to koi whose skin does not have these qualities. Young koi

Some of the winners of the 1995 All Japan Nishikigoi Competition held in Tokyo.

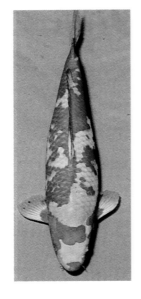
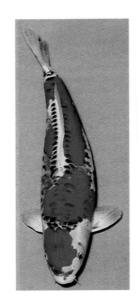

Some of the winners of the 1995 All Japan Nishikigoi Competition held in Tokyo, Japan.

almost always have this bright, lustrous skin quality. As the fish gets older, so does the skin lose much of its luster. There are exceptions and some of the most successful breeders of jumbo koi say they have a *secret* vitamin which keeps the skin in excellent condition. I doubt that this is true because when I visit many of these experts not all their koi have lustrous skin. Most koi exhibitors are of the opinion that the skin luster is a result of proper diet. I believe it is a genetic characteristic.

SLIME COVERING

Neither the skin nor the scales are touched by the water in which the koi swim. The entire body of the fish is covered with slime. This highly nutritious slime is almost pure protein and might very well be the element in the healthy *skin* which judges prefer. This being the case, a high protein diet should be tried if your koi do NOT have a shining, lustrous appearance. Look at the labels of the fish food containers; there should be a protein, fat, fiber, moisture and ash content statement. The most important food factor is probably the protein content.

The slime covering protects the fish from infections and many other problems. Yet, when I artificially spawn koi, I put the koi to sleep and then wipe off all the slime I can with a rough towel. This enables me to handle the koi more easily (it doesn't slip in my hands), and to make the egg or sperm squeezing process a lot neater and more sanitary.

As with all aspects of koi beauty, you have to have experience, a clear idea of what koi beauty means to you, and a thorough knowledge of koi color standards. Many skins have a basic color. That is, if you remove all the scales on a given fish, the skin would have a basic color. There are two basic skin colors: the wild color, which is referred to in the koi trade as *blue*, and the clean, clear color, which is referred to as *white*. The scales upon these skin colors forms the contrast which defines the quality of the particular fish. In each of these two skin colors there

Views at the 1995 All Japan Nishikigoi Competition held in Tokyo. The judges select the best fish and they are placed together so they can be judged against each other.

The winners line up for the *class* photo. Then each gigantic award is delivered personally to the winners. This is the highlight of the world koi show circuit.

are qualities. The white skin color must be clear, soft white. The Japanese talk about porcelain from which dishes are made in China (chinaware), while the blue is likened to the Korean dishes (Korean chinaware). These are favorite reference colors for Japanese judges. In Israel the breeders rely more on contrasting the white or blue with the scale colors. This high contrast makes the fish brighter. Perhaps it would be fair to say the Israelis like brash, startling, bright colors with contrast, while Japanese koi judges prefer the subtle difference but still with contrast. When you see Israeli and Japanese koi side by side, this contrast is very obvious. In humans, the blue-black hair of young Oriental people is very different than the black hair of the Mediterranean peoples (Italy, Spain, etc.).

Each color class of koi has its own skin, scales and pigment requirements. These requirements (standards) will be discussed separately under each of the recognized color varieties. In reality there are more than 80 varieties of koi NOT counting the long-finned varieties!

JUDGING KOI

It has already been stated (more than once in this book), that *beauty lies in the eyes of the beholder*. That doesn't change and never will. Perhaps it might be easier if we compare the koi to a ladies dress. A ladies dress has **style**, **color** and **pattern**. Perhaps even **price** can be included because a cheap fish is expected to be inferior in some quality. **Size**, of course, comes into consideration. Dresses of large sizes are rarely as colorful and attractive as small sizes; the same is true of koi. Young fish must be more beautiful than old, larger fish to have the same relative value.

At the present time koi judges around the world use the characteristics of style, color and markings as the bases of judging koi and awarding points. Typically in Europe and the USA, 40 points out of 100 are given for style (or *figure* as *style* is sometimes called), 20 points for color, 20 points for marking or pattern, and the balance of 20 points for such things as deportment, swimming ability or elegance. In the excellent book **THE CULT OF THE KOI** by Michugo Tamadachi (A TFH book, catalogue number TS-132, ISBN 1-85279-002-4) the author states on page 176 of the second edition, that *Shape (style) is most important to a*

Masao Kato, owner of Japan's top koi breeders, startled the show with this Grand Champion Kohaku. The judge, Natsuji Anabuki, who was certified by ZNA as an Honorary Certified Judge, wrote: *This koi has a wonderful body shape for a jumbo-sized koi of 90 cm (about 36 inches) in length. It gives us a youthful and fresh impression. The plump body has an atmosphere of a champion. The head Hi is preferably arranged and has much variation. The second Hi spreads deeply to the abdominal part. The third Hi patch is big in the right part and small in the left part, which shows the taste of artificial and elaborate work. This koi with dense Hi markings looks like a scaleless koi. The edge of the Hi patches are clear as if red papers were patched. It is a promising koi.*

Judges' Commentary

1st Place in Size 10, Kohaku

ZNA Certified Judge Koremichi Ito
At first sight, this koi with a straight Hi patch looks like a Taisho Sanshoku, but it has Tsubo-Sumi (well-placed black spots) at the important places. It has a white area cutting into the red marking and a dense Tsubo-Sumi spot on the white skin of the right shoulder. The similar Tsubo-Sumi at the tail region gives the dignity of Taisho Sanshoku.

1st Place in Size 9, Showa Sanshoku

ZNA Certified Judge Koremichi Ito
This koi has a big and clear Maruten (a round patch on the head). The Sumi markings are nicely arranged on the Sandan (three-stepped) Hi pattern. Especially, the Sumi on the mouth and the shoulder are the highlights of this koi. The neat tail region gives it a gracious impression of a modern Showa Sanshoku.

1st Place in Size 8, Aigoromo

ZNA Certified Judge Kenichi Kizawa
This is an elegant, vivid and exquisite koi. In spite of being a koi in size 8, it has such a beautiful white ground, Hi patches of high quality and indigo-blue Sumi of Asagi lineage.
   Even the Big Three (Kohaku, Showa and Sanke) could not compete with it.

1st Place in Size 7, Kohaku

ZNA Certified Judge Susumu Fujita
The body ground showing a good growth and high quality Hi markings are the most attractive point in this koi. As to the pattern, I would like it to have more white skin, but this koi has a bright future because of its excellent quality. It has a neat body, deep Hi markings and sharply defined edges.

1st Place in Size 6, Kohaku

ZNA Honorary Certificated Judge
Kaneko   Tadao Kaneko
At first, this koi has an excellent foundation. The thick Hi markings are nicely refined and sharply cut. It also has an interesting stepped pattern all over the body. Especially the head Hi and the big Hi patch appeared from the head to the shoulder are the highlights of this koi.

1st Place in Size 5, Kinginrin Kohaku

ZNA Certified Judge Hideaki Eto
This is a picturesque koi with typical white ground. It is quite a "performance koi" that I have been looking for for a long time. The brightness of the ground makes me imagine spacious silvery mountain ridges. The koi with vivid, mysterious red Hi markings and a simple, irregular Hi pattern will make an ideal Ginrin Kohaku in the near future.

1st Place in Size 4, Kohaku

ZNA Certified Judge Hiroyuki Funakoshi
This is a Sandan (three-stepped) Kohaku with a simple pattern. Although the third Hi patch reaches the tail joint, however, the positional relation of the second and the third patches is good enough. The bright Hi is preferably refined. The white skin seen between the first and the second Hi patches may be a little bare, but the clear and white skin becomes a charming point.

1st Place in Size 3, Kohaku

ZNA Certified Judge Hiroyuki Taniguchi
Everything is perfect in its color, pattern, white skin, edges and luster. Especially the sharply defined edges and the white skin are the most outstanding of all. The first Hi marking in the shape of the figure 8 is arranged from the head to the front dorsal fin, the second Hi patch runs from the right to the left slanting to the left and the third Hi makes an ideal stop at its tail region.

1st Place in Size 2, Kohaku

ZNA Certified Judge Takeo Ito
Apparently this is a plain Kohaku with a little heavy Hi markings on its body. But the defined appearance of the longish and round head Hi and the following white skin are the highlight of this koi. The well-finished body in a good shape appeals its excellent tail joint. More sharply cut edges are required on the second and third Hi patches.

1st Place in Size 1, Kohaku

ZNA Certified Judge Takemasa Kuroki
This koi, which was big enough, was barely qualified to enter the size 1 grouping.
   It has a typical Sandan (three-stepped) pattern. The whole pattern is clearly embossed owing to the excellent edges and the white ground. It is too beautiful to be identified as a koi in size 1. It also has some disadvantageous points, but has obtained this position with superiority to the others.

These remarks were made by the judges who selected the champions shown on the facing page.

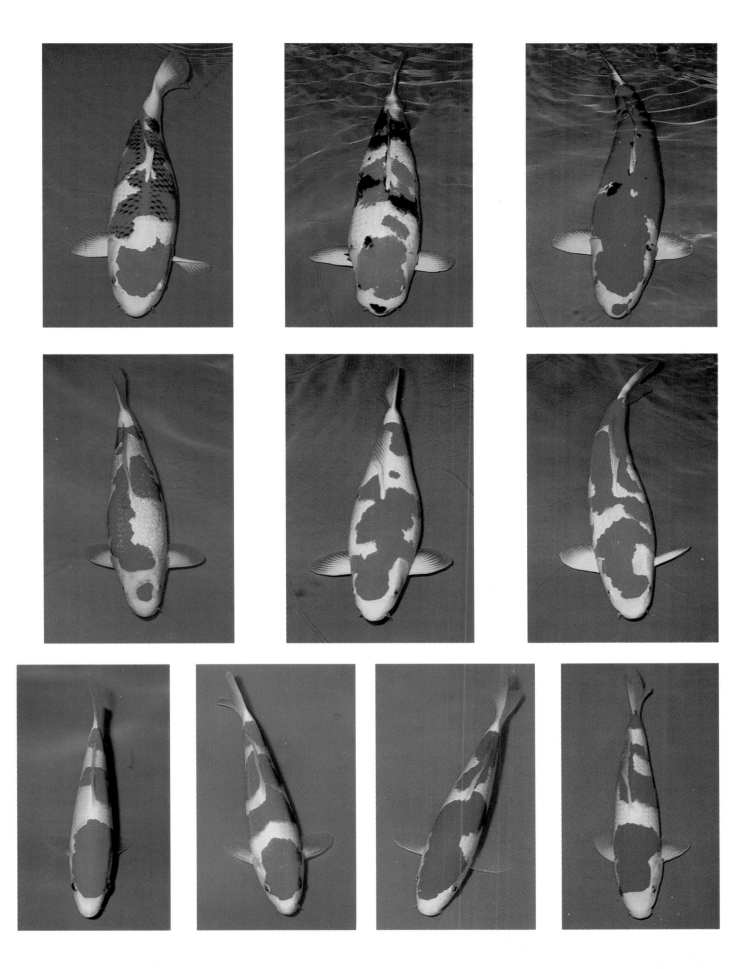

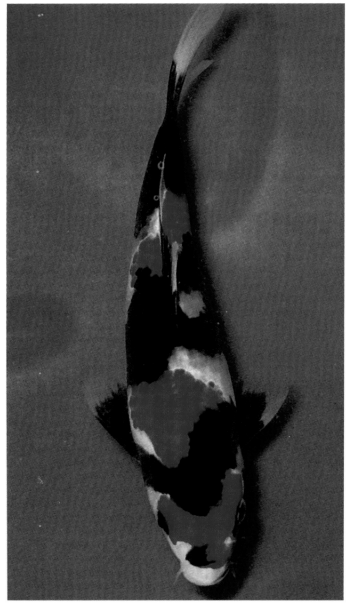

This young champion is a Showa Sanshoku in Size 2. The ZNA Certified Judge Takeo Ito wrote the following: *This is an ideal koi as a Showa Sanshoku variety. Seeing is believing. It has less amount of white skin, but has top quality Hi and Sumi markings. This is the first time for the koi in size 2 to be elected as a Young Championship in the nationwide shows. This koi defeated the Kohaku in sizes 3 and 4, and won the prize.*

koi and scores more points than any other single feature: 30. Color is awarded 20 points as is pattern. Quality earns 10 and elegance 10 also, as does imposing appearance. These latter terms leave much room for individual thoughts. So you can see that Orientals allow 30 points to non-objective characteristics while Western judges only allow 20 points. Style, color and pattern are OBJECTIVE, measurable, standardized and easily understood; the SUBJECTIVE characteristics such as *dignity* and *elegance*, even deportment and behavior, are almost impossible to measure. If a fish is nasty, chases other fish, stays quiet on the bottom, or doesn't join the school when they

swim in formation, then the fish is eliminated. But if 10 points are for deportment, how much is the penalty for laying on the bottom or chasing other fish? This is what makes beauty contests so difficult to predict. And don't think that a single judge can judge the same group of fish exactly the same day after day. They cannot.

PATTERN

When koi only have one color, there cannot be a judgment given for *pattern*, so the 20 points may be applied somewhere else. I usually add the points to the intensity of the color (10 points) and the style or figure of the fish.

Judging the relative value of one koi's pattern against another is a matter of taste. I have NEVER seen a colored pattern on a koi which didn't have some redeeming features. When viewed from above, the color pattern, whatever the colors, must be interesting, attractive and distinct (so they can be fit into a color variety category). If you think of a modern painting that just has splashes of color, so it is with many koi varieties. Either you like the splashes of color or you don't.

Since a koi is bilaterally symmetrical, the ideal is to have the color pattern bilaterally symmetrical. This is a rare occurrence, so you judge the pattern against that hypothetical possibility.

The interesting body parts of a koi, namely the head, the edible part (the trunk), and the tail are the three general areas of size and shape contrast. So the markings on these body parts should be characteristics. Since the tail is small, the marking on the back part of the fish (the caudal peduncle) should be small. The trunk is the largest part, so the markings on this part should be the largest. The head is in the middle (size-wise), so its markings should be in between the tail markings and the trunk markings in size. For Kohaku, the most popular variety of koi, the red markings on the white skin should be easily categorized into two basic color marking groups. The *dan-moyo* or *step pattern* is to resemble the stones in a Japanese garden. These stones are used for stepping to view the pond without getting your feet muddy. The *renzoku-moyo* is the continuous pattern, like lightening, and is continuous from the tip of the snout to the tail. Fishes exactly fitting these guides are very rare (I have never seen any), so points are awarded for closeness to the ideal.

The ideal patterns will be discussed under the descriptions of the individual color varieties.

From time to time, **RINKO** magazine published beautiful paintings of koi. This Kohaku depicts the dream fish!

1995 WINNERS

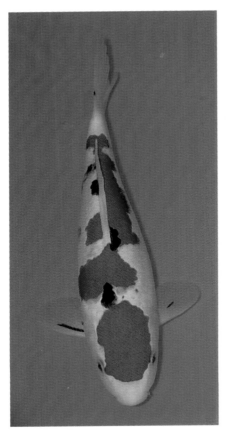

4 Bu Champion Taisho Sanshoku
Owned by Yoshimi Okada

6 Bu Champion Kohaku
Owned by Morio Soda

8 Bu Champion Kohaku
Owned by Yukio Niimi

The famous Japanese koi expert
Yoshifumi Iwata.

A judging scene.

1 Bu Champion Kohaku
Owned by Masaru Hishida

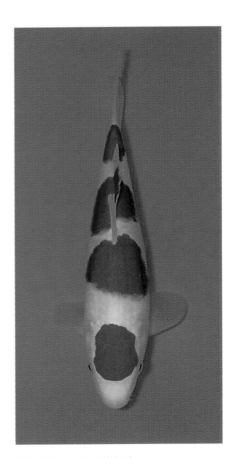

2 Bu Champion Kohaku
Owned by Masaru Hishida

THE NATURAL HISTORY OF NISHIKIGOI

As with almost all natural history, the evolution and development of the nishikigoi is clouded in doubt and theory. Almost everyone agrees that the nishikigoi, which we will refer to as **koi** in most of this book, was derived from the wild carp, *Cyprinus carpio*. There are, however, serious differences between the wild carp and the present koi. Not only is the basic color different, but their profile is also different.

sides of their bodies). Their gill rakers may be significant in differentiating subspecies: the wild carp from Eastern Europe usually has 23-27 outside and 30-34 inside. Sex cannot be determined by the variation in gill raker counts.

The nishikigoi differs from the *normal* European carp in that its streamlined, torpedo-shaped body has become elongated, thinner

An early scientific drawing of *Cyprinus carpio* as it appeared in a Russian book (Berg).

The wild carp of Eastern Europe are always described as *torpedo-shaped and gold colored*. Their elongated profile does not accommodate the usual notch between the head and the rest of the body. Their regular scales are large and the edges have intense melanophores giving the scale a dark tip which when it appears as a pattern on the fish is reminiscent of a net. It has a barely visible lateral line running through the middle of the sides. It has a fin count of

D, III-IV, 18-21; A, III, 4-5; C, IV-VIII, 16-18; PEC, I, 15-19; PEL, II, 7-9. They have 34-40 scale rows along the sides and they are bilaterally symmetrical as to scale rows and sex (both sexes have an equal number of scales on both

and hump-backed. The regularity of the scalation on the wild form has given way to irregularity, reduced scale counts and even scaleless forms. The golden body color has changed to white or blue. Interestingly, if the koi are released into a large pond, as was done here in Neptune, New Jersey, their future generations eventually regress back into the wild carp form. This regression is the most convincing evidence of the origin of the koi, since it is accepted that the wild carp originated in Asia.

Having originated in western central Asia, the wild carp spread in both directions, sticking to the temperate waters, to inhabit

Siberia and China in the east and Europe up to the Danube River in the west.

The Danube fish were collected by the Romans about 150 A.D. This has been proven by the discovery of carp fish bones in the ruins of the fortresses in areas across the Danube River. Many fish bones were unearthed during excavations of old Roman forts and in almost every case the *majority* of the bones were carp bones. The others fishes' bones were sturgeon (*Acipenser)* and catfish (*Silurus*).

While carp are considered to be freshwater fish, there are documented examples of carp living in both brackish and fully saline (marine) water. The Romans brought them to Italy right after Christ's arrival (the first century A.D.), and they were cultivated there. Due to the periodic floods for which Italy is famous, many carp escaped into the waters of Italy and gradually supported a natural population west of the Danube.

The establishment of Christianity after the downfall of the Roman empire, lead to the establishment of monasteries. The monks at that time were interested in doing something with all their free time, so they developed skills in making wines (Dom Perignon champagne, for example)

INTERNATIONAL HERALD TRIBUNE, FRIDAY, APRIL 28,

INTERNATIONAL

Vladimir Mashatin/Agence France-Presse

CHECHEN COMMERCE — A street vendor selling fish in Grozny. President Boris N. Yeltsin of Russia has signed a decree ordering a cease-fire in the southern republic.

The *Herald Tribune* of April 28, 1995 showed this vendor selling carp in Grozny during the height of the rebellion against Russian rule.

A fishing competition held in Belgium for children from 8 to 17 years of age features a photo of a large size wild carp still to be found in Belgian ponds.

and in breeding carp. According to Dr. Eugene Balon, the earliest record (of carp rearing) is by the secretary to King Theodorus (475-526 A.D.) of Ravenna, Cassiodorus, who was ordered to transport the wild carp from the Danube to Italy, thus imitating and continuing Roman tastes and habits.

Since the Catholic church ordered about 100 days per year during which fish must be eaten (every Friday plus holidays), the carp became a commercial entity which could be available in quantity on any given day since they were the only edible fish cultivated. Even to this day, many orthodox Catholics refrain from eating meat on Friday and celebrate Easter and Christmas with a meal of carp which they usually buy alive (especially in eastern Europe). Failure to observe the dietary restrictions often led to death penalties during the Middle

A modern Chinese silk painting showing koi.

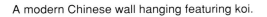
A modern Chinese wall hanging featuring koi.

PONDS FOR YOUR KOI

A natural koi pond. The koi are fed from the rocks.

A natural koi pond with the koi being viewed and fed from a bridge.

Aeration and filtration can be accomplished in many ways but none is so beautiful as a waterfall.

There are three basic kinds of ponds in which koi may successfully be maintained. Before you make a decision about which kind of pond you will use, consider the following:

1. **AVAILABLE SPACE.** If you have a lot of ground space around your home for a pond, you should consider this as the best of all worlds. For with a lot of space, you can have almost any kind of koi pond you want with the possible exception of the natural pond. Don't let lack of space hinder your plans, though, because small plastic pre-formed ponds are available from your pet shop or garden supply store suitable for keeping on a small balcony in an apartment house! Regardless of the amount of space available, there is surely a place for keeping koi and goldfish.

   However, keep in mind that the koi pond must have an equal amount of space dedicated to filtration, walking paths and protection against small children and animals falling in! There are many styles in ponds built on your own grounds, from original designs made from cement and poured by master concrete workers to plastic liners which you do yourself. The latest koi pond fad (and the one I use), is the second-hand swimming pool. Most swimming pool dealers have used or repaired swimming pools. They have the experience to set them into the ground and attach the necessary plumbing and filtration.

2. **AVAILABLE MONEY.** This is always a consideration. Certainly the least expensive koi pond is one made from a sheet of plastic. These are available at most pet shops or garden supply stores that specialize in water lilies and goldfish. I have several friends who keep a water garden made from plastic sheeting. These same ponds could keep koi equally well. There is NO most expensive koi pond. You can make a huge formal pond, extending above the ground (which is the best design of all). The above the ground feature allows you a natural protection from children or animals falling in, and it brings the fish to your height so you can

Above-the-Ground Ponds

Concrete and stone masons are very skillful in making above-the-ground koi ponds or water gardens. They use many materials including concrete block, facing stones, and concrete forms into which concrete is poured to form the pond. This type of pond is most likely the most expensive and usually cannot be too deep. A good design might be one that is 4-5 feet deep with half of the depth below ground level. The edge of the pond then becomes a seat for people to use when feeding or studying the fish.

To construct an above-the-ground pond you MUST have skill in laying concrete. The concrete must be reinforced with steel rods, mesh or whatever else the size of the pond calls for. It is not a handyman's job but the job of an expert. Don't try to save money in the construction of an above-the-ground pond by hiring inexperienced workers.

Above: A koi pond inside a shopping mall.

Right: Terraced rocks aerate and decorate this koi pond.

Below: The stones go right into the water where you can wade barefoot among the koi.

The owner of a vegetable market in China kept a koi pond to entertain himself while he waited for customers. Many customers came to feed the koi while they awaited their turn for service.

These three levels each have a koi pond.

These ponds can be formal and, if you think about it, abound all over the world as a decorative **three-coins-in-a-fountain** type. Almost all have sprays and/or water falls, and are very decorative. There is no reason why fishes cannot be kept in such ponds except for the copper sulfate or chlorine which is dumped into the pond to keep it clear of algae and bacterial growth. Most of these decorative above-the-ground ponds are semi-sunk in the ground.

Natural Ponds

By far the most beautiful and ideal pond for

This huge pond is filtered with a huge pumping system and the water is return to the pond over a series of stones.

koi is the natural pond. This is usually easily constructed if your home is on a hill, or sets on marshy, poorly drained topsoil. Merely bring in a suitable machine, dig a hole 6-8 feet deep and as large as possible. The hole should fill with water naturally. Plant the pond with fringe and water plants and you have a wonderful natural pond. There are many disadvantages of the natural pond. Usually it is difficult or even impossible at times to see the through their walls in which you can locate drains. The water drained from the pond usually goes into a series of settling tanks or mini-ponds. Thus the water containing the droppings and uneaten food particles is removed from the koi pond and diverted into a settling pond where it settles to the bottom and is flushed out of the system with a toilet-type of debris removal system. Some of these settling ponds have been equipped with a biological filtration system wherein the organic material is broken down by bacteria as the pond water drips through it. The settling tanks usually take care of the larger particles of dirt. After having these large particles removed, the water then goes through mechanical filtration in a series of procedures which may send the water through a thick bed of sand and/or through filtering materials which have to be washed, cleaned or replaced. There are literally thousands of filtering

Left: This fountain set is for individual areas of application. EHEIM offers four complete sets with different performances and spray heights. **Right:** The EHEIM pond pump is suited for all applications and pond sizes. They are ideal for fountains, cascades, decorative stones, waterfalls and streams.

EHEIM fountain sets and pond pumps.

schemes and designs. A few of them are shown here so you have some examples of the various schemes.

If you are very serious about a koi pond, ask your koi supplier for the names and addresses of people who have established koi ponds and get their views of how to start right. Koi clubs are extremely helpful in getting started properly.

It is very tempting to write that *you cannot clean your water too thoroughly,* but we have to define the word *clean* first. A filtration system *cleans* water by removing from it all waste and toxic

The 3460 EHEIM compact filter is for ponds up to 9 cubic meters (= 12 cubic yards) with a maximum depth of 80 cm (=36 inches).

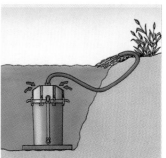

Three different fountain effects available from EHEIM fountain sets.

The EHEIM 3451 is a ready-to-use, complete filter. It has a practical carrying handle, is easy to maintain and is easy to operate.

materials, making it fit to be returned to the pond. Toxic materials include dissolved chemicals gases, cigarette butts and anything *foreign* to the pond. In the process of filtration and settling, the wastes are usually flushed away with the old water so that new water must be continually added to the pond. This water may have to be conditioned, too, so perhaps you don't want a system that adds water directly to your pond but perhaps is better added to the last stage of water purification (filtering) in your filtering system. Hard and fast rules are difficult to make. To overcome possible problems from adding water directly from the tap, I have the water *constantly* dripping into the pond. This keeps the pipes from freezing in the winter, and it allows any buildup of chlorine, fluorine or other chemicals to dissipate from the water. It also compensates

for temperature differences, especially in the summertime. By having the water dripping from as high as possible, the turbulence helps rid the water of gaseous chemicals and aids the pond's surface to rid the pond itself of poisonous carbon dioxide and other harmful gases.

READ, READ, READ

TFH Publications specializes in fish books and publishes more koi books than ALL other publishers combined. But read whatever books you can get your hands on. One book is a must.

The Atlas of Garden Ponds by Axelrod, Benoist and Kelsey-Wood, TFH number TS-178, ISBN number 0-86622-343-6, contains plans and discussions of koi ponds and filters. Albert Spalding Benoist is a certified architect who specializes in koi ponds! He has done a unique and admirable job.

A schematic showing the elaborate filtration system necessary to maintain a pond meticulously clear. For more details see the book **The Atlas of Garden Ponds** by Axelrod, Benoist and Kelsey-Wood., TS-178.

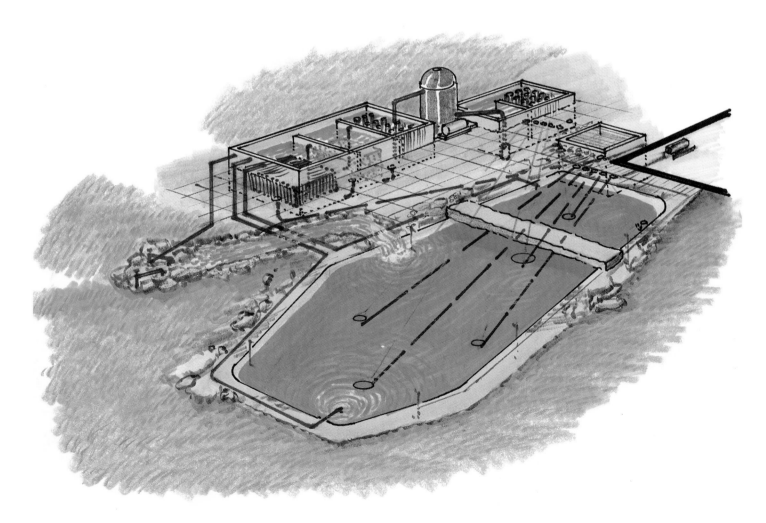

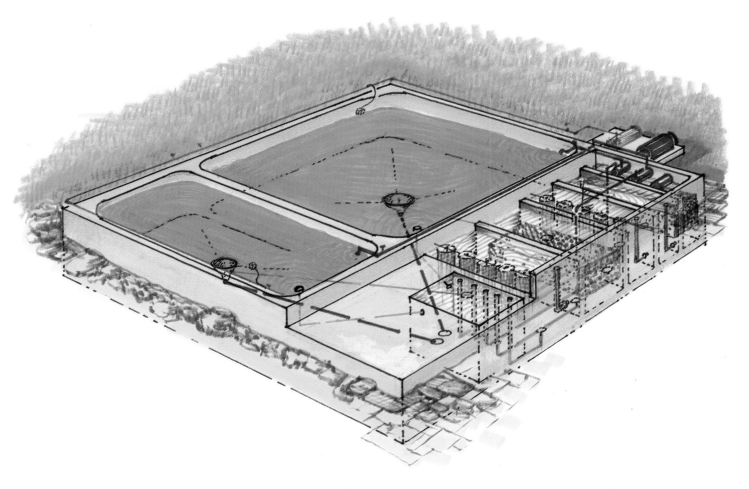

The two drawings shown here are ideas for koi ponds with filtering systems that have proven to be workable. See the **Atlas of Garden Ponds** for complete details of the construction.

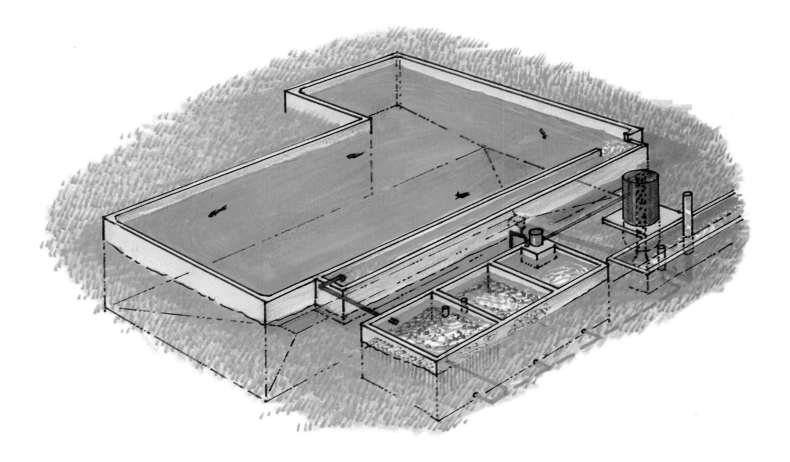

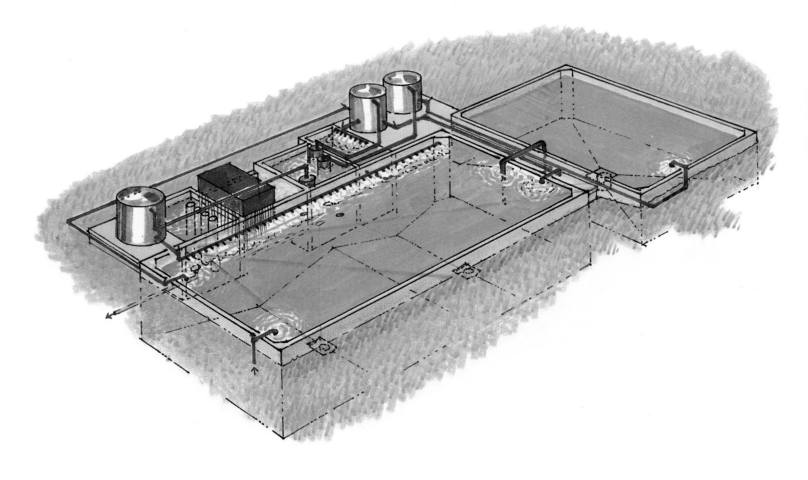

Two drawings of koi ponds with their accompanying filter systems.

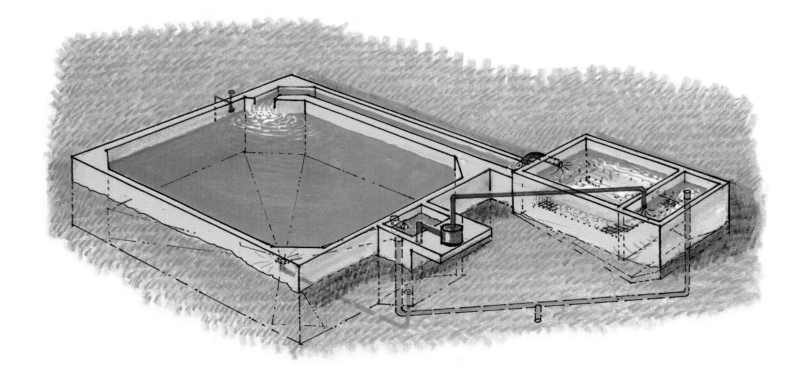

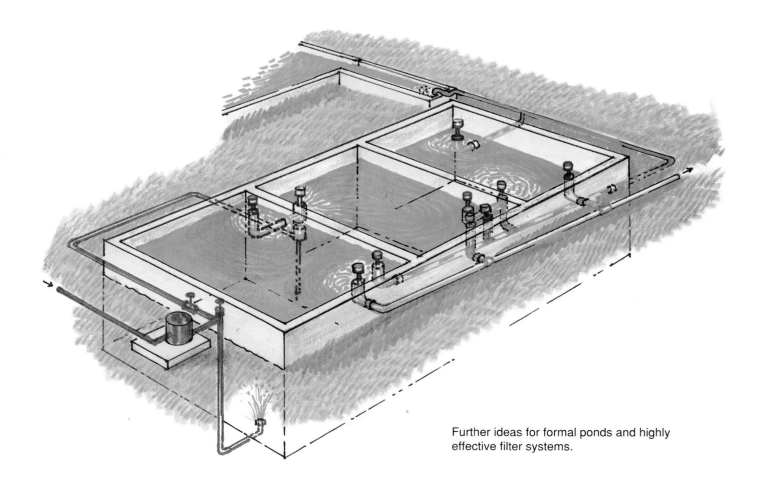

Further ideas for formal ponds and highly effective filter systems.

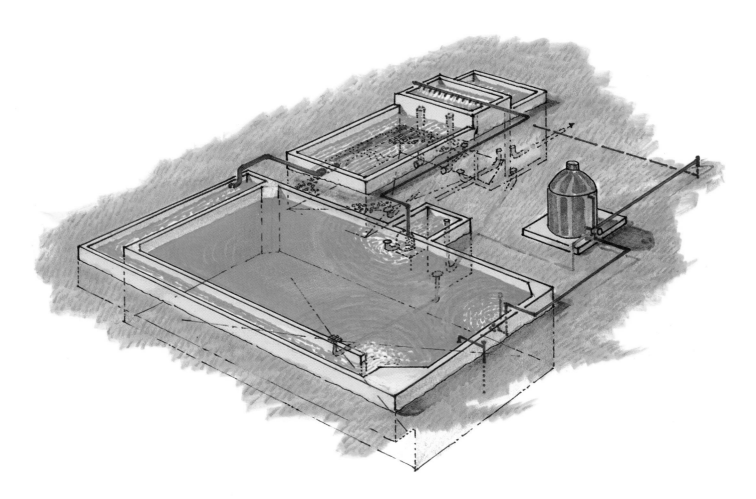

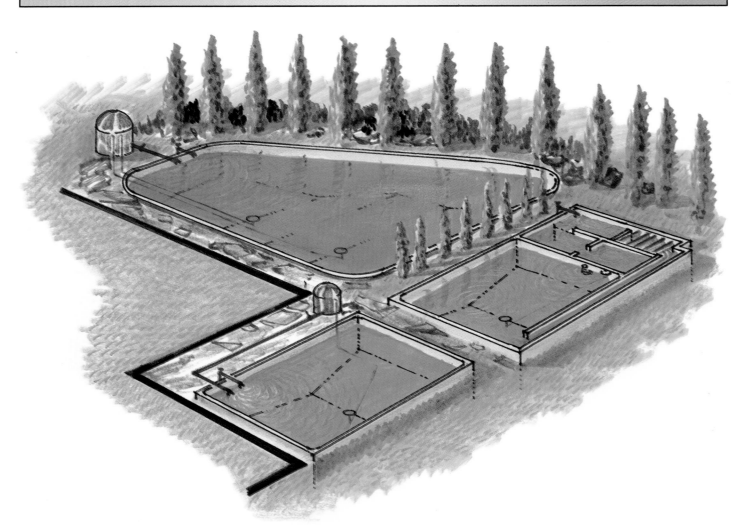

Above: It is possible to use three ponds by keeping and maintaining adult fish in the largest pond and yearling fish in the medium-sized pond. The smaller pond has baffles for removing debris and for bacterial degradation of biological material. Newly hatched fish do well in this pond because of the microscopic food available in such and environment. **Below:** This layout features a pitched pool bottom for the accumulation of debris. The debris is pumped to biological filters and settling tanks. Full explanations of all of these designs is available in the **Atlas of Garden Ponds** by Axelrod, Benoist and Kelsey-Wood

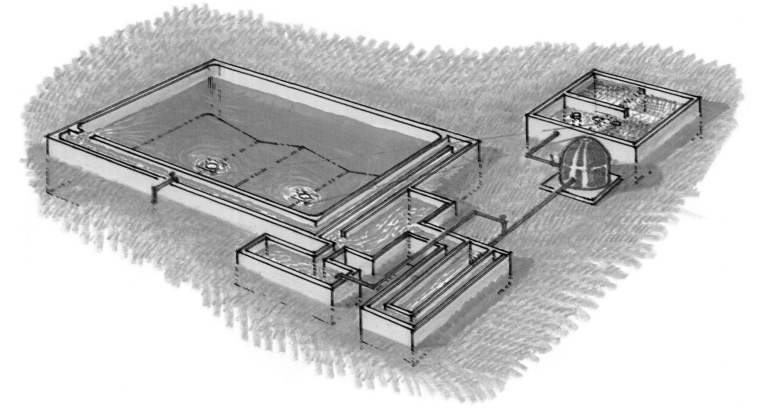

PLANTS FOR YOUR GARDEN POND

There is almost no limit for selecting plants suitable for decorating your koi garden pond. It is customary and usual to use plants in the pond water itself that both float and are rooted. It is also very common to have edge plants which are planted around the edges of the pond but with their roots in the water. Then, of course, there are those plants which are terrestrial plants that can be used for decoration or as fencing. One word of advice

The dream pond surrounded by beautiful flowering plants that come up every year (irises) and multi-colored water lilies.

don't use water plants you pick up in the local stream or pond. Such plants are almost always the hiding places of dangerous pests, parasites or pesticides. Only use plants you buy from your local pet shop or garden supply store.

TFH publishes three great books on garden ponds. These carefully cover the great variety of plants which succeed in temperate, subtropical and tropical climates. The best book is, of course, *The Atlas of Garden Ponds* by Axelrod, Benoist and Kelsey-Wood TS-178. There are two additional books: TT-034 *Designing Garden Ponds* and TT-035 *Garden Ponds for Everyone.* These books can be found in every garden or pet shop specializing in water gardens.

Pet shops sell many varieties of aquatic plants. Most of them are bog plants that thrive only under tropical conditions. While most of these plants are maintained under-

Floating plants and suitable filtration keep a pond's water crystal clear. The koi are visible in clear water and the easiest way to keep the water clear is with the assistance of living plants.

water, they are usually propagated with their foliage protruding out of the water. The best of these by far are those aquatic plants that have rooted in rock wool and are sold in miniature plastic pots. These are hydroponically (chemically) grown and are free of all parasites that are harmful to fishes or other plants.

Bunch Plants

The best aquatic plants for your koi pond are the soft-leafed aquatic plants that thrive under all weather conditions. These are commonly referred to as *bunch plants* because they are sold in bunches and are

This lovely koi pond was constructed from plastic sheeting and stones.

To get aquatic plants to grow quickly, they should be fortified with a plant plug. Photo courtesy of Aquarium Products.

Elodea nuttalli.

Bacopa monnieri.

Large natural ponds depend upon running water to keep the water clear.

Egeria densa.

Myriophyllum brasiliense.

Fontinalis antipyretica.

Ceratophyllum demersum.

Eleocharis minima.

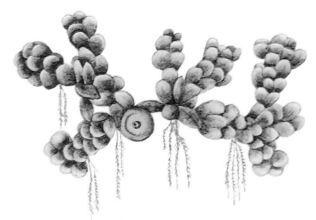

Azolla caroliniana.

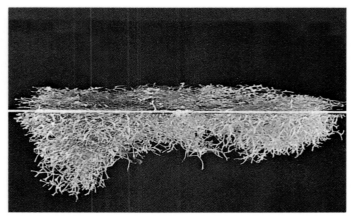

Riccia fluitans.

usually grown outdoors and harvested. They are then tied in small bunches with a rubber band around the bottom. If they are planted into the substrata of the pond, they will root and eventually cover the whole pond. Koi eat their soft leaves and spawn in the thicker growths of the bunch plants. When they become too thick, harvest them and pack them into bunches. Your local pet or garden supplier will usually be happy to buy them.

The most common bunch plants belong to the genera *Bacopa, Ceratophyllum, Egeria, Eleocharis, Fontinalis, Myriophyllum* and *Elodea.*

Floating Plants

Of the utmost necessity are floating plants. They provide food for the koi and ducks which may be attracted to the pond, a hiding place for the fry, and, most importantly, SHADE to keep the sun from reaching the algae.

Floating plants are simple to grow and propagate IF THEY GET ENOUGH DIRECT SUNLIGHT. The smaller the floating plant, the better. The most popular genera are

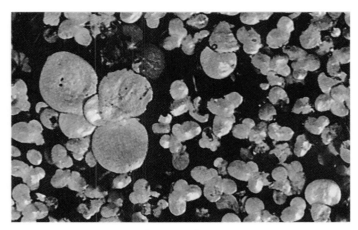

Lemna minor.

Water Hyacinth, *Eichhornia crassipes,* can grow so thickly, that it impedes water transportation.

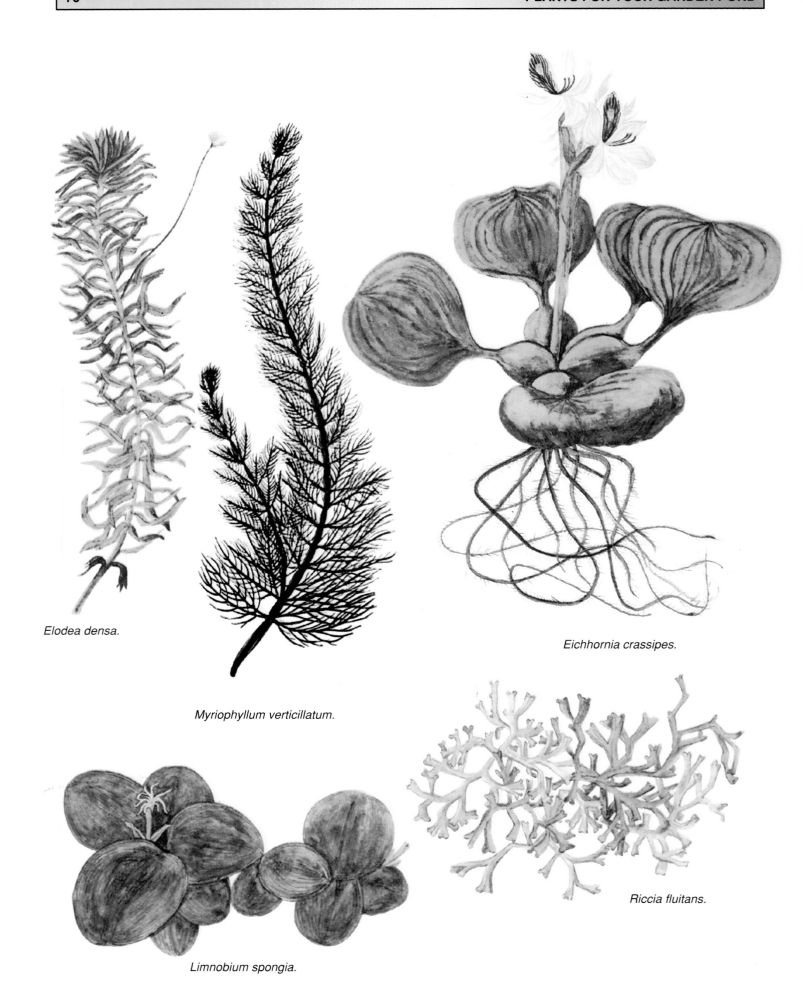

Elodea densa.

Myriophyllum verticillatum.

Eichhornia crassipes.

Riccia fluitans.

Limnobium spongia.

Lemna, Hydrocharis, Limnobium, Riccia and *Azolla.* The larger floating plants are the Water Hyacinth, *Eichhornia crassipes,* Water Lettuce and the Water Lilies.

Under ideal conditions these plants quickly cover the tops of the smaller ponds. Water Hyacinth is such a fast growing plant that I have seen them cover huge lakes in Brazil. Once I was trapped for three days in a lake where the Water Hyacinth covered the top and I could not find my way out. In Florida, small creeks are often completely clogged with Water Hyacinth. In Cuba, where it is also found, the farmers collect the Water Hyacinth, grind it up, boil it and then feed it to their pigs.

Rooted Plants

Obviously most of the plants already mentioned have roots, but those mentioned can thrive WITHOUT the roots being buried in the soil (except for Water Lilies). Rooted plants are not satisfactory as submerged plants in the pond because their beauty is their leaves and you can't admire their leaves from above. Therefore it is best to do without aquatic plants such as *Vallisneria,* Amazon Swordplants, and the like. Some of my friends grow these plants outdoors in their ponds so they can harvest them in September (which coincides with a busy season for tropical fish stores) and sell them to their garden suppliers or pet shops.

There are more artificial categories of aquatic plants. However, you would be best advised to visit your garden pond supplier and order the plants he knows will grow best in your area and under your individual conditions.

MARGINAL PLANTS

The plants placed along the margins of the pond are called *marginal plants.* The usual marginal plants are the Cattails or Reedmace, *Typha,* Irises, Sedges, *Lobelia,* Pickerel Weed, and Marsh Marigold. Your local supplier might well have others, too.

These plants go into a resting phase every winter and come back with vigor in the early summer, as do the hardy water lilies.

The plants mentioned above are happy with their roots planted in shallow water.

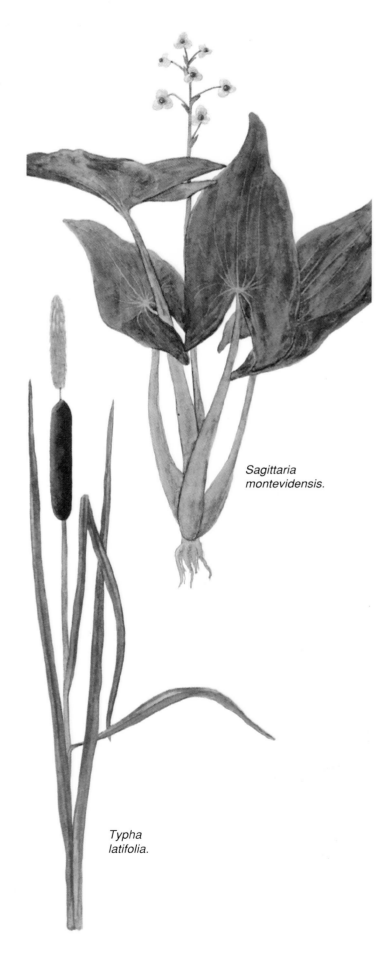

Sagittaria montevidensis.

Typha latifolia.

Water lilies planted in baskets can be moved indoors to protect them if they are tropical.

There are hundreds of different kinds of water lilies available through your local pond fish supplier. Some are perennial, others annual or tropical.

Some gardeners like to plant roses, hedges or even grapes around their pond. The grapes are woven around a trestle which goes over the top of the pond and protects it from the direct rays of the sun.

In general, you are much better off buying plants from your local supplier. While there are many mail order companies offering their services, you are really buying in the dark if you are not familiar with the plants you may be ordering. There are some VERY ethical garden suppliers who specialize in helping the garden pond hobbyist. These suppliers advertise in

Tropical Fish Hobbyist and similar magazines. Many pond fishes are also aquarium fishes so articles about koi and water gardening are frequently found in these magazines. So your hobbyist magazine is the place to look for the name and address of a good mail order supplier.

A well planted pond offers security for your koi and encourages spawning in the springtime. It also protects the pond from unwelcome algae.

This is a true water garden, including lotus! It may be hard to find the koi, but its a great way to cure a swamp problem.

A pond filled with magnificent long-finned koi.

toads, newts and salamanders. These are all welcome guests because they are all insect eaters. Frog larvae, called *tadpoles,* are great consumers of algae, so even they are welcome guests, but don't fret when some wet night hundreds of small frogs are jumping round in your garden! Obviously, the kind of amphibian that visits will depend upon where you live.

Daphnia are ideal foods for small koi. They are about 10% of the size shown and they are often referred to as *water fleas*.

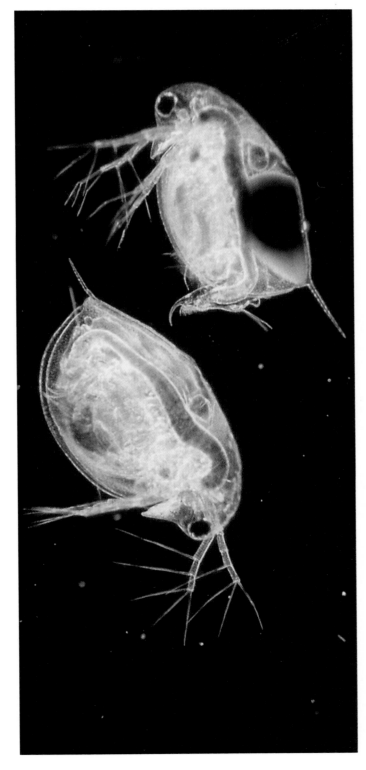

Tadpoles are welcome in the pond as they eat algae. When they grow up they may be dangerous to fry as some frogs eat fish.

Raccoons are everywhere in New Jersey. Other parts of the world have their own predatory mammals. It's very difficult to protect your pond from these predators but they are not very successful in catching fish that swim in water over one foot deep.

If your pond is large enough, you might see some skimmers, like this Black Skimmer, *Rynchops nigra*, go after the fry that swim on the top of the water.

PREDATORS

The raccoon, in New Jersey especially, is a constant dread. They greedily attack fishes and once they find the garden pond, they constantly re-visit the place. They rank above cats, kingfisher birds and the neighborhood kids when it comes to stealing fishes. How often have I found the neighbors' kids fishing in my pond and taking large koi home for dinner. Their Mom would often bring back my dead koi and tell me how sorry they were that Junior caught my koi. They expected me to eat it.

Last year on my New Jersey pond I had the great pleasure while visiting my backyard koi garden pond to find a 6 feet high blue heron poised to catch my three month old koi! Since I prefer losing koi to shooting a beautiful blue heron, I bought a long fishing seine and covered the pond with it. That didn't stop the heron. He kept biting the seine until he had a fishing hole. He merely waited for a koi to swim by the hole

Kingfishers rarely attack koi ponds but they might if they get hungry. This is the Ringed Kingfisher from Brazil.

Egrets can be very dangerous to koi ponds if they discover them. This is *Egretta garzetta*, a particularly large egret that seems to love koi.

Cormorants are birds that can dive into your pond and swim underwater until they catch a fish. The only way to protect against all bird predators is to use a net fastened slightly above the water's surface.

Fish eagles or fish hawks may also prey on your koi. They rarely attack ponds that have a dense plant cover.

and ZAP! the koi was swallowed. The heron visited my pond every year and stayed from April until November. I finally found out how to get rid of it. I bought a cheap plastic copy of the heron. The kind that are used for garden decorations. It was about 4 feet high. I stuck it into the ground adjacent to my pond and the other heron never returned. It seems that herons respect each others fishing grounds and would never think of fishing along with another heron.

Herons are the most destructive of the birds, though kingfishers do a thorough job

The Wood Frog, *Rana sylvatica*, is welcome around the koi pond, but they make a lot of croaking noises during breeding time.

on the fry. There are many other fish-eating birds to worry about, especially the fish eagles and cormorants. These are mostly found in tropical areas. In almost all cases, the laws protect these animals from being shot. But shooting them is terrible and you are advised against killing any animal. Rather learn their habits and frighten them away. Having a few large cats prowling around will usually keep the birds away. My poodle successfully keeps all the birds away with his loud barking and his running after them when they land. Once a wounded bird landed and he ran up to it screaming loudly. The poor bird merely cowered and awaited its doom. But my dog Oliver merely sniffed it and kept barking. He didn't harm it in any way. I picked up the sea gull and brought it to William Starika, the expert bird editor for T.F.H.Publications. He nursed it back to health and released it in our local marshy swamp (Shark River).

Spotted Salamanders can be as interesting as koi in your pond. They only prey on very small fish.

FISHES FOR THE GARDEN POND

There are many fishes that can be kept in your garden pond. The variety depends upon the climate where you live, how protected your pond is and how much you know about fishes. Your local garden pond supplier or aquarium shop can supply you with many kinds of fishes. Since most cold water fishes can live in the semi-tropics, but warm water fishes cannot live in the temperate zone, the evolution of garden pond fishes has tended to favor using cold water fishes as pond fishes and not tropical fishes. For those who KNOW, though, many so-called tropical fishes come from colder waters and can thrive in waters that don't go below 50° F. Certainly the White Cloud Mountain Minnow, *Tanichthys albonubes*, from around

Golden Orfe, *Leuciscus idus.*

White Cloud Mountain Fish, *Tanichthys albonubes*, are beautiful small fishes that thrive outdoors in temperate climates.

Tench, *Tinca tinca.*

The original wild carp of Eastern Europe, *Cyprinus carpio*, photographed by the author (HRA) in the Berlin Aquarium.

Canton, China can be a beautiful but small fish for the pond, as also are the more popular Korean Paradise Fish, Sticklebacks and, of course, the hardy sunfishes. Many sunfish, especially those from New Jersey, like the Black-banded Sunfish or the Pumpkinseed Sunfish, are well established as both pond and aquarium fishes.

Larger, but less colorful pond fishes are the Roach, *Rutilus rutilus*; the Golden Orfe, *Leuciscus idus*; Tench, *Tinca tinca*; Rudd, *Scardineus erythrophthalmus*; and such local fishes as small trout, catfishes or suckers.

The king and queen of the pond are the goldfishes and koi.

Phoxinus phoxinus

Acanthorhodeus asmussi

Scardineus erythrophthalmus

Rhodeus sericeus

Vimba vimba

Tinca tinca

Sarcocheilichthys czerskii

Sarcocheilichthys czerskii

Coldwater fishes suitable for the koi pond.

Leucaspius delineatus

Phoxinus phoxinus

Scardineus erythrophthalmus

Rhodeus sericeus

Rutilus rutilus

Chondrostoma nasus

Ctenopharyngodon idella

Leuciscus idus

Coldwater fishes suitable for the koi pond.

GOLDFISH

The most popular of all aquarium fishes is the goldfish. They are probably the most hardy and least expensive of all domesticated fishes. Over the hundreds of years of their domestication, many varieties have been developed. These developments in Japan, China and the USA, are mostly concerned with the variation in eye form, fin and body shapes. They do NOT possess the potential for color variations as do the koi because their domestication and production has been more recent and more controlled than the koi. Remember the koi were developed in Europe and the Middle East for a thousand years or more, spreading out further and further until most of the temperate world had their own supplies of carp from which the koi developed. Goldfish were developed primarily in China a few hundred years ago, then Japan, and finally the USA and the UK.

Not all goldfish are suitable for life in the pond. Many have such absurd body shapes that they can hardly swim and could not reach the surface of the water if they had to feed from the top. Others have eye defects. In any case very fancy goldfish varieties are best kept in protected shallow pools, or in aquaria.

Wardley makes a goldfish food in flake form which has proven extremely beneficial for pond goldfish as well as aquarium fishes. Koi also thrive on the Wardley goldfish product.

The basic goldfish are fine for the pond, even if they lack the dramatic colors of koi. Koi and goldfish get along well together in the same pond. Koi stop eating when the water is about 50° F., but goldfish even eat when the ice covers the top of the pond. The varieties of goldfish that are recommended for the pond are the Common, the London Shubunkin, the Bristol Shubunkin and the Comet.

Veiltails, Fantails, Moors, Celestials, Bubble-eyes, Pompons, Lionheads, Orandas, Pearlscales and Gill Curled Goldfish do not thrive in ponds.

The three goldfish shown here are, top to bottom, Comets, Common and Shubunkin. These varieties can live with koi. They even feed when there is ice on the pond while koi stop feeding at about 50°F.

The fancy goldfish, clockwise from top left, are Veiltail, Pearlscale, Lionhead and Water Bubble-eye.

Shubunkin goldfish are wonderful in a koi pond.

The needs of goldfish and koi are the same, though goldfish are more hardy than koi. They both spawn at about the same time and produce huge quantities of eggs so it is very easy to over-populate your garden pond with either species. You should make plans to dispose of the fry to prevent overcrowding which might mean losing all the fish in the pond.

The best way to dispose of unwanted pond fishes is to sell them to the dealers who originally supplied you. Remember that early spring is the best time to sell your fishes, so fishes bred the previous year are just the right size for sale through dealers.

KOI OR NISHIKIGOI

The most popular of all pond fishes is now the koi. Koi were developed to their perfection in Japan, even though they originated as ornamental fish in China. They are, of course, merely colored carp, *Cyprinus carpio*. At least 100 different varieties of koi have been recognized, but very few varieties breed true. Usually when you have two fish which are identical in visual appearance (phenotype), when they are bred together, you would be lucky to get more than 20% that look like their parents. (This is clarified in Dr. Rothbard's chapter in this book.)

Since raising koi is a competitive hobby and business, the Japanese have taken the 100-or-so varieties and reduced them to 13 major varieties. In Israel and some other countries, a few more varieties may be recognized for selling purposes, but for shows only 13 classes are recognized. Within each of the 13 classes are groups according to their size; usually

there are 14-16 size groups. In local shows outside Japan, or in Japan where there are few entrants, the groups are classified into as few as six sizes.

Variations in fin length or body shape are not accepted in Japan, but that will probably change soon as more and more long-finned varieties are appearing, especially in the USA.

The recognized 13 varieties are:

1. **kohaku**, a white fish with red markings. There are many kinds of kohaku depending on the pattern of the red.
2. **taisho-sanke**, is a three-colored fish. Its basic colors are the same as the kohaku but there is an added black color. The black should be the least obvious color. There must be a large red mark on the head with no black.

Grand Champion over 70 Bu (=over 70 cm, or about 28 inches) Kohaku, owned by Sakai Fish Farm.

3. **showa-sanshoku**, is another three colored fish but its basic color is black and there are red and white patterns on a mostly black fish.

4. **bekko**, is a bi-colored fish with small black markings on another color. The kind of bekko depends upon the second color. Shiro-bekko, for example, is a black and white fish, etc.

Runner-up Grand Champion 70 Bu Taisho Sanshoku owned by Tamaura Fish Farm.

Grand Champion over 75 Bu Showa Sanshoku owned by Hiroyuki Kawakami.

12. **kinginrin**, are koi with shining or silvery scalation.

13. **tancho**, are koi with the beautiful red patch on their head.

Grand Champion Kawarimono in the 80 Bu category.

Grand Champion A-Ginrin, a Kinginrin in the 70 Bu category.

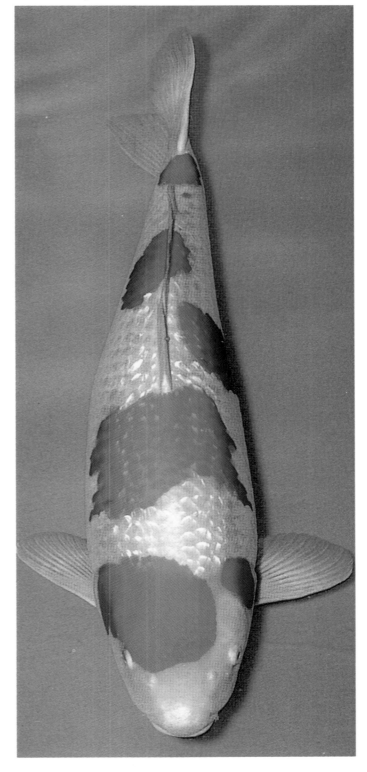

A Grand Champion 75 Bu koi with a beautiful tancho marking on its head.

A Grand Champion Kohaku like this can be entered either as a tancho or a kohaku. It is a 40 Bu category in size.

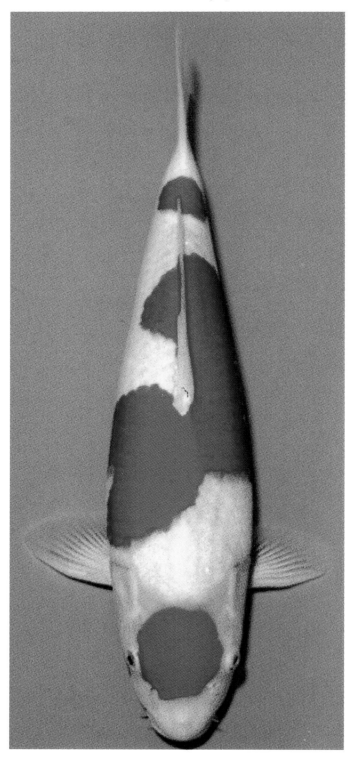

KOI VARIETIES

There are literally thousands of kinds of koi if we consider color varieties, scalation and fin shapes. Were these varieties propagated there would be mass confusion as there was with the Guppy when it began to have the same varied background as the nishikigoi, or koi as English-speaking people call them. Eventually the Guppies were categorized into general colors, general patterns and general shapes of the fins. The same is true of the koi.

While all koi are derived from the wild fish, *Cyprinus carpio,* and all wild *Cyprinus carpio* look alike, except for extremely rare sports or hybrids, our domesticated koi are different. Like Guppies and Discus, koi do not reproduce according to prediction. If you cross two red and white koi (kohaku are white koi with red markings), you'd be surprised at how FEW red and white koi are produced, and how dissimilar they are to their parents! A good percentage of look-alikes would be 20%.

Obviously, the judging of koi has to be organized in such a way that it would be humanly possible to judge the koi and this judgment could be replicated. This means that if you have three sets of judges judge the same koi, you should expect the same results. This is basically true though there are lots of minor exceptions since *beauty* lies in the eyes of the beholder.

The Japanese have evolved a basic system of 13 categories, with some sub-categories. They accept the German carp with its ugly scalation, or rather *lack* of scalation, but they do not accept the long-finned varieties developed in the USA. This is a shame since the long-finned koi are much more graceful and attractive than the normally finned koi.

The thirteen categories are *kohaku, taisho-sanke, showa-sanshoku, bekko, utsurimono, asagi shusui, koromo, ogon, hikari-moyomono, hikari-utsurimono, kawarimono, kinginrin,* and *tancho.* These categories were defined in the previous chapter and will be studied separately in the pages that follow.

But before we become involved in the color varieties, let's look at the scale variations.

This is a color variety of koi called the kumonryu. This champion was a 70 Bu size.

GERMAN CARP

German carp or, as the Japanese call them, *doitsugoi,* was the term applied to the food fish which was imported from Germany. These carp were easily recognized by the genetic deformation or loss of scales. The Japanese admired this scalation, especially since it was German and they admire many German things, and bred it into their line of colored carp (koi). From the point of view of the author, the German scalation is not attractive and should not be carried in the ornamental carp lines. The long-finned carp are much more beautiful. But judge for yourself by the accompanying photos!

Above, left Magnificent long finned koi with German scalation. They are not accepted by the Japanese koi societies.

Left: The fake Sweetheart Koi, which has had red scales transplanted from the head to the sides to form a heart. You can put your initial on a carp, too, but eventually the scales fall off (perhaps months later).

Below: A German carp called *doitsugoi* by the Japanese on display at the Steinhart Aquarium in San Francisco, California.

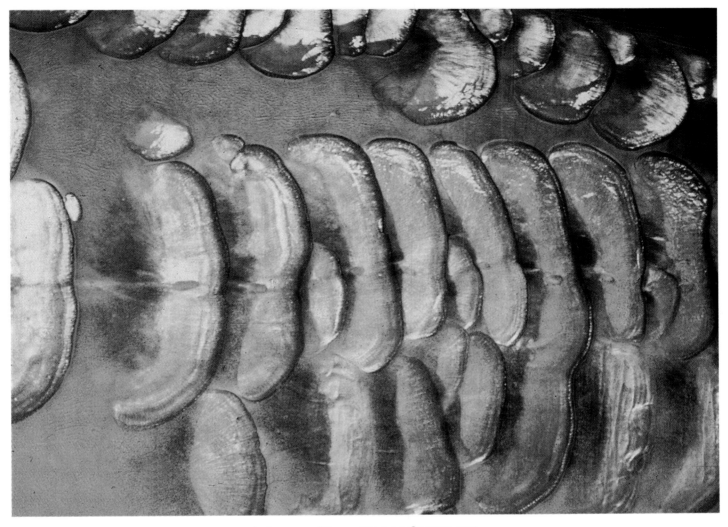

A close-up of the scales on a German carp.

There are three kinds of doitsugoi (German carp) scale arrangements. The LEATHER carp is the most scaleless of all carp. They are allowed a few scales at the base of the dorsal (top) fin, but if these few scales are missing, all the better.

The MIRROR carp have several rows of scales on each side of its body. Bilateral symmetry is admired. A row runs down the middle of the back while another row runs along the same course as the lateral line.

The ARMORED carp are carp trying to go from the *mirror* carp to the normal carp. So they have the basic *mirror* carp scale pattern of parallel rows of scales along the sides and dorsal edge, plus some random patches. Because *armored* carp are not symmetrical, this is the least desirable variety and it is rarely found at koi shows. The word *symmetry* is the key word when judging doitsugoi. The term *doitsugoi*, by the way, comes from the Japanese pronunciation of

the German word *deutsche* which means *German* and of, course, the Japanese word *goi* for *carp*.

According to Dr. Takeo Kuroki, Japan's leading writer on the subject of koi and a man much admired by the author, the German carp arrived in Japan about 1904 when 40 German carp were imported. Only four females and one male survived to breeding age and these five carp became the basis of the whole German carp introduction to the nishikigoi.

Many Japanese koi breeders see a lot of value in scaleless koi because the skin colors are brighter and not obscured or diminished by the overlaying scales. But this is true only of certain color varieties. This is especially true of the metallic-bodied koi which are called *hikarimonos*. But the traditional kohaku (red and white) and sanke (red, white and black) are far from attractive and are never to be found in serious koi shows.

This type of Doitsu Chagoi was common a long time ago. Contrary to its name, its body color is green.

This yellow Doitsu has a good balance of the yellow body color with the large, dark blue scales of the German carp.

Markings of a great Kohaku appear on this Doitsu. This is the equal of a refined Wagoi.

This orange koi has a great balance between the dark German scales and the dull orange color.

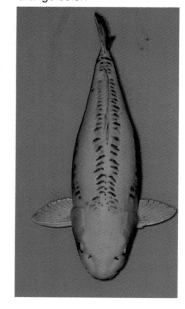

KOI SIZES AND SHAPES

Japanese are small people living in small houses. Most things in their homes are smaller than those found in Western homes because space and land in Japan are by far the most expensive in the world. But, when it comes to koi, the larger the koi the better it is. If you have two exactly identical koi (which admittedly is hard to find), the larger one would always win over the smaller. This being the case, Japanese koi shows are divided into size categories. Each category is called a *bu*. A *bu* was a small denomination of Japanese currency and would be the verbal equivalent of a penny. In koi size categories, a *bu* is 4 inches (actually the Japanese use the metric system, so the *bu* is 4 cm). Minor shows where there are fewer entries may use a 2 inch *bu*, but 4 inches is normal. When koi are measured the distance from the tip of the mouth to the tip of the tail is measured. So if you put the koi into a box with a movable partition, the nose and the tail would just touch at a distance equivalent to the size of the fish.

When a koi gets over 30 inches it is called a *jumbo*. In most, if not all, cases the body shape and dimensions change as the koi gets larger, much like human beings who get fatter as they become older, but they don't get taller to distribute the fat more evenly over their body. So large bellies might be the result both in fishes and in humans. In koi, a jumbo must be svelte, i.e., slender (except for egg-laden females), active, graceful and beautiful. Understandably, these characteristics are subjective and not objective. It would be difficult to replicate judges' response to evaluating any jumbo koi because of the difference in the concept of *beauty*. The same with its swimming. Jumbo koi are judged both at rest and while active. Judges try to make their tasks easier by eliminating candidates on the bases of split fins, torn fins, missing fins, kinky fins, even injuries are enough to disqualify a fish. Judges have often disqualified jumbo koi because they are either unequal in size, or too small for such a large fish category. Usually after all the disqualifications, a single fish is left to be proclaimed *champion*.

Judging jumbo koi is a grand art, not for beginning judges. But as better fish foods for koi are developed, the koi will grow larger and more and more jumbos will be seen in the competitions.

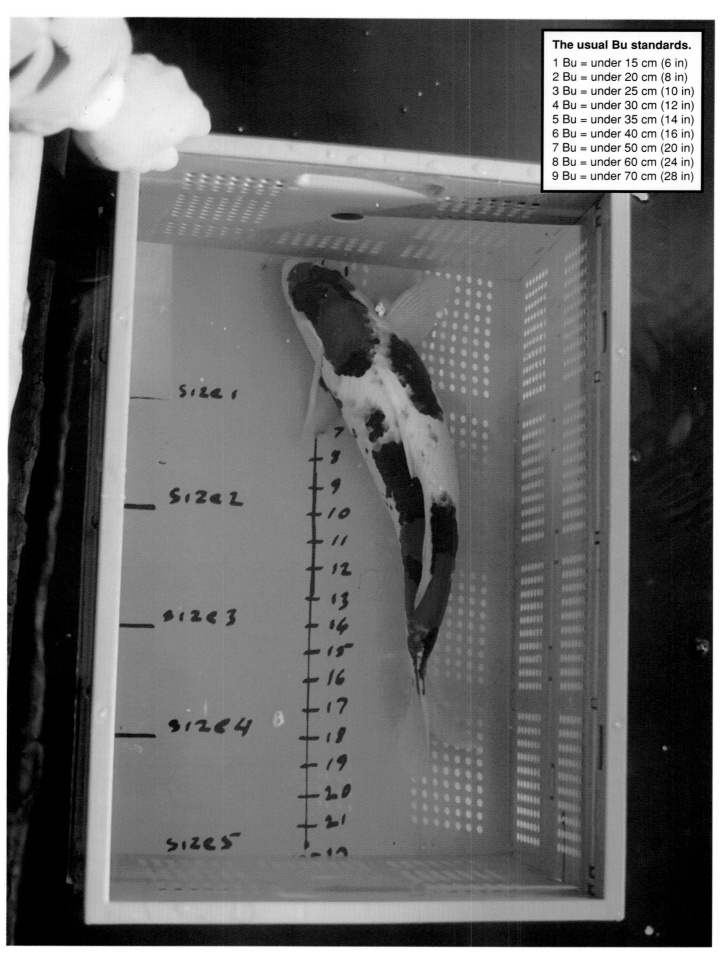

The usual Bu standards.
1 Bu = under 15 cm (6 in)
2 Bu = under 20 cm (8 in)
3 Bu = under 25 cm (10 in)
4 Bu = under 30 cm (12 in)
5 Bu = under 35 cm (14 in)
6 Bu = under 40 cm (16 in)
7 Bu = under 50 cm (20 in)
8 Bu = under 60 cm (24 in)
9 Bu = under 70 cm (28 in)

During competitions, koi are measured in a box like the one shown here. The markings can be in inches, centimeters or in Bu specifications.

THE FACE OF THE KOHAKU

An idealized Kohaku. This is a two color fish, red and white, and is the most popular color variety to be found in Japanese koi shows.

If you first observe any animal, humans included, your glance is primarily directed at the face, more specifically, at the eyes. The same is true for the kohaku strain of colored Japanese carp (koi or goi, whichever you prefer). The kohaku strain must have red (hi) on its face. For good quality show koi, the red should be above the eyes and certainly below the lateral line. All kohaku's color patterns begin with the red on the head.

If the kohaku has only red on the head and this red resembles an isolated circle, square, diamond, oval or shield, then this strain of kohaku is referred to the tancho group. But to be a tancho, the kohaku may not have even a single scale of red anywhere else on the body. A kohaku with the tancho on the head is called a *tancho kohaku*. That is, first of all it is a tancho, and the fact that it has only red and white makes it a kohaku.

For good quality in terms of modern standards (and most of the world uses Japanese standards), kohaku must possess all their color in the top 50% of the body. This requirement originates with the realization that koi are observed from the top and ALL color must be visible from above. While it is quite true that MOST koi are viewed from above in ponds from the banks or from bridges, there are koi that are on display in public aquariums or in homes where they are usually viewed from the side. Ultimately, you must decide. Most koi keepers do not enter koi competitions, so they want a koi with as much color and as interesting a color pattern as possible.

The ideal tancho spot is a true circle, but very few kohaku varieties have true circles. An interesting variety of kohaku is the tancho with other red. The red can be on the lips, in which case the fish is called a *kuchibeni*, or it can run from the tancho spot to the snout in which case it can be referred to as a *hanatsuki*. The *maruten kohaku* is a kohaku which has a tancho on the head and other red on the body.

While you might have two absolutely perfect *kuchibeni* lipstick kohaku with beautiful tanchos, breeding them together is far from a guarantee of any look-alikes. Koi do not breed in colors according to our expected Mendelian ratios. Some characteristics, like German scalation, is fairly predictable.

The Body of the Kohaku

The idea of red markings on a white body, plus red on the head is what kohaku are all about. The head red marking must be separated from the body marking if you care about show standards. While very interesting kohaku patterns are possible with continuous red markings from the head to the tail, usually a separation is appreciated.

Where the red markings are spots and not large blotches, the correct definition of these markings is *komoyo*. When you wish to refer to large blotches of red, you call these blotches *omoyo*. Since we have nothing but Japanese names for these characteristics we are locked into the Japanese language. They have the same problem with baseball...the words *strike, walk, ball, home run, etc.* are all words in the Japanese vocabulary.

Kohaku with a single large blotch from head to tail are referred to as *ippon hi*, which means *single or one red*. There are dozens of further adjectives to describe the red markings on a kohaku. The *tobihi* is a splashed pattern and some fancy pigeons in Japan are also referred to in the same way. In the USA we call these pigeons *splashes*.

One of the first words you learn in Japanese when you live there as an American (like the author did), is the term *ichi ban*. Ichi ban means *number one*. For a koi to be *ichi ban* means it is top notch, a champion. The Japanese words for number two are *ni ban*. *San ban* would be number three but the Japanese do not go further than *ni ban*. A *ni ban* is the most polite term for junk, garbage, or *feed it to the piranhas*. Depending upon where you go in Japan, there are other words...many not so polite, though most Japanese koi breeders are polite to the extreme. As a rule they are farmers and without great formal education, but there are some brilliant minds which are also dedicated to koi and Dr. Takeo Kuroki, a physician, immediately comes to mind.

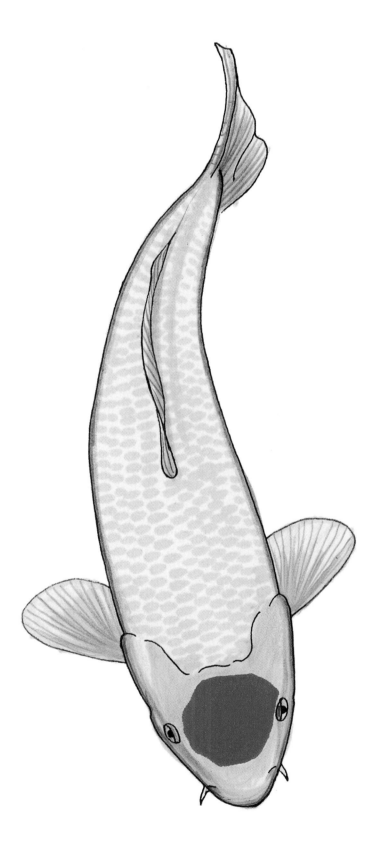

If the Kohaku only has red on the head and the red resembles a circle, square or rectangle, the fish is called a Tancho Kohaku.

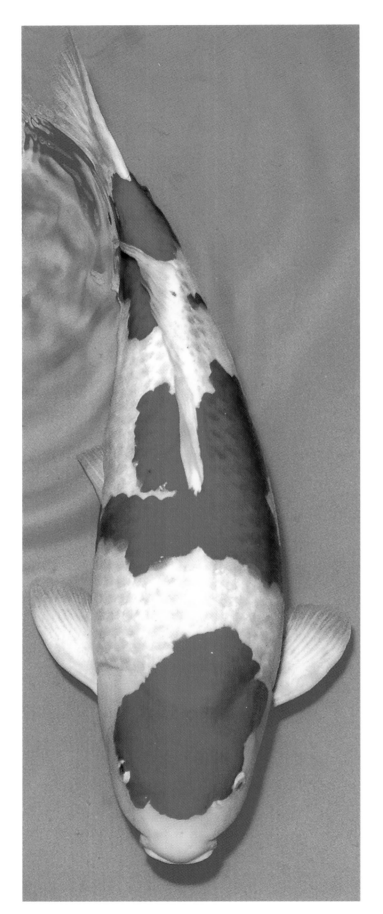

A champion Kohaku over 75 cm (30 in) long.

Kohaku Color Patterns

There are dozens, hundreds perhaps even thousands of kohaku color patterns. But all of these patterns fall into one of two categories.

INAZUMA KOHAKU are ippon hi kohaku which means they have one large blotch and this blotch runs from the head to the tail (not THROUGH the tail...only to the tail.) Koi like this are fairly rare but they are not more valuable than the disconnected patterns. As a matter of fact they are even less appreciated.

Good kohaku should not have red in the tail, but they should have red markings on the caudal peduncle, which is the area immediately before the tail fin begins. If a kohaku has no color on its caudal peduncle it is called a *bongiri* and is usually disqualified from major competitions.

STEPPING STONE KOHAKU are kohaku with blotches along the back which remind one of the stones used in Japanese gardens for walking on the usually wet mud. These blotches are usually referred to as *dangara*. Kohaku with two dangara are referred to as *nidan kohaku*. The Japanese have many ways of numbering something. The third floor of a building would be called *sankei* because the *kei* is the ending

Two champion Kohaku with very beautiful markings and a deep red color on lovely white skin.

This glorious Tancho Kohaku won the Grand Prize in the Wakagoi (Young Carp) Section. It was 40 cm (16 inches) long.

In 1995 this magnificent male Kohaku won the Grand Prize in the Kyogoi (Big Carp) Section (Males). The fish was over 75 cm (30 in).

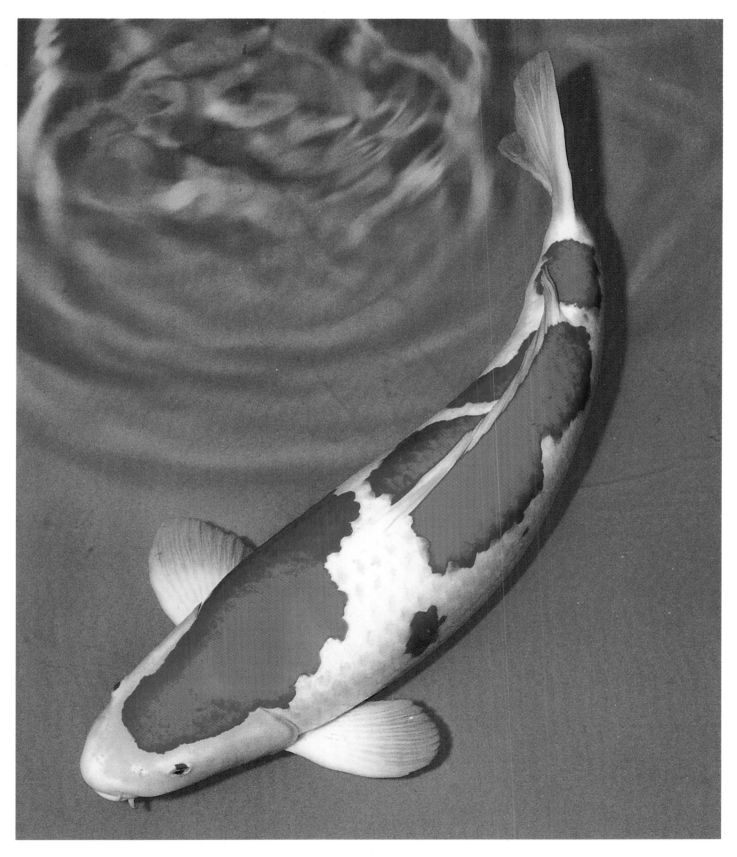

The Grand Prize in 1995 All-Japan Show in Tokyo went to this lovely Kohaku in the Seigyo (Adult Carp) Section (Males). The fish measured 70 cm (28 in).

This gorgeously colored champion Kohaku won the top prize in the female section for large carp. She was over 80 cm (32 in).

for counting things that are flat. *Sandan* is what kohaku with three dangara are called. I recall there are a dozen or more ways to count, but usually more than four dangara are not acceptable because the red blotches would be too small then and would hardly be recognizable as a stepping stone pattern when viewed from above in anything but the most sparkling clear water. The four step kohaku, perfectly balanced with the same amount of red on both sides of the fish, is the most highly prized.

Like all red markings on a kohaku, it is necessary to have balance. This is *artistic* balance and need not be geometrical, though geometrical would be greatly appreciated because it almost never exists on kohaku.

The Lightning Pattern
About 1989 when I visited the All-Japan Nishikigoi Competition in Tokyo, I was impressed by a man they called *Osaki-san*. I couldn't tell if they were referring to the city of Osaka or the drink *Sake*. Anyway, Osaki-san had a fish which had a lightning bolt running down its back, crossing the top of the dorsal so it was almost even on both sides of the body. I was told this fish was sold for $50,000!!!

The Kohaku's Fins.
In general any color at all in a kohaku's fins is disqualifying. There are circumstances, however, when the kohaku is of such fine quality in all other regards, that a little spot on the fins is forgivable.

Unfortunately, there are dyes available which enable you to put color where it wasn't meant to be. It is also possible to take the red scales from a hi patch and transplant it into a mismark. I was able to take some of the red scales from the hi tancho of a kohaku and transplant them into the scale pockets of scales I removed from the side of the fish, thus spelling my initials. This fish-doctoring is frowned upon but is not forbidden specifically by most club rules since there is no way to prove that a transplant has taken place.

The technique, by the way, is simple. Simply anesthetize a koi with MS-222. Then carefully remove the scales you wish to replace. Then remove the scales you want to transplant, one at a time, and put them into the empty sockets from which the objectionable scales were removed. It may take a little practice, but it certainly doesn't bother the koi as I've done hundreds of these transplants and have yet to get an infection or death among the participating koi. I was never satisfied with transplanted scales from one fish to another, though some people have told me they have done it successfully.

FINAL WORDS ABOUT THE KOHAKU COLOR VARIETY

Perhaps the most simple of color combinations for koi development is the kohaku, a strain of red and white. The Japanese favor this variety for two important reasons: their flag is red on white, like the kohaku, and this was the first color variety to be *fixed* genetically. But, while producing red and white koi is not difficult, getting one that measures up to the strict standards of the breed is something else. The Japanese koi breeders have strict standards. No kohaku is good unless it has red (hi) on the head; it should not have hi on the belly; etc.

Even when the strict standards are met can a kohaku be judged for its beauty and grace and this is where the judge's art begins. For this reason raising great kohaku is VERY difficult. As a matter of fact, great kohaku may well be the most difficult variety to breed. An often quoted statement is something like *Great koi breeders start with the kohaku and end with the kohaku*, insinuating that they tried other color varieties but the only REAL challenge was in breeding great kohaku.

Dr. Takeo Kuroki wrote (in *Tropical Fish Hobbyist Magazine*, October, 1993) about the problems in breeding great kohaku. Following is an extract of this article:

...the kohaku is so important that it demands more detail (than other breeds). First, let's talk about the best patterns for the head, body, tail and fins. We should keep in mind that few koi will fulfill all of the fundamental points which follow; they are not necessarily worthless because of this. Very few koi are perfect.

As far as he head is concerned, a red marking (hi) is indispensable here. Even if it has beautiful markings on the body, a kohaku without a head marking will be culled. The ideal shape of the head marking is something like a U-shape, with the curve of the U forward. Some irregular shapes can be quite pleasing too, however. The hi should

The fake Kohaku with German scalation. The scales of this so-called Sweetheart Koi were transplanted.

be confined to the top of the head; if it covers too much of the head we refer to it as a red mask, and these are not preferable.

The head hi should come nearly all the way to the tip of the snout and down to the eyes. The region around the mouth should be clear. Some koi have a red marking around the mouth; these are called lipstick koi *and are generally disliked. Only when the head hi does not come down to the level of the eyes does the lipstick produce the necessary balance.*

The back should have a pattern that is well balanced on both sides. A large marking in the shoulder region makes a kohaku look especially attractive. A V-shaped white cut on the shoulders is especially desirable. A continuous pattern from head to shoulders without any cuts looks dull.

It used to be that only the pattern on the back was highly appreciated, but now that which spreads down somewhat toward the abdomen is praised. This is called deep wrapping. *Mind you we do not want any red markings on the belly itself.*

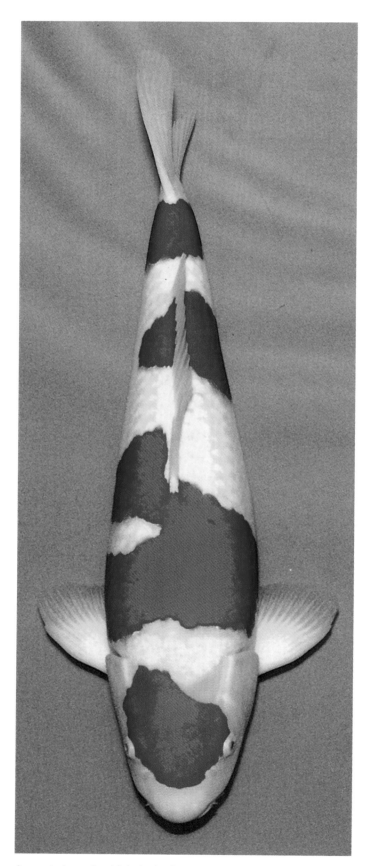

A great champion Kohaku in the 60 cm (24 in) size group. The very white skin, the deep red and the sharp edges make this a truly remarkable Kohaku.

A small red marking called the last hi *or* tail stop *is desirable on the top of the caudal peduncle. Ideally, there should be about a 2-centimeter (one inch = 2.54 cm) break between the tail stop and the tail itself. At any rate, the red must never extend onto the tail. In addition, none of the other fins should carry any red color, particularly the pectoral fins.*

We can summarize the important features of a fine kohaku in the following five points:

    1. Bright hi.

    2. Clear edges.

    3. No hi over the eyes or fins.

    4. No hi markings spreading below the lateral line.

    5. A head hi not spreading below the nose, and a tail hi not spreading onto the caudal fin.

All of these five factors are important, but there can be a bit of a leeway on point 4. to allow for the deep wrapping which is preferred today. However, there is nothing at all wrong with nishikigois whose markings are confined above the lateral line, and in fact these are more traditional. (N.B. Most koi shows held outside of Japan disqualify kohaku with red markings below the lateral line).

There is a tendency today that strange and unique koi are highly prized. This is good but such koi can only be appreciated by comparison to the standard type.

Remember there are kohaku of both Japanese and German (doitsu-goi) *lineage. Most of the Japanese type are fairly traditional in appearance, while the German lineage are often a bit more experimental. The doitsu-kohaku often look very fine when young, with sharp, clear edges to their hi markings. The mirror koi with their neatly arranged scale rows look much better than the leather koi with their random scalation. Still, both types of doitsu-goi often lack imposing appearance when they are larger and generally lose to the fully-scaled Japanese-type kohaku in koi shows.*

Although it is not always easy to evaluate koi of any variety, especially kohaku, if you can memorize and apply the five fundamental points you will be well on your way to knowing a good kohaku when you see it.

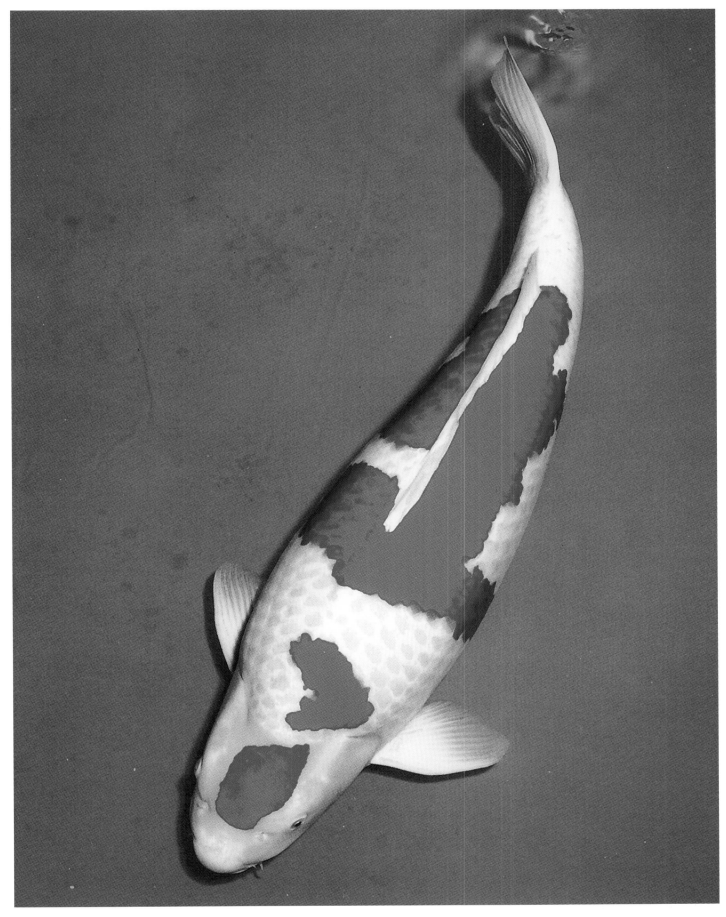

This Kohaku was the Grand Champion in the 24th All-Japan Nishikigoi Show held in Tokyo in 1955. It was an 85 Bu (85 cm = 34 in).

The Grand Prize in the Kyogoi (Big Carp) Section went to this huge Kohaku of 85 cm (34 in).

Here she is...considered by some to be the Taisho Sanke of the Year, this 85 cm (= 34 in) fish won the Grand Championship in the 26th All-Japan Nishiki-Goi Show held in Tokyo in 1994.

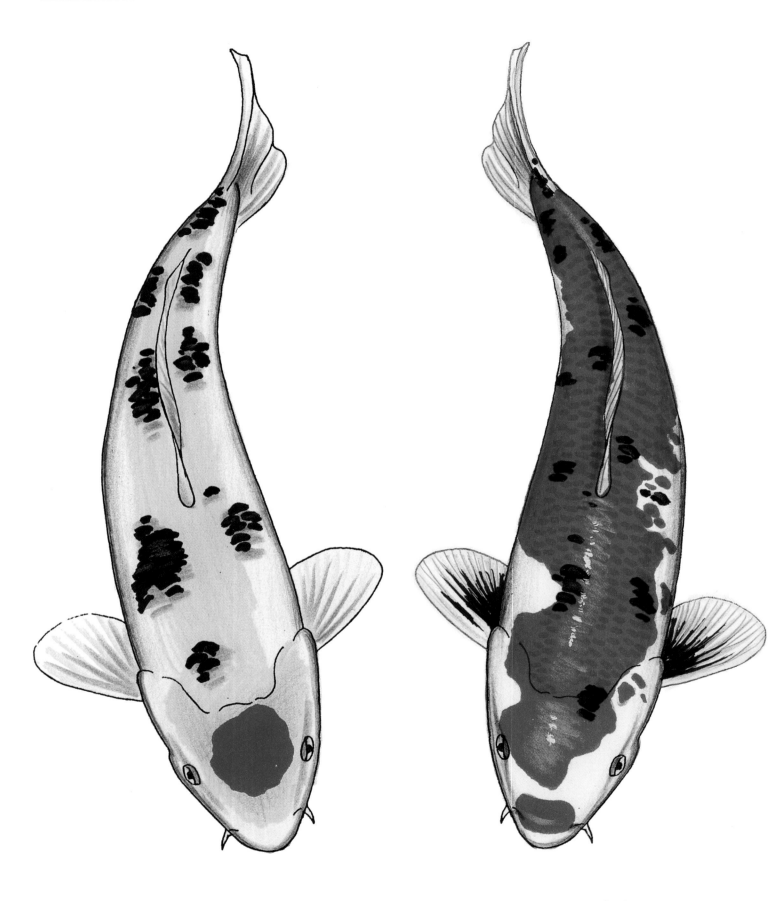

Idealized Tancho Sanke.   Idealized Aka Sanke.

kohaku but the red should be enhanced by the black markings and not compete with it. This is a tough call for the judges.

The black or sumi must be deep black or even slightly purple when they are large. They must never show white underneath the black scales and the black must NEVER be visible on the head! A real fault is when the sumi overlay the red. Fish with this characteristic are usually culled.

While this color variety is the second most popular, as evidenced by the numbers entered into koi shows, they are much more difficult to produce than kohaku. Often great taisho sanke are more expensive than excellent kohaku, but great kohaku are more readily available than excellent taisho sanke.

There are many adjectives added to the *taisho sanke* designation. The *maruten sanke* is a tancho (red mark isolated on the head). The *aka sanke* is a taisho sanke whose black is found spread unevenly throughout the body when viewed from above. There should be no color or black on the belly.

The fins should have some black streaks. Some breeders claim that if the tail and pectorals have good sumi markings, the rest of the sumi markings will be more permanent, as a loss of sumi with size and age is a detestable characteristic of many taisho sanke strains.

Many other strains also show taisho sanke characteristics:

The *kanoko goi sanke kawarimono* is a freakish fish which is only allowed in shows in the Miscellaneous (kawarimono) Class. The terms kanoko goi means fawn-colored koi. The black markings are randomly scattered over the fish's body. The overlapping of the black and red marks produces the purple. The black usually extends onto the head. All in all this is a very handsome fish but not one universally accepted as a good koi type.

The koromo sanke is a three-colored fish derived from taisho sanke and ai-goromo. The ai-goromo is a kohaku with most of the red overlayed with a black scalation giving the fish a reticulated pattern. Most green fishes, like wild guppies, have the reticulated pattern. This is also found in wild carp. A good koromo sanke is a beautiful fish but rarely seen at shows.

The *tancho sanke* is basically a tancho which has the red marking on the head isolated from

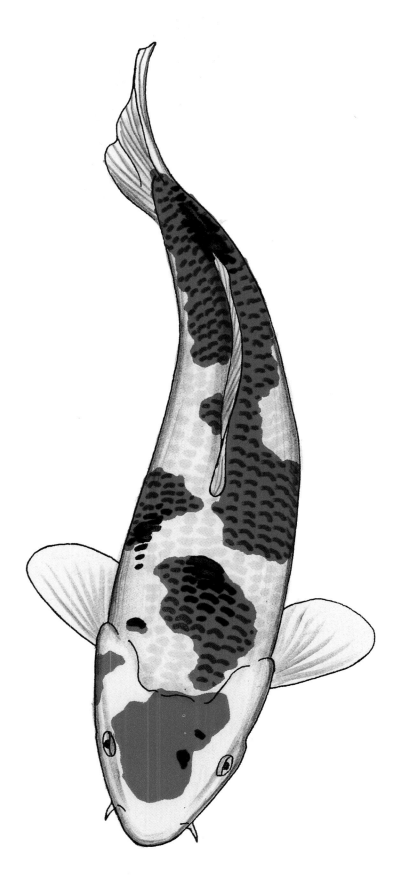

Idealized Sumi Goromo.

This champion Taisho Sanke took the Grand Prize in the Seigyo (Adult Carp) Section.

A champion Taisho Sanke 55 cm (=22 in) in length.

 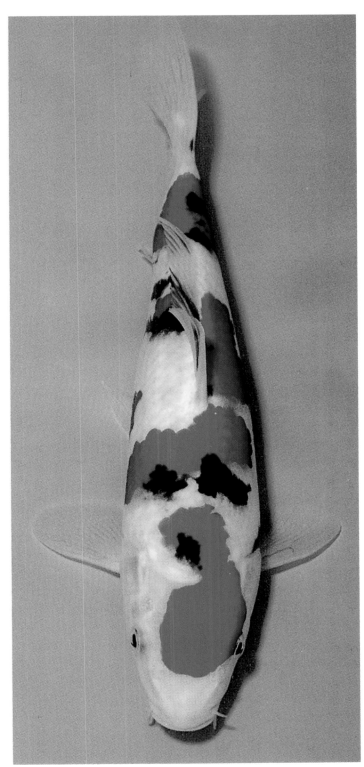

Two young winners of the Taisho Sanke prizes were the 20 cm (= 8 in) koi on the left and the 25 cm (= 10 in) one on the right. These are well marked fish with bright colors and such intensity is rare among small carp.

Two young winners of the Taisho Sanke prizes were the 30 cm (= 12 in) fish on the left and the 35 cm (= 14 in) fish on the right.

In the larger Taisho Sanke sections of the All-Japan Show, these two Taisho Sanke won prizes. The fish on the left is 50 cm (=20 in) and the fish on the right is 55 cm (=22 in).

This jumbo Taisho Sanke champion is 85 cm (34 in).

This champion Taisho Sanke features extremely contrasting colors and a white skin. This rare fish is 75 cm (= 30 inches) long.

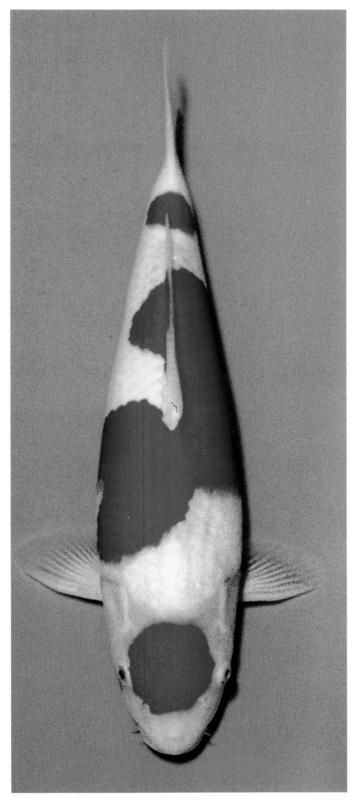 

Left: A champion Kohaku with a nice Tancho on its head. This fish should be compared with the Showa Sanshoku **(Right)** so you can appreciate the similarity of the two color varieties. Add black to the Kohaku or subtract black from the Showa Sanshoku. The Kohaku is 40 cm (= 16 in). The Showa Sanshoku is 45 cm (= 18 in).

Idealized Showa Sanshoku.   Idealized Tancho Showa Sanshoku.

the acceptable standards for this variety. If a taisho sanke has black on the head it is a cull! For people who have their koi spawning in the springtime, they might notice that the hatchlings of kohaku and taisho sanke are very light colored while the hatchlings of showa sanshoku are solid black. Therefore we think of showa sanshoku as black fish.

The black mark on the head of a showa sanshoku is very important. The most acceptable, and most common, is the head where the black will be an oblique, irregular line running from the snout region to the back of the head. This location then separates the colors white and/or red into distinct areas. The shape of this black is often remarked upon by judges and their imagination of this ink-blotch might make interesting study for an educational psychologist. When this black marking splits the red pattern on the head it has a special name, *menware*. The word *menware* (pronounced *men-wahr-eh*) means *divided head region* in Japanese. It does NOT mean *men's clothing* as I heard one expert(?) say.

It is standard that a taisho sanke should have no black (sumi) on the head, or very, VERY little, if at all. The showa sanshoku that has only the menware on the head are specially prized and exceedingly rare. The difference in the sumi (black) markings is also very different in these two color varieties. The black markings on the taisho sanke are rounded and usually are found on the back. The black markings on the showa sanshoku are large, extended blotches which usually pass deeply into the belly of the fish. I think about these type of markings as having a totally black fish and dropping globs of white or red paint on its back. These kinds of similes often run through the minds of the judges.

There are also differences in the fin markings of these two tri-colored varieties. In the taisho sanke, black markings are expected in the pectoral fins. The pectoral fins are the most important fins for koi lovers because they are the most visible when observed from above. In the taisho sanke, these black pectoral fin markings are limited to stripes running parallel to the rays of the fin, if, indeed, they are found at all. In the showa sanshoku the black markings are blotches which usually radiate from the insertion of the pectoral. This

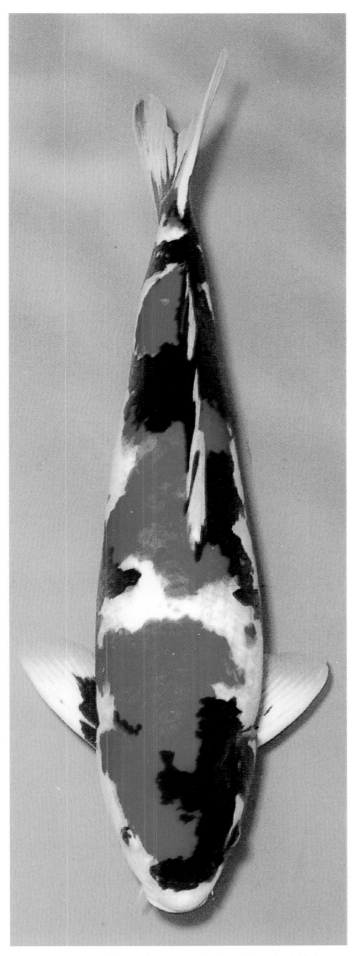

A champion Showa Sanshoku in size 60 cm (= 24 in).

The Grand Champion Showa Sanshoku in 1995 was 70 cm (= 28 in).

Left: Showa Sanshoku champion of 70 cm (= 28 in). **Right:** A super champion Showa Sanshoku in the jumbo class of 75 cm (30 in). Showa have to give the impression of being mostly a black fish

This grand champion Showa Sanshoku took the top prize in 1995. It was the Grand Prize Winner in the Sogyo (Adult Carp) Section at a size of 55 cm (= 22 in). The facial pattern seemed ugly to the author (HRA), but that's what makes judges necessary!

means the blotches are located at the base of these paired fins. They have no symmetry with the rays of the pectoral fins. The markings on the pectorals should be the same, but they are usually slightly different. During judging, the similarity of the markings may or may not carry a lot of weight, depending on the judge. The author has often been impressed by the blotches when several showa sanshoku are almost of equal quality when their other characteristics are evaluated.

The Japanese term for this black blotch at the base of the pectorals is *motoguro,* which literally means *black base.*

Frequently, a desirable shading affect called *checkering* (in Japanese the term is ichimatsu-moyo) can be seen usually beginning at the shoulder and ending in an intense sumi (black) mark.

History of the Showa Sanshoku.

Everybody concerned with the history of this color variety of koi seems to agree with Dr. Kuroki's story because it is available in English. He wrote:

The first showa sanshoku was bred by Jyukichi Hoshino of Takezawa in 1927. He crossed a ki utsuri (a black fish with golden markings which are often tainted with black specks) with a kohaku. The color of the hi in the first showa sanshoku had a distinct yellowish brown tinge. It was Tomji Kobayashi who first tried to make it scarlet by crossing with yagozen kohaku. He has been breeding excellent showa sanshoku since 1964.

It is the excellent colors found in the Kobayashi strain that have been credited with the extreme popularity of this magnificent color variety of koi.

Color Patterns Acceptable in Showa Sanshoku

The ideal showa sanshoku has an interesting menware black stripe splitting the head. When this stripe looks like a bolt of lightning, all the better. A Y-shaped pattern on the head is also acceptable providing it isolates the white and red coloring that might exist.

The pectoral fins must have black blotches on the bases of the pectoral fins. These blotches must never be striped or elongated. They must be deep black and they need not be the same on each of the pectoral fins in the same fish.

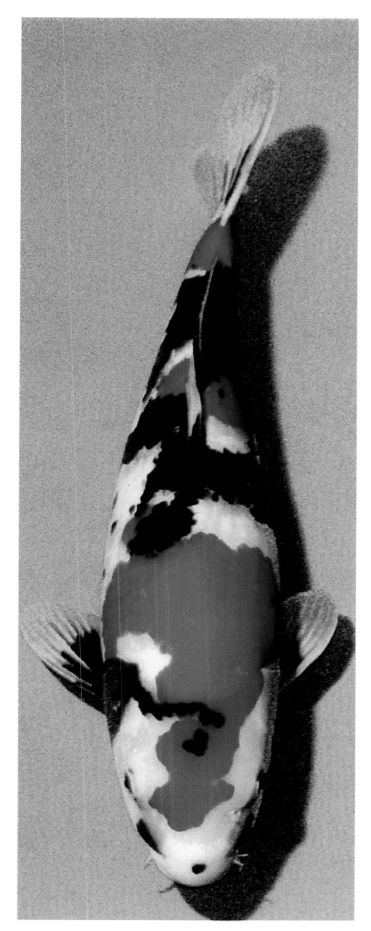

A champion Showa Sanshoku of 45 cm (=18 in).

A beautifully marked young champion Showa Sanshoku only 20 cm (= 8 in) in length.

The body black blotches must be arrogant, imposing, spectacular and deep black in color. You can best judge the meaning of these superlatives by looking at the accompanying photographs of champion koi.

The black markings on the body have to be interesting, too. A strain of showa sanshoku has an exceptional lightning bolt running down the back, separated by the dorsal fin, but very thick and deeply colored black. The black should be smooth and not disjointed. The edges of the black should not be gray. The more usual markings are shaped like clouds. That is, they must be thick, contrasting edged and continuous. These *clouds* of black should float in a sky which is red and white. The larger these black markings, the better.

The red (hi) color must be intense and follow the same general standards as in the kohaku color variety. The head must be emphatically colored red, just like a kohaku, but in the showa sanshoku the red can run over, around and below the eye, coloring the cheeks, chin and jaw. A colorful snout is also appreciated. Basically, it should have as much red as possible as long as there is still room for the necessary black. The red on the head should be intensely colored and not orange. In many English showa sanshoku, the head hi has a nice pattern, but for some reason the red is not uniform and greatly distracts from the total impression of the fish. The edges of the red color must be emphatic, clean and not shaded.

The white coloration is the key, because it accentuates the black and red areas. A good showa sanshoku should have about 25% of its body covered with white and the back should have 40% at most. The white MUST be pure milk white. It should not be tinged with yellow. Lovely showa sanshoku have a dorsal edge fully colored with red and black but in the middle is a cloud of white which isolates a deep black mark, making it an island in the sky. The white cheeks are often startling and the white on the caudal peduncle is almost a necessity, as it is for the kohaku and the taisho sanke.

There are at least a dozen sub-varieties of

Compare these two champion Showa Sanshoku. The fish on the left is 70 cm (= 28 in); the fish on the right is 75 cm (= 30 in).

This champion Showa Sanshoku is 55 cm (= 22 in).

showa sanshoku. All the German carps (doitsu-goi) can be colored like a showa sanshoku, as well as the following varieties:

The *hi showa sanshoku* is an intensely red fish that has more red than black. It should have no white on the dorsal edge so that red and black cover the entire top of the fish. Other than that, it should be a normal showa sanshoku.

The *boke showa sanshoku* is not an acceptable color variety in many countries, though the UK allows it into many of its shows. The black in this variety is not emphatic. It is grayish, pale and lackluster.

The *tancho showa sanshoku* is another faulty fish. Basically it is a tri-colored showa sanshoku with the tancho spot on the head. Depending on local rules, the black should be present on the head, but I have seen some tancho showa sanshoku with only a hint of black.

The *kin showa sanshoku* is a scale variation which glistens with metallic gold. Otherwise, the basic showa sanshoku standards apply.

The *gin showa sanshoku* is another scale variation. This variety has metallic silver scales. It,too, must follow the basic standards of the showa sanshoku. The kin and gin showa varieties are rare, expensive and often combined in show programs because there are always so few entries in these categories.

The *kanoko showa sanshoku* is a Miscellaneous Class (kawarimono) variety which has the fawn color instead of the black. The scales are edged. To find even a decent specimen of this color variety is an event.

The *kage showa sanshoku* features white scales which have black or gray centers. The edges of the scales are white and the centers are dark, making a net-like appearance in the white areas. This, too, is a very rare color variety.

The *koroma showa sanshoku* is similar to the kage showa except the white is pure and the center of the red scales is black while the scale edges are red. Of course, the black must extend onto the head as in all showas.

BEKKO

The *bekko* is a two-color variety of koi that usually appears as a by-product of taisho sanshoku. When these bi-colored fish appear they are inbred for the purpose of producing better quality fish, but this rarely happens.

By definition of the original Japanese standard, the *bekko* is a solid color fish with a color which contrasts with sumi (black). This background color, to be contrasting, must be yellow, red or white. Since the fish derives from taisho sanshoku (taisho sanke), the sumi markings should be judged according to that standard where these black markings are strategically placed to give the pattern an even balance. There are major differences between the taisho sanke (=taisho sanshoku) and the bekko in terms of the sumi markings.

In taisho sanke, the head must never have any sumi markings. In the bekko, while the black on the head is frowned upon, its appearance does not disqualify the fish because several champion koi with bekko coloration have had black marks on their heads *because these minor black markings balanced the black markings on the body of the fish.* Whereas striped sumi are required (or almost so), they are welcomed but not required in the bekko strains. In the taisho sanke, the pectoral fins should have striped black rays, in the bekko they can be anything... striped, blotched or white.

Because the bekko is such a simple fish, it is severely judged and even the most minor infraction eliminates it from championship. This is especially true of the aka bekko (*red bekko*) and the ki bekko (*yellow bekko*). For this reason the appearance of the ki bekko and the aka bekko at major koi shows is rare.

On the other hand, the shiro bekko (*white bekko*), is not uncommonly seen at large koi shows. They are so representative of the bekko family of two-colored koi that when people talk about bekkos, they always mean the white bekko.

What is said about the shiro bekko also applies to the other color varieties of bekko. All colors must be uniform, intense and of a single shade. You cannot have orange and blood red in an aka bekko. The standard calls for the most white background in the

A champion Bekko in the size 60 cm (= 24 in) class. A *bekko* is a solid colored fish with contrasting black markings.

An idealized Shiro Bekko is a black on white koi.   An idealized Aka Bekko is a black on red fish.

shiro bekko, certainly the same as in the kohaku. For some unknown reason, most bekko have a shadow around the head. This shadow is especially annoying when a beautiful white bekko (*shiro bekko*) with great sumi markings, is spoiled by a yellow head.

Color Patterns

The pattern of contrasting colors is always important in koi. Perhaps it is most important in the bekko because the fish is essentially a solid color with MINOR black markings. The colors cannot be metallic and must be as lackluster, uniform and flat as possible. This would then act nicely as a background of the densely pigmented melanophores which group together to form the small blotches for which the bekko is appreciated.

As with most koi varieties, the black markings should be visible from above, which means that they should occur on the dorsal edge of the body and not on the belly. Markings on the pectorals are judged with the balance of the body. They are not required.

Some standards dictate that the sumi (black) markings end before they abut the tail, while some recite that the sumi markings should stop before the tail. So, *at the tail* or *before the tail* is open for the judges' interpretation, but the sumi pattern should float in the background color, therefore it looks better if the sumi is very distinct from the tail and stops a respectable distance from the insertion of the caudal fin. Small sumi markings are ugly on this fish. These so-called *black heads* are never seen on show fish.

Unfortunately, as the fish grows, so do the sumi change. Sometimes they change for the worse, but more often they change for the better. For this reason, small bekko are more valuable than many other small koi.

For those who like exactitude, the black (sumi) on a bekko should be about 10% of the top half of the fish (between lateral lines). A fish with more than that requires a very strong background color and perfectly uniform sumi markings.

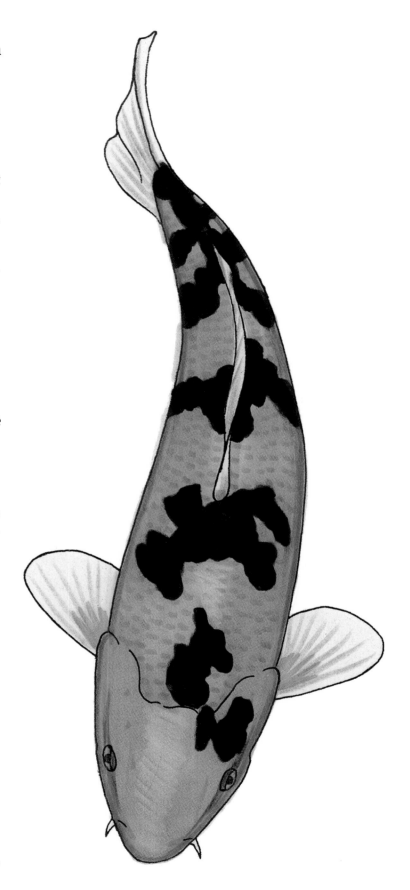

An idealized Ki Bekko is a black on orange koi.

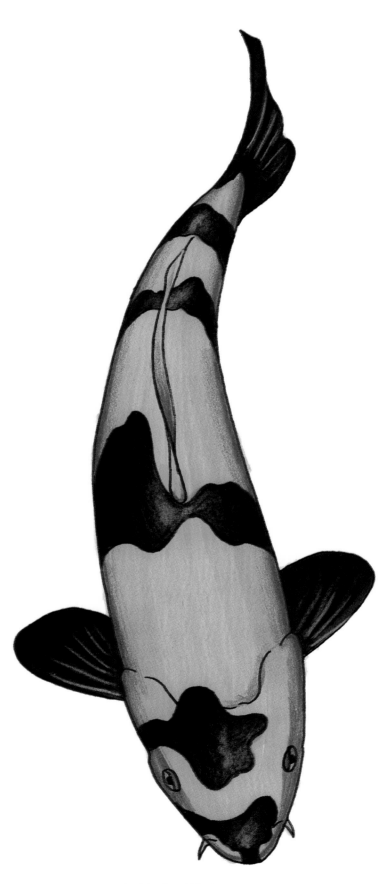

An idealized Kin Ki Utsuri.

UTSURI

Utsuri are usually (and originally) produced as by-products of the showa sanshoku. They are also originally derived from black koi. Now, as a matter of fact, they are produced directly from one or both parents being good utsuri to begin with. Like in the bekko, the yellow utsuri, *ki utsuri*, is very difficult to produce and they are rarely seen at shows. They are, in fact, the opposite of the bekko. Where the bekko had yellow, red and white background colors with black markings, the utsuri has black with contrasting markings in red, yellow and white. The same names apply to these color varieties, namely, the *shiro utsuri* is white with black markings; the *hi utsuri* is red with black markings; and the *ki utsuri* is yellow with black markings.

Beginners often confuse the shiro bekko and the shiro utsuri, but they should always keep in mind that in the utsurimono, the black is the predominant color and should always be at least 50% of the fish's color.

Color Patterns

In the same standard as the showa sanshoku, the black markings should cover the snout, the cheeks and jaws, a menware splitting the head, and a motoguro splash pattern at the base of the caudal fins. The demands on the hi utsuri and the ki utsuri as far as black markings are concerned is identical except for the motoguro on the pectoral fins. In the hi utsuri and the ki utsuri, the pectoral fins should have striped markings.

A shiro (white) utsuri must have large, outstanding sumi markings contrasting with milk white (=snow white) skin. Small sumi marks, unevenly spread over the fish, or even localized, are unattractive from the standard's point of view. A very desirable characteristic is the menware, a lightning shaped head sumi that divides the skull into at least two parts.

During the 1945-1950 period, fish that were mostly black were preferred, especially in the white utsuri. At that time people spoke about 10% of the fish being white. Now (1995), the last Tokyo show indicated that there was a decided preference for a 60/40 balance between the white and black, with more black showing than white. This often leads to considerable confusion when separating the two varieties, especially at pet shops and local koi shows.

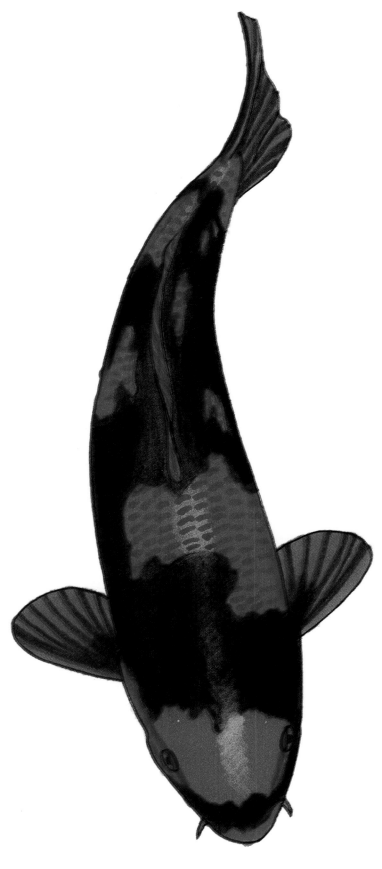

An idealized Hi Utsuri.

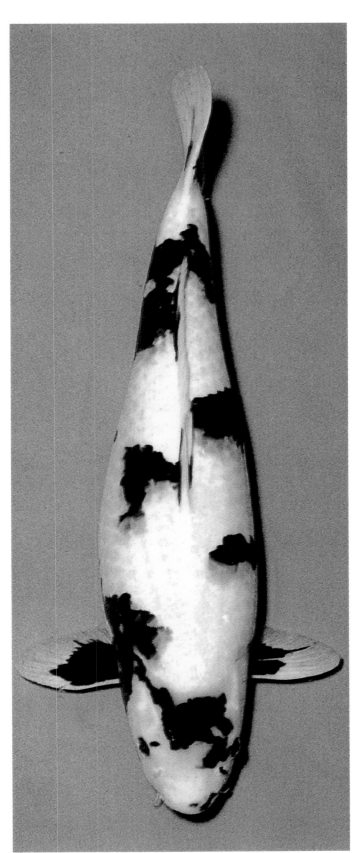

A champion Utsuri in the 60 cm (= 24 in) class.

A jumbo Utsuri in the 75 cm (= 30 in) class.

Shiro Utsuri

Sumi on the head.

The body is draped with blacks and whites. The black is restricted to the back, top, bottom and sides.

The pectoral fins should have major black motoguro striped or white or even be completely black.

According to Dr. Kuroki, during the Meiji period, 120 years ago, a ki utsuri existed and was prized. The Japanese koi breeders referred to this fish as *kuro ki han,* which is a black fish with yellow markings. It is interesting that *kuro ki* is the name of Japan's illustrious koi writer Dr. Kuroki (=kuro ki)! The equally famous historical figure, Elizaburo Hoshino, fixed the strain and presented standards for the variety. At the same time he named it *ki utsuri.* These fish, which are still around today, have intensely dense black markings, many of which are V-shaped. They even have some with metallic yellow markings (*kin ki utsuri*) (which are spectacular and highly prized.)

The dread of all utsuri breeders is black heads, which are small, irregular black markings spread over the body without apparent pattern. These are culls in Japan, but they are seen commonly at small koi shows.

In the red/black hi utsuri, the black markings in the pectoral fins, *motoguro,* are an absolute necessity. These motoguro should be balanced against each other, or as similar as possible.

Dr. Kuroki advises that fine hi utsuri effectively compete with kohaku and taisho sanshoku when they are all competing at large Japanese koi shows.

An interesting observation made by the author (who has written many books about freshwater and marine aquarium fishes) is that utsuri are colored more like domesticated mammals (dogs, cats, cows, pigs, etc.), than like naturally occurring fishes. Is there some genetic lesson to be learned from this? Certainly horses can be colored like shiro utsuri, but not humans! When black and white people have children, the children are darker than the white parent and lighter than the dark parent. In domesticated animals this is

Six examples of champion Utsuri koi which took prizes at the 1995 All-Japan Nishiki-goi Show held in Tokyo.

This champion Asagi won lots of prizes but the red is not very visible from above and it is doubtful that this author would have made a champion out of this fish.

usually not the case.

ASAGI

This color variety displays a blue scalation with a white belly and red below the lateral line, on the cheeks below the eye and perhaps some red in all the fins. It is not a very attractive fish but when many koi are kept in a pond or pool, they offer a welcome change.

The asagi is a very old color variety of koi, almost 175 years old. It first appeared, as did all color varieties of koi, among the offspring of the black or *magoi*. There are three recognized types of magoi. The tetsu (*iron*) magoi, the doro (*mud*) magoi, and the asagi magoi. None of these fish are startling, nor are they attractive unless shown with more colorful varieties.

The asagi magoi (which is really its proper name), now referred to simply as the *asagi*, has a blue back with a reticulated or net-like appearance. Each scale should be uniform with a darker center and lighter edges. This is what gives it the reticulated pattern. There are many shades of blue or gray depending upon many factors, diet being important, but genetic lineage becoming supreme. There hasn't been much improvement in this fish during its 175 year domestication and propagation because it is not an expensive fish. While each scale has its characteristic dark center and light edge, there are many variations of this separation, even with strains where the separation is indistinct and not contrasting. In all cases, the lighter the color blue or gray, the better.

Asagi Color Patterns

Aside from the blue reticulated back which is characteristic, an intense red or hi must predominate the cheeks, sides and pectoral fins. The other fins MAY have red, but the pectorals MUST have red. The red must be a blotch and the same color as the red on the sides and cheek. This red, or hi, must be an intense blood red. The more brilliant the red, the better the fish. Dull, brownish red koi are culls. The red pectoral fins, called *shusui* fins, should be outstanding and basically even. There may be some striated red patterns radiating from the blotch of red at the base of the pectorals. The preferred color of the pectoral should be dirty rather than snow white, but snow white pectorals with the red are acceptable.

Six examples of champion Asagi which took prizes at various All-Japan Nishiki-goi Shows held in Japan.

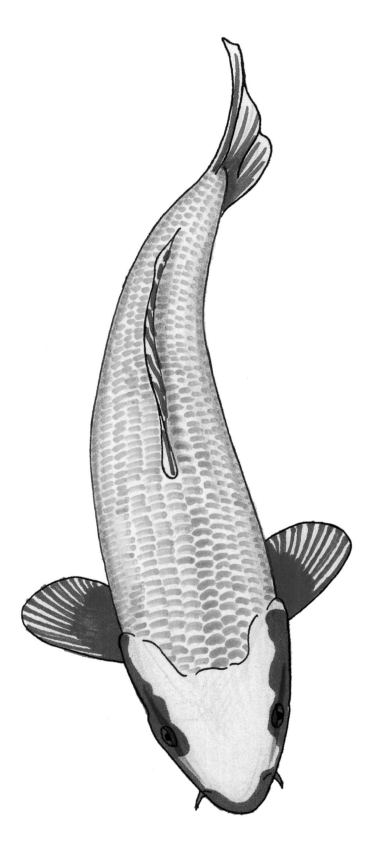

Idealized Asagi.

There should be an equal amount of blue and red with the red below the lateral line and blue above it. Larger, older asagi sometimes develop hi markings on the back where it should only be blue. This is a fault. Another common fault is the appearance of a black margin between the hi and the blue.

The head must be clear, being light blue to match the lighter parts of the scales. This is not difficult because the skin of this variety is light blue. The scales lack pigment on their edges and this is how the light blue edging of the scales originates. Any pigmentation on the head, even a tiny black or red mark, is totally unsuitable and fish showing head markings are culled.

The belly of the asagi should be a snow white. Because much of the skin is blue, the white is usually polluted, thus its value when it is white. There are several color varieties of the asagi, as follows:

The *konjyo* or *konyo asagi* has the same black as the original magoi.

The *narumi asagi* is a dark fish with heavy blue gray pigmentation in the center of the scales with white scale edges.

The *akebei asagi* is quite similar to the narumi asagi except the centers of the scales are light blue. This sub-variety is often called the *mizu asagi*.

The *taki asagi* is a koi with a white border between the blue back and the red abdomen. If this dividing line is black it is a major fault.

The *hi asagi* is a koi whose red is greater than the blue. The red may even run from the abdomen to the top of the fish. This is appreciated by some and culled by others. It depends upon the standards in the particular club. In major Japanese shows this variety is not usually accepted.

The *asagi sanshoku* may well be the most beautiful asagi color variety of koi. It features the typical blue, reticulated back of the asagi, but it has the magnificent red markings on the head and sides and a snow white belly. This is the strain which is crossed with the German scaled varieties (doitsugoi) to effectuate the shusui.

SHUSUI

The color varieties of koi that are called *shusui* are derived from the asagi. In 1909, Professor Yoshigoro Akiyama of the National Fisheries Institute produced the first shusui by crossing asagi with German *doitsugoi*. The types used were the mirror carp which were noted for the symmetry of the rows of scales running from the back of the head to the end of the caudal peduncle, with one row of scales on each side of the dorsal fin. Because the scales are large and easily seen, and are the only scales produced by this genetic defect, it is extremely difficult for the shusui variety to live up to the proscribed standard established in 1910 by Professor Akiyama.

Color Patterns

Basically, the shusui must have a head as light blue as possible, but not white. The two rows of scales MUST be blue. If they are any other color, judges usually disqualify them even though they are more beautiful than the blue scales. If the skin on the back is anything but light blue the fish is penalized. It cannot have the asagi colored skin, which is substantially darker. This is especially true of those shusui whose backs may be gray or black. Individual spots are frequently observed on the shusui's back and sides. These are faults.

The snout, cheeks and fins must have hi. The hi should be an intense, bright red. The pectorals should have as much hi as possible and should be balanced, one against the other. Too much red in one pectoral fin (or too little, for that matter) makes the fish look unbalanced.

Scales on any part of the body except the two rows is frowned upon and the shusui may be penalized if there are better shusui in the same competition. Sometimes there are bilaterally symmetrical clumps of scales on the shoulder which are found to be charming, but the specimen is better without them. It is really the call of the judge.

Some shusui have scales with silver margins. This is allowable under most show rules.

The fine shusui should have two huge bands of red running from the belly to the lateral line and from the snout and mouth THROUGH to the tail (and into the tail).

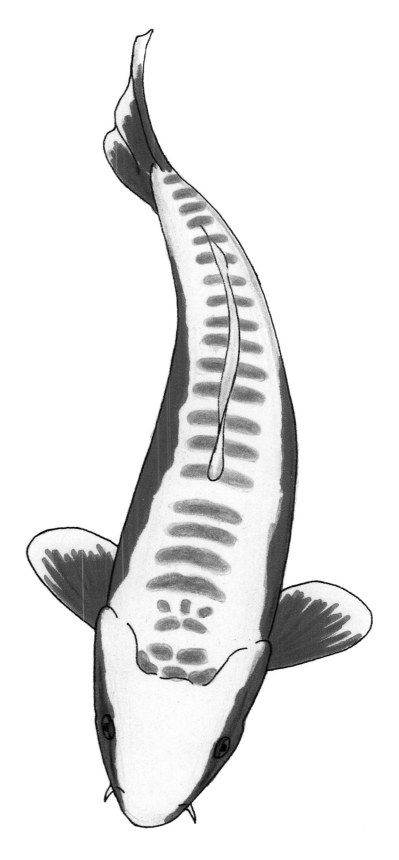

Idealized Shusui.

 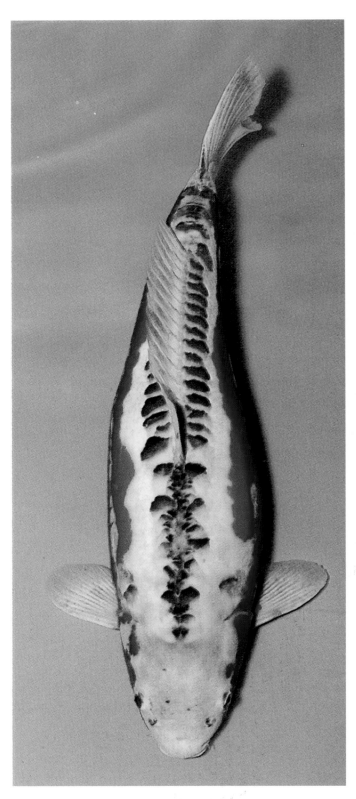

Left: A superb champion Shusui in the jumbo class at 85 cm (= 34 in). Compare this fish to the German scaled Doitsu Shusui (**Right).**

This should be a vivid red for a prized fish. If the color is orange, the shusui is usual. Not infrequently, as the normal shusui gets older, it becomes a hi shusui with the red creeping above the lateral line to the rows of scales, and sometimes even around them to cover the whole back. Of course you cannot see the hi under the scales.

Color Varieties

There are many sub-varieties of the shusui. Just a few of them are as follows:

The *hana shusui* has rotund red markings on the side like the petals of a rose. *Hana* in Japanese means *flower*.

The *hi shusui* is a red fish with bright red flames running from the belly to the back.

The *ki shusui* is a normal shusui except that instead of red, the hi areas are golden yellow.

There are also *sanshoku shusui, showa shusui, fuji shusui, bunka shusui* and *goshiki shusui.*

In the Miscellaneous Class (kawarimono) there are two famous examples. The *ginsui* and the *kinsui* were developed by crossing them with *ogon.* The ogon are bright, shining metallic scales which are extremely effective in koi coloration. They are best-sellers when they are small (up to about 6 inches = 15 cm) because as they get older their metallic iridescence becomes faded and may even disappear. Were there such fishes as 24 inch (60 cm) long ginsui (silver shusui) or kinsui (golden shusui), they would be extremely popular.

Two Doitsu Shusui in the young fish size below 30 cm (= 12 in).

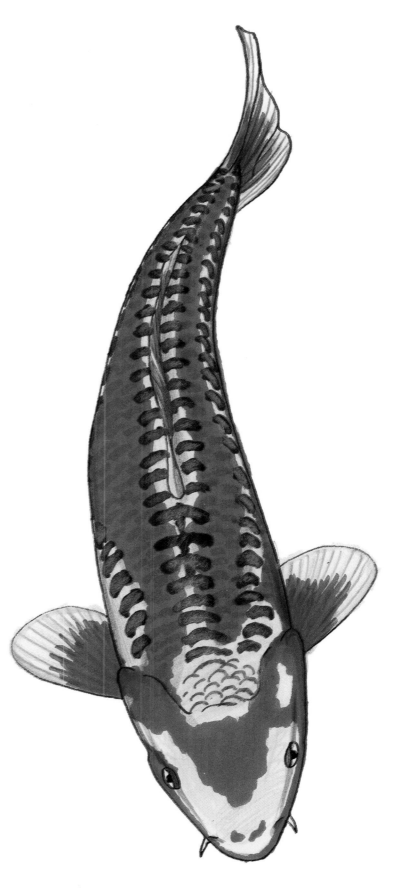

An idealized Hana Shusui. *Hana* in Japanese means *flower*.

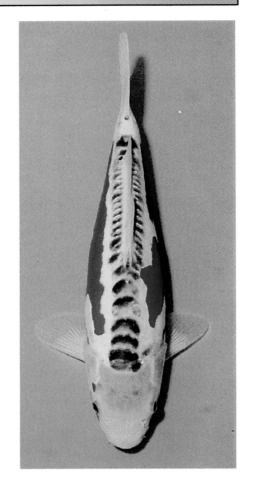
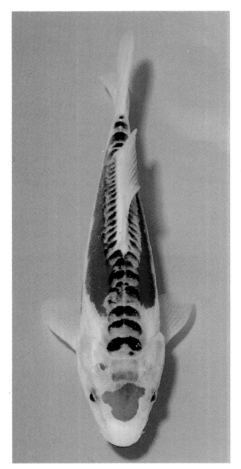
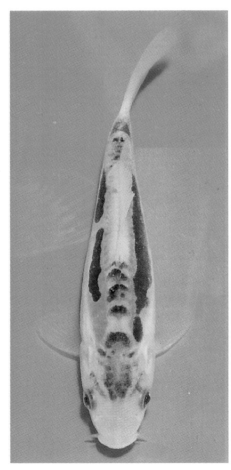
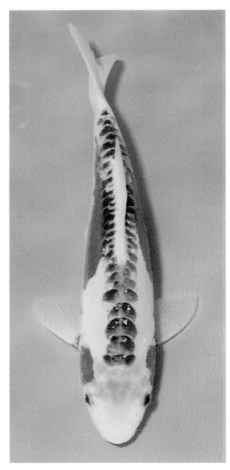

Six wonderful examples of Shusui with German scalation. All of these fish have excellent red/white separation. The lack of contrast in some fish is a result of poor photography.

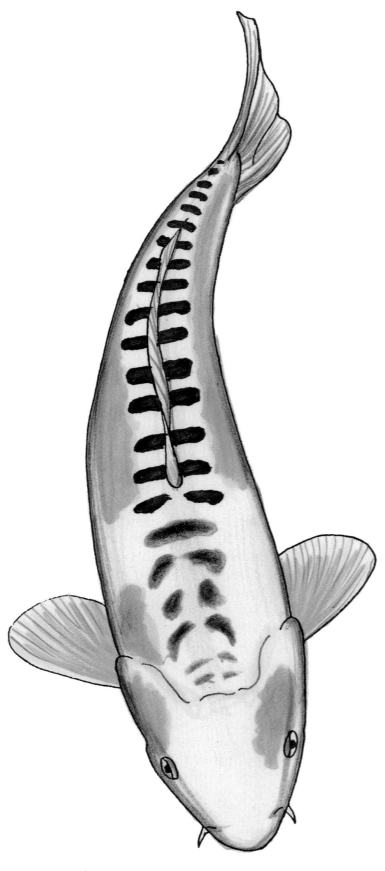

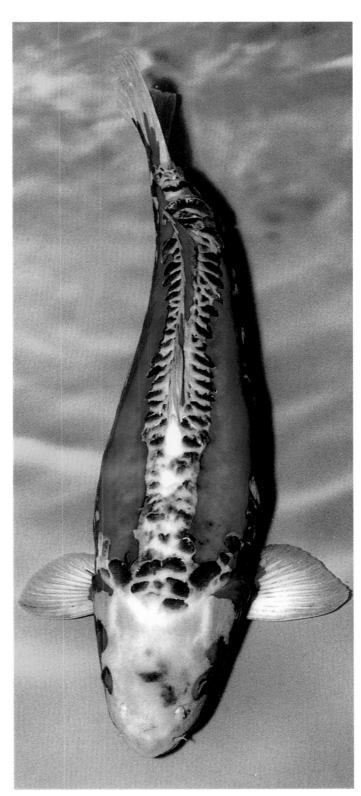

An idealized Kinsui. The Kinsui and the Ginsui are kawarimono (miscellaneous class).

A young Shusui showing wonderful color. This fish is only 14 cm (= 6 in).

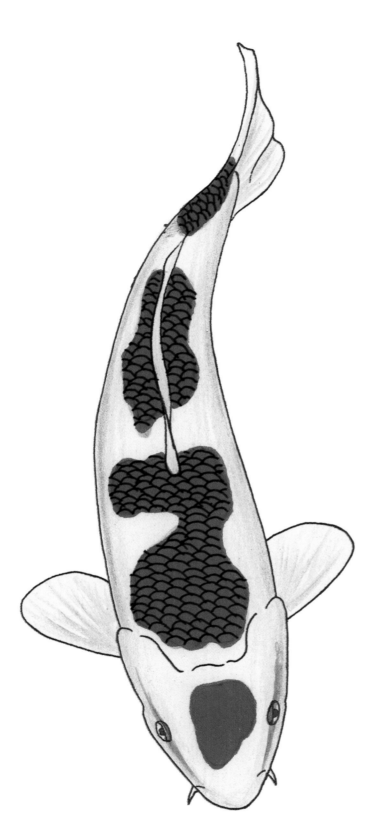

An idealized Aigoromo.

KOROMO

The koromo is one of the more rare varieties of koi. According to legend, someone crossed a male kohaku and a female asagi and produced fish which had an indigo blue reticulated pattern in the pigmented areas. The word *koromo* means a *garment* or something to wear. Thus, the veil of blue reticulated scales is referred to as koromo. There are many koromo (often spelled as *goromo*). The individual breeds will be discussed in more detail, but suffice it to say that such varieties as kohaku, taisho sanke and showa sanshoku, which have indigo-tinged patterns emphasizing the hi (red), are all called *aigoromo*.

Koromo have been available in Japan since 1950 when I bought some from a small breeder at the local Tokyo koi show. I was unsuccessful in producing any of these fish in Florida or New Jersey.

Aigoromo

The blue scales found on many varieties of koi are collectively referred to as koromo. The most popular of the group is the *aigoromo*. The prefix *ai* means *blue* in Japanese. This blue nomenclature refers to the blue scales which cover the red (hi) markings. The head of the aigoromo, though, must not have any blue reticulation.

The description of the color pattern of an aigoromo starts with comparing it to a kohaku. The aigoromo must have a good kohaku hi color pattern. The red must be intense, dense and cloud-like. These hi patches should be NEATLY, UNIFORMLY overlaid with the blue scales. The blue scales should NEVER appear on the white skin; only on top of the red, and better specimens even have the blue overlay falling slightly short of reaching the edges of the hi patches.

The fins of the aigoromo are usually white, but very charming aigoromo have red pigmentation in their pectorals, and, after all, red is the color of choice, and the pectoral fins are the koi's most outstanding appendage. So red pectorals are fully appreciated on aigoromo. Black in any of the fins is detested!

Most koi lovers buy koi when they are young, say 4-6 inches (10-15 cm) in length. This is not a wise practice when buying aigoromo as the blue netting becomes more intense and elaborate as the fish grows older

A champion Aigoromo.

A champion Aigoromo.

and larger. On the other hand, when the young show extremely well developed blue, the chances are that this will degenerate with age. The best aigoromo develop from youngsters that looked like excellent kohaku. Fine examples of aigoromo are rare, but they seem to be of exceptionally good quality when you do find them. They are often prize winners when placed into competition at local koi shows.

Exotic and Rare Koromo Types

There are quite a few different koromo types besides the aigoromo. It is theoretically possible, that any color variety of koi that has well defined large color patches could have these patches overlaid with the netting of the koromo, providing the base color is light enough for the netting to be seen. The koromo are not usual koi, but the most popular of the exotic and rare koromo types are as follows.

Sumigoromo

The substitution of the prefix *ai* for *sumi* indicates that the overlaid koromo netting is black and not blue. Not only is this webbing an intense black, or sumi, but it is a solid black, whereas the blue in the aigoromo is not solid. Thus the sumigoromo is a much more dramatic fish than the aigoromo.

Starting with a basic kohaku that has excellent hi markings, good sumi markings over the hi (but not quite reaching the edges of the red) seem to be constantly changing. Acceptable sumigoromo have nice head hi markings which are also laced with the koromo markings. If the markings are excellent in young fish, then it is usual that the markings fade when the fish grows older and larger. In contrast, when the sumigoromo started out as a young fish with no sumi at all, just a good kohaku, the sumi develop in a very pronounced fashion as the fish gets older and larger. Notice that the words *older and larger* are used in conjunction with one another. Poorly kept fish may get older, but not larger. Some may even shrink in body weight and thickness if fed improper food. An English lady once bragged to the author that she fed her koi dog food pellets because they were a lot cheaper than koi pellets. I asked her if she was training her koi to bark! She was insulted and complained to the authorities sponsoring the

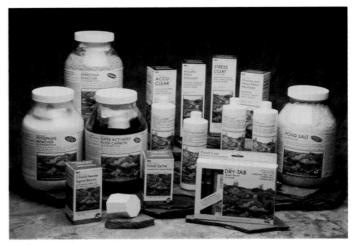

There are many fine products available at your local aquarium shop which can assist you in pond maintenance. Photo courtesy of Aquarium Pharmaceuticals.

show in which I was lecturing. I returned two years later and this very same woman came straight at me from across the room. I wasn't looking forward to seeing her again, but she walked up to me, stuck out her hand and apologized. She admitted that her koi suffered from lack of growth, loss of egg production in the females, and general color loss due to the dog food diet. I smiled when I replied: *...and they didn't even learn to bark!* This time she laughed with me.

The lesson to be learned here is that if you want to keep show-quality koi, you must provide excellent selection, care and feeding. Selection is important. If your collection of young is poor, you will have poor older fish. *GIGO* is the phrase word...*garbage in, garbage*

Water test kits are available at your local aquarium store. The kits can test for nitrates, nitrites, pH, ammonia and other parameters necessary for a healthy koi pond. Photo courtesy of Aquarium Pharmaceuticals.

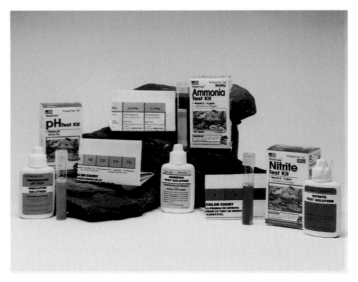

out. The care koi need is clean water, free of decaying vegetation and chemicals, and suitable light. The feeding is easy. Get a good brand of koi food from the shop that sold you the koi, or your local pet shop. BE SURE IT IS A NATIONALLY ADVERTISED BRAND as some suppliers buy trout or catfish pellets and weigh them out in plastic bags to be sold to the unsuspecting koi hobbyist. Most laws require that the package contain protein, fat, fiber, moisture and ash content. If the koi food you buy does not have a label indicating the nutrients and country of origin, don't buy it!

Obviously, proper development of the

Koi's color depends heavily on a well balanced diet. Special foods are available to enhance the color. Ask your local pet shop for special koi foods. Photo courtesy of Ocean Nutrition.

koromo types depends heavily on their care, and this is especially true of the sumigoromo.

Budo Sanshoku Goromo

The Japanese word *budo* means *grape* and in this variety the markings are both purple colored and look like a bunch of grapes hanging from a vine. The whole idea of koi keeping is the peace and harmony they can bring to your life. Each koi is studied and your imagination is free to depict the markings in any way that pleases you. The budo sanshoku is a good case in point because the pattern of the budo is the *least* obvious of the color patterns of the budo sanshoku.

Breeders produce budo sanshoku by crossing asagi and kohaku. This is the same way that aigoromo are produced, so in reality budo

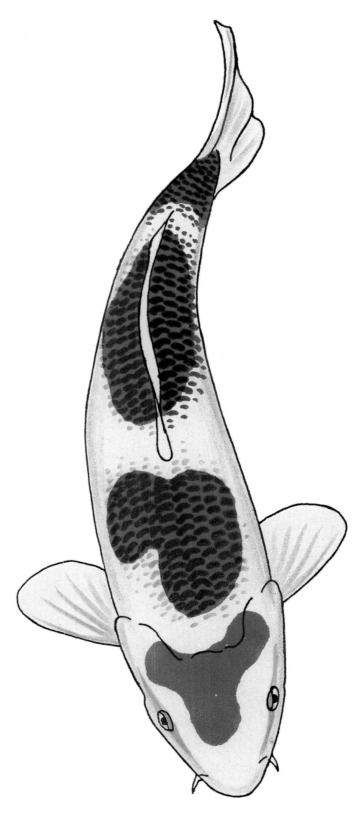

An idealized Budo Goromo. The Japanese word *budo* means *grape*.

A magnificent hagoromo. Unfortunately, this fish was created electronically to show an idealized specimen.

sanshoku are both by-products of the asagi/ kohaku cross-breeding programs at many fish farms.

The budo sanshoku is very similar to the aigoromo except that the blue is not intense in the budo sanshoku, thus it causes a more purple color. Light blue on top of red is the way artists create purple in the 4-color lithographic process where the only colors available are yellow, red (magenta), blue (cyan) and black. From these four basic colors, thousands of shades can be created.

A nice strain of budo sanshoku colors is available with German scalation.

As with all koi color varieties based upon the kohaku, the white should be snow white and not yellow. The hi (red) mark on the head should be red and not purple, as the koromo should not overlay the red.

In budo sanke, you have purple sanke (three-color) koi which are produced by the blue overlaying the basic red blotches. The head should be white and clear of all markings.

The koromo sanke has the netting over the scales giving it the well known reticulated pattern, but it is not purple like the budo sanke. Instead, the koromo net is tight, thin black lines. The more distinct these lines are, the better. The sumi (black) should cover all the hi (red) blotches except on the head. The head hi must be pure, intense and as tancho-looking as possible.

Of the many koromo types available, the hagoromo is especially attractive...and very rare. The hagoromo is very similar to the aigoromo with its blue body, but the hagoromo has flaming red cheeks and pectoral fins which are extremely attention-getting when it swims past you in clear water. This strain, according to Dr. Kuroki, was created by Masanaga Kataoka in 1956 by crossing a female asagi with a male ogon.

Lately (1995), many of the Japanese exhibits had many more koromo than in the past. German scaled koromo (doitsugoromo) with various intensity of the netting were on display. The netting is, of course, caused by the incomplete markings on some scales. It is expected that this increased visibility of the koromo color variety of koi will enable progress to the standards developed for these various strain.

Wonderful examples of koromo types. If you can remove all coloration except red and white, you should be left with a fine Kohaku. It is said that this fish derived from an Asagi and a Kohaku.

KAWARIMONO

According to the standards presented by Zen Nippon Airinkai, the Japanese official koi society, and the standards by which the important *All Japan Show* annual competitions are judged, the basic 12 koi groups are completed by the thirteenth group called the kawarimono. At the January, 1995 All Japan Show this grouping was changed and renamed the KAWARIGOI to contain the old Kawarimono and another group. Other organizations both in Japan and world-wide, have added additional categories (such as the long-finned koi, which are not recognized in Japan at all). In order to make the categories as complete as possible and, as a result of political infighting, the Airinkai established the kawarimono. This section includes *many* of the koi that are not included in the other twelve categories. The key word is *many* since not *all* other koi varieties are acceptable for the All Japan Show held in January every year.

having quite a time of categorizing the newer varieties. In 1994 they had 23 different categories. In 1995 they only had 21 categories.

Since this is a catch-all category, it can be described as the Miscellaneous Class in the show. A great many kawarimono have been produced by crossing the well established koi varieties with each other. Sometimes kawarimono have more than two breeds involved with the cross; others may be very complicated.

Kawarimono almost never win major shows because there are usually few standards for these exceptional varieties. Thus the usual winners are the kohaku or taisho sanke, which have very complete standards and very experienced judges. But the kawarimono are very popular and may very well be the best selling group since commercial breeders and

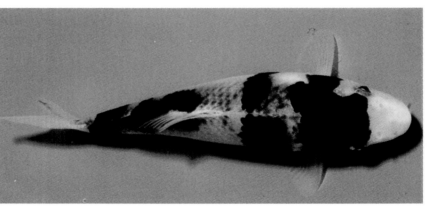

Examples of champion kawarimono.

Because this book will not be used for the All-Japan Show, but rather for the thousands of shows outside Japan, we'll stick with the *kawarimono* grouping. Most of the smaller shows in Japan have also opted for the kawarimono grouping instead of the kawarigoi. By the way, the All-Japan Show is

retailers of koi sell the non-standard breeds under the Japanese name *kawarimono* to impress their potential customers. Then, too, many kawarimono are very colorful and interestingly marked so they make welcome additions to the mixed population of regulation koi.

Examples of champion kawarimonos in varying sizes. The koi upper left is 25 cm (=10 inches); the center upper fish is 35 cm (= 14 in); the fish top right is 40 cm (= 16 in); the fish lower left is 45 cm (= 18 in); the center below is a kawarimono of 50 cm (= 20 in) and the bottom right kawarimono is 55 cm (= 22 in).

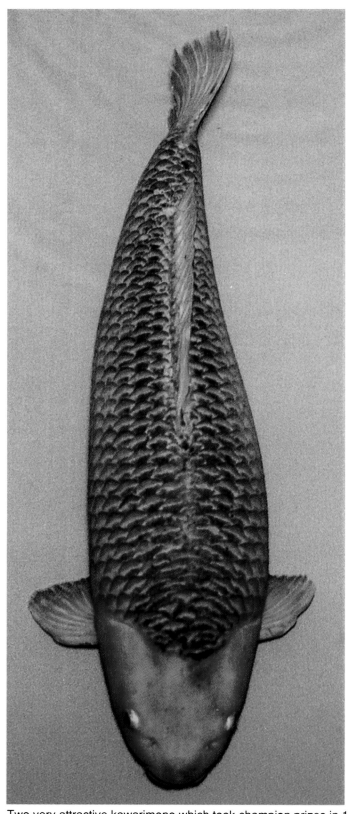

Two very attractive kawarimono which took champion prizes in 1993 at the All Japan Nishiki-goi Show held in Tokyo.

Dr. Kuroki said it right: *They* (kawarimono) *add spice to any collection of koi.*

Like the other koi varieties, there are many, many sub-varieties of kawarimono. The sub-varieties are almost limitless depending upon the rules of the particular show-sponsoring organization. Following are some of the more usual kawarimono.

Kigoi and Chagoi

Over the years there have been two categories of kawarimono that habitually appear at major Japanese koi shows. These are the *kigoi* and the *chagoi*.

The *kigoi* is a brilliant golden yellow koi. It shows no other body color. They are very popular with koi hobbyists who have ponds with dark bottoms and sides (as almost all hobbyists have) because they stand out against a dark background.

Not genetically related to the *kigoi* are the *akame* kigoi. These are albinos with the albino pink eyes. Thus an akamuji, benigoi, or aka hajiro, which are deep red koi with no other colors except white, can have an albino form which would not be called an *albino akamuji* but would be called an albino kigoi! When crossing any albino kigoi with each other, it doesn't matter which is the origin of the albino specimen. All the offspring will be albino. But if you out–cross an albino kigoi with a normal kigoi or any of the red fish (akamuji, benigoi or aka hajiro), the resultant offspring look like the normal parent. For experienced koi keepers, the yellow of the albinos from the three red varieties is not *golden* yellow but more a mustard yellow.

Albino kohaku have the same mustard colored hi (red), which is very unusual appearing.

Chagoi

Cha means *tea*. It can also mean *brown*, or honey or mustard color. Thus a chagoi is a tea-colored, non-metallic, single color koi. It is said that when you produce a chagoi with a doitsu scale pattern, it will be your most friendly koi. Many pet shops have large indoor koi ponds. They usually sell small packets of koi pellets so the koi can be fed by children (adults, too!). In studying the tameness of different color koi, the author has concluded

An idealized Kigoi is a bright, golden yellow and must not have any other body color.

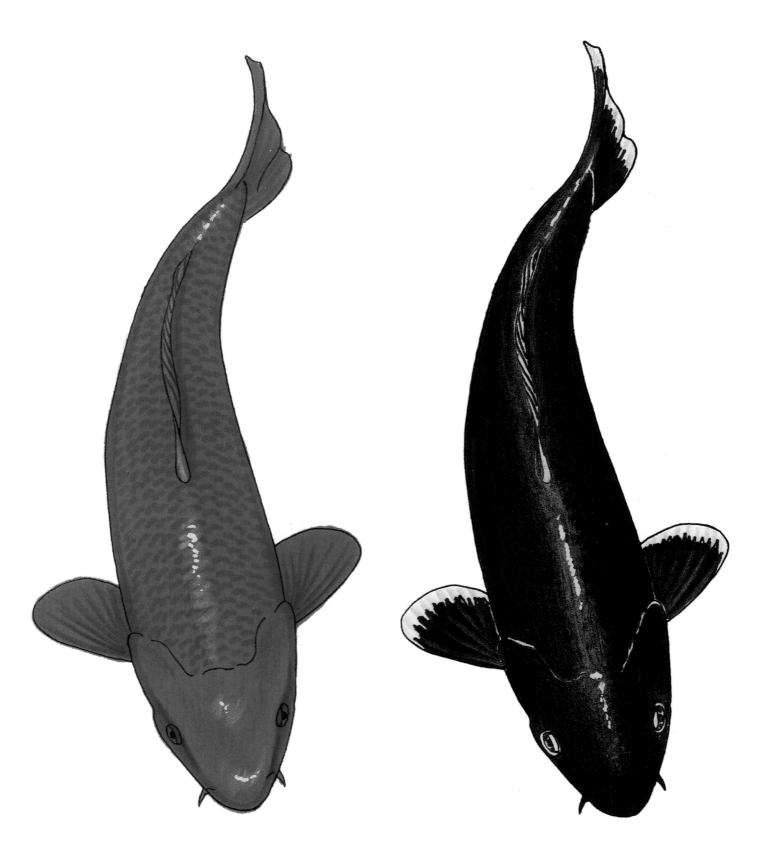

An idealized Benigoi should be all red.   An idealized Karasugoi should be all black like a raven.

that the color of the koi has little to do with their tameness. The really significant characteristic is the size (=age) of the koi because the older they are, the more contact they have had with human kindness.

Chagoi look like wild-colored carp during their first year. After wintering, they start to become tea-colored and at the end of their second summer they are fully colored. Many chagoi have dark ends to their body scales. This develops into a net-like, reticulate pattern which does not enhance the color but rather makes the chagoi more somber.

Karasugoi

The terms *karasu* refers to a solid black bird found in Japan. It might be a black crow. Thus the *karasugoi* is a koi whose entire body is black. Therefore it is the opposite of the albino koi in which the gene for the black melanophore is missing. This is a melanistic fish. Some of them even develop melanoma, which is a black cancer.

Further qualifiers are added to the karasugoi's name, such as the *hajiro karasugoi*, which has a totally black body but white tips on the pectoral fins. Then there is the *hageshiro karasugoi*, which has an all black body except for the head and pectoral fin tips, both of which are white. Additionally, there is the *yotsushiro karasugoi*, whose head, pectorals and *tail fin* are white. Another amazing fish is the *matsukawabake* karasugoi. This fish has melanophores (black pigment cells) that are very sensitive to water temperature. They are white in the winter and black in the summer.

The black fish are not very popular because they are almost invisible in the usual koi pond whose sides and bottom are covered with dead algae. But when you see them in a pet shop's light-blue bottomed plastic koi pond, they are extremely attractive.

The *dragon koi*, kumonryu, is also a karasu variety. (Since the karasu itself is a sub-variety of the kawarimono, the kumonryu karasugoi is a sub-sub-variety...or something like that!) This is a white-headed splashed fish whose body has white markings on a black base. The dorsal, tail and ALL other fins are white and it has lots of doitsu scales along the sides and top, usually following the dorsal edge and lateral line.

The suminagashi karasugoi is a weird and rare black koi. It has black scales but the edges of the scales become faded and turn white. It then looks like an asagi but it derives from a different genetic line. They are sometimes listed under two categories, the *suminagashi karasugoi* and the *asagi suminagashi* without reference to the karasu. The suminagashi scale often has a raised relief appearance, which is very attractive when viewed in a blue-bottomed pool. But like all black koi, it gets lost in an outdoor environment.

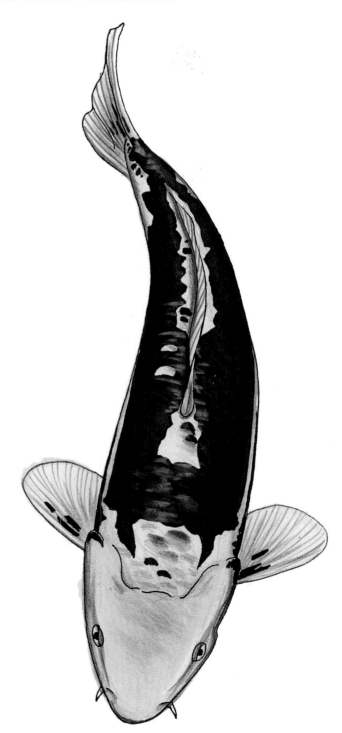

The Dragon Koi, Kumonryu.

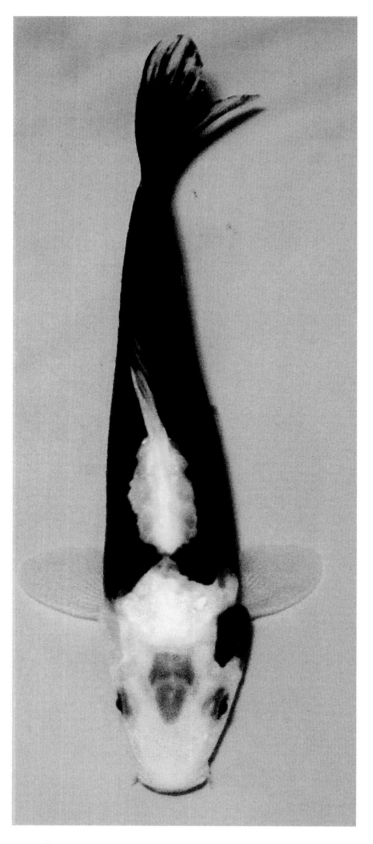 

Two magnificently colored kawarimono in black and white. The fish on the right has German scalation and is a Doitsugoi.

Two wonderful kawarimonos! The fish on the left has the colors of a killer whale and was very popular at the All-Japan Nishiki-goi Show in which it won a prize. The fish on the right is a kawarimono with German scales.

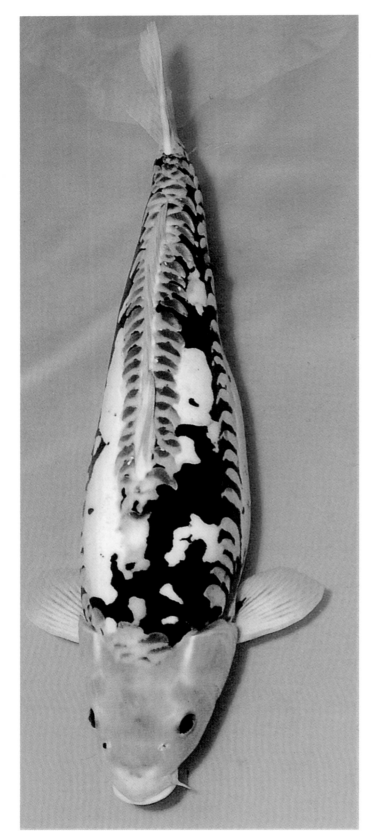 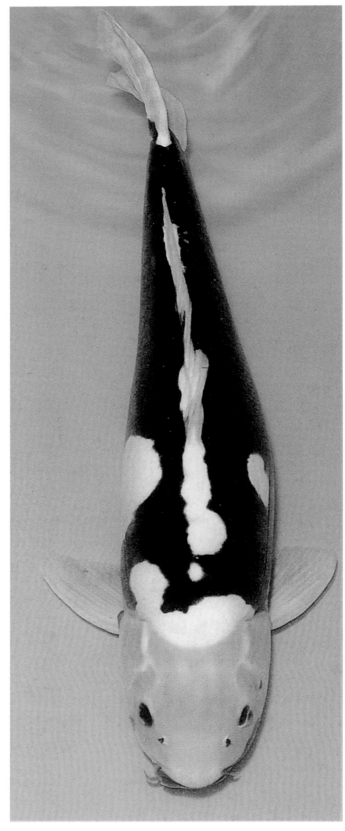

Two wonderful kawarimono in black and white. The fish on the left has very effective German scalation.

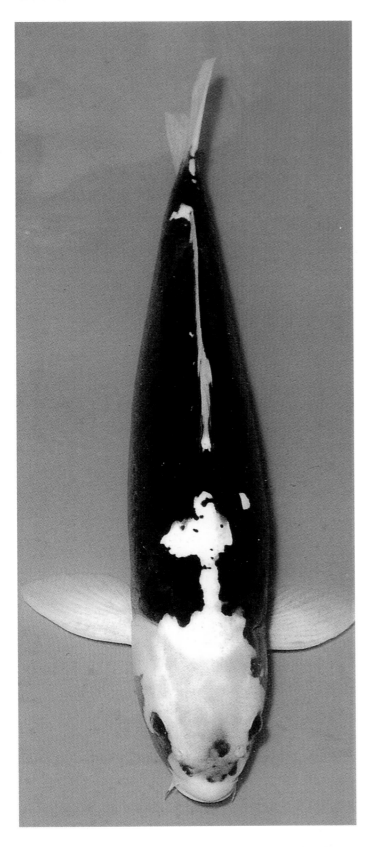

The depth of black on this kawarimono is exceptional.

This idealized Karasugoi was created electronically.

An idealized Akamatsuba which is a solid red matsuba.

MATSUBAGOI

The term *matsuba* means *pine cone* and it is used to describe a kawarimono whose scales have black centers and light edges giving an impression of a pine cone. The cause of the lighter edges is the sculptured relief of the scale centers. Think of the scale having a pyramid on it. The greater amount of pigment is in the center, but fades to the edges, the way a pyramid has fewer stones at the base than it does in the center. Only the scales visible from above are affected. The belly scales are normal.

Japanese koi history teaches us that these fish are derived from the asagi and have been around as long as the asagi, or almost 175 years. There are many color varieties of matsubagoi and each of the color varieties are also recognized with doitsu scalation, which makes a rather large congregation in this matsubagoi grouping.

The red matsuba are called *akamatsuba*. Dr. Kuroki advises that they have almost disappeared from the koi scene in Japan. Consequently, they are bred in Israel, and are very expensive to come by. The Israelis use cloning techniques, so their koi are more *pure*, if that is a good descriptive adjective. These red koi have black markings in the centers of the scales caused by the density of the pigmentation in the pyramiding effect of the chromatophores.

The *yellow matsuba* is an akamatsuba without red pigment cells. It is called a *ki matsuba*.

The *shiro matsuba* is a white akamatsuba. It has white scales with a dark center to the sculptured scales running on the upper half of the body.

None of the matsuba kawarimono can have metallic scales. The matsuba pattern is very interesting from a geometric point of view and close analyses of the patterns on different color varieties can produce some interesting studies. The matsuba will eventually become a category recognized along with the other standards, but since they are not recognized and have little chance of winning top prizes (=money), most koi breeders don't *waste their time* producing them for the market.

The *matsuba doitsugoi* are extremely beautiful and interesting matsubagoi. The monster scales on the side (lateral line) and dorsal edge are called the *mirror* type of doitsu

An idealized yellow matsuba which is a Ki Matsuba.

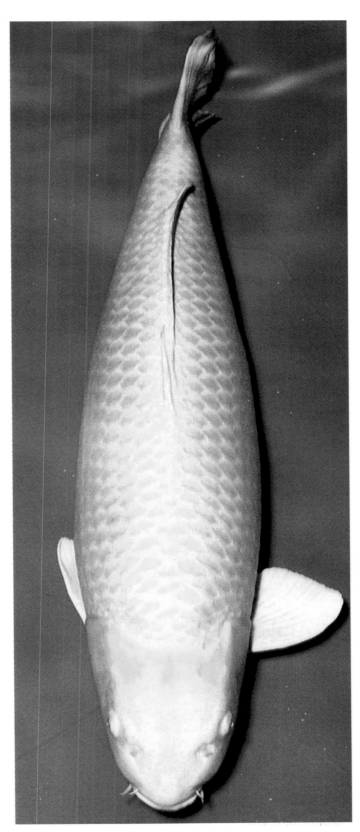

A magnificent Gin Matsuba.

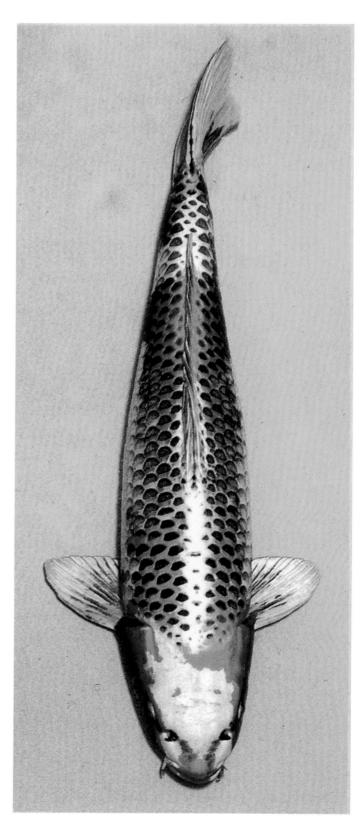

This magnificent fish is a Pine Cone Kohaku, which means it is a kawarimono with a nice Kohaku pattern overlaid with pyramid-shaped scales that appear darker in the center and lighter on the edges, thus giving the pine cone effect.

This champion (1990) Hikarimono is a beautiful matsuba with metallic scales.

The fins on this lovely kawarimono, along with the head, are stark white. The basic Kohaku pattern is weak but the overlaid blue matsuba scales make this a real beauty. The Japanese word *kage* means *indistinct* and that word aptly describes this fish since, except for the white, it has no outstanding colors.

scalation. There are no leather type of doitsu scales in matsubagoi. A perennial favorite is the yellow *ki matsuba doitsu*. It was produced from the shusui many years ago. It is still, however, a very rare variety as are all matsubagoi.

Kage Utsuri and Kage Showa

The word *kage* in Japanese means *indistinct*. It can also mean *blurred, phantom* or *shadow*. In this case it refers to the blurred, reticulated dark pattern which surprints over the basic red or white koi. It is very similar to the matsuba (pine cone) pattern. The obvious difference between the kage and the matsuba is the solid black blotches which distinguish the kage.

The *kage showa* has the standard showa pattern with kage covering *some* of the white. This is basically a showa sanshoku with the blurred reticulated pattern. It is necessary for the black pattern to be dense and articulated. This is a beautiful but rare combination.

The *kage shiro utsuri* has the usual black and white utsuri markings with kage. Of course you can't see the kage over the black because the sumi (black) is too dense in pigmentation.

The *kage hi utsuri* is basically a hi utsuri, which is a red and black fish, with the center of the red scales having dark pigmentation. The demarcation between the red and black patches should be sharp and clean, without red scales overlapping the red where the black scales might be a bit lighter than normal. The reticulated markings should be extremely clear or the fish looks badly and is culled. This makes the show fish of this variety very rare.

Goshiki

The Japanese word *go* means *five*. Thus *goshiki* means *five colors*. Initially appearing at a Tokyo show in 1918, this variety resulted from crossing an aka bekko with an asagi or an aka sanshoku. Modern breeders use an asagi/taisho sanke cross. This produces a goshiki with two colors of blue...light blue and dark blue...as in the asagi, and the red, white and black of the taisho sanke. The overall impression of the fish is purple! Fine specimens of this variety have deep, blood red markings with the three step pattern. An outstanding head is also important.

This 7 Bu champion Goshiki was the hit of the 1990 All-Japan Show held in Tokyo.

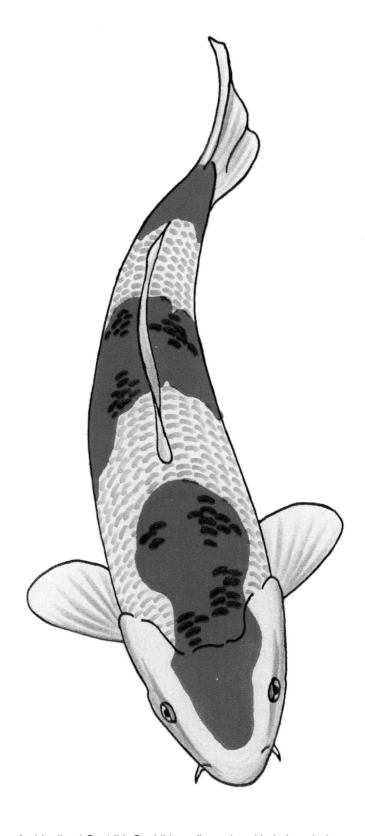

An idealized Goshiki. Goshiki are five colored koi, though the colors are made up of overlapping colors.

A champion Goshiki 65 cm (= 26 in) long.

True magnificence.! A wonderful four step red pattern, making it's Kohaku basis very obvious, plus a lovely reddish brown tinge. A real rarity.

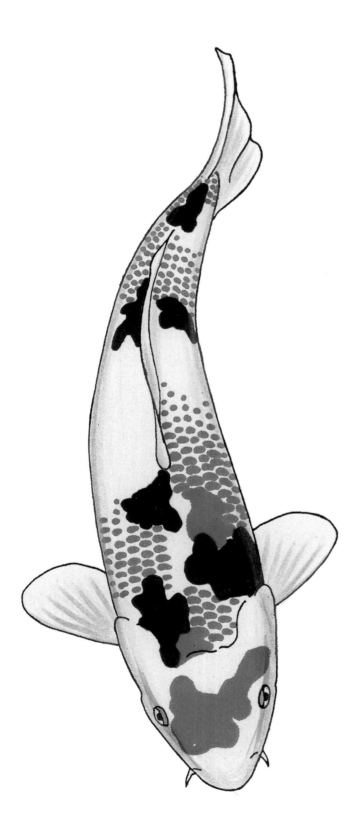

An idealistic Kanokogoi.

This variety is water temperature sensitive. It is at its best when the pond is warm; when it gets below 50° F. the colors darken. In near freezing waters, the fish may turn black! Several new varieties of goshiki make rare appearances.

Kanokogoi

If a koi has red scales with white edges, giving the scales an individual, separated appearance, this is called *dappled.* The Japanese word for *dappled* is *kanoko.* There are several kinds of kanoko, but the most common is the kanoko kohaku.

The term *kanokogoi* refers to the fawn coloring in the scales.

The *kanoko kohaku* is a kohaku which keeps the head hi (red) outstanding without fawn (kanoko) markings. The kanoko is found on the top half of the fish, which is the part visible when viewed from above.

The *kanoko kohaku* with an iridescent shine is referred to as a *sakura ogon,* while a *kinzakura* is a gotenzakura with shiny scales.

The *kanoko showa* is a showa wherein the hi (red) blotches are light purple (fawn).

The *kanoko sanke* is a sanke with uneven red markings.

Standards for all of the goshiki varies greatly from show to show because they are so rarely entered. They never take first prizes at major shows so they are not produced in great quantities.

The *gotenzakura* is a koi whose red dapples (kanoko) resemble a bunch of grapes. They may appear at shows under the *kohaku* category, but they suffer in comparison with a fine kohaku. It is usual practice to enter them in the Miscellaneous Class (kawarimono).

Ochibashigure

A very interesting and rare color variety is the *ochibashigure.* This term means *dead leaves floating on the water* referring to the leaves that fall onto the pond when the weather turns cold. The fish is derived from the chagoi line. It became famous when it was on display at the Rin-Rin Park, Ehime Prefecture. When it was a yard (36 inches) long, it took the jumbo koi first prize at the 18th Imabari Koi Show. Dr. Kuroki calls it *a national treasure.* It occurs in normal scalation as well as doitsu. It has green, gray basic colors with a filigree reticula-

This is an idealized Kinzakura. It is actually a Gotenzakura whose appearance is enhanced with metallic sheen.

tion of brown from which the allusion to dead leaves floating on the water originates. It is a very expensive variety when fine specimens are available; there are many less-than-fine specimens to be seen.

There are still dozens of kawarimono which could be described here, but they are so rare, and are found under so many aliases, that listings would be meaningless until proper standards evolved. It is quite probable that as koi keeping keeps growing worldwide, these rare color varieties will eventually develop into standard varieties at which time exact definitions would evolve as interest in the variety grows.

HIKARIMONO

This is a very popular koi variety. It has metallic scales and is a one color koi. The most popular variety of hikarimono is the *ogon*. It is a favorite as pond koi because its high luster is highly visible against the dark bottom and sides of the usual koi pond. It is a koi variety that looks expensive but in reality is affordable. This variety appeared in Japan about 1921 and is generally credited to Aoki-san who inbred the gold for five years in order to develop the strain we now know as the golden ogon. He also developed other metallic varieties including the golden (kin kabuto), the gin kabuto (silver), the ginbo (black with silver metallic sheen) and the kinbo (black with golden metallic sheen).

The *kin kabuto* is a black ogon whose scales have golden, metallic edges. The head is metallic gold with black markings like a cap.

The *gin kabuto* is a black koi which has silver edges to the scales. The head is metallic silver with a black cap-like marking.

Both the kin kabuto and the gin kabuto are held in contempt by the serious breeder because technically they are not single-colored koi.

The *kinbo* and *ginbo* are related to the gin and kin kabutos. They have a similar metallic sheen but they are blacker. These two varieties are also rejected because of their being two-colored instead of one-colored.

Proceeding from Sawat Aoki's pioneering efforts, professional breeders finally developed show quality, solid colored golden ogons. They became immediate hits with the hobby and were produced in huge quantities. They are so

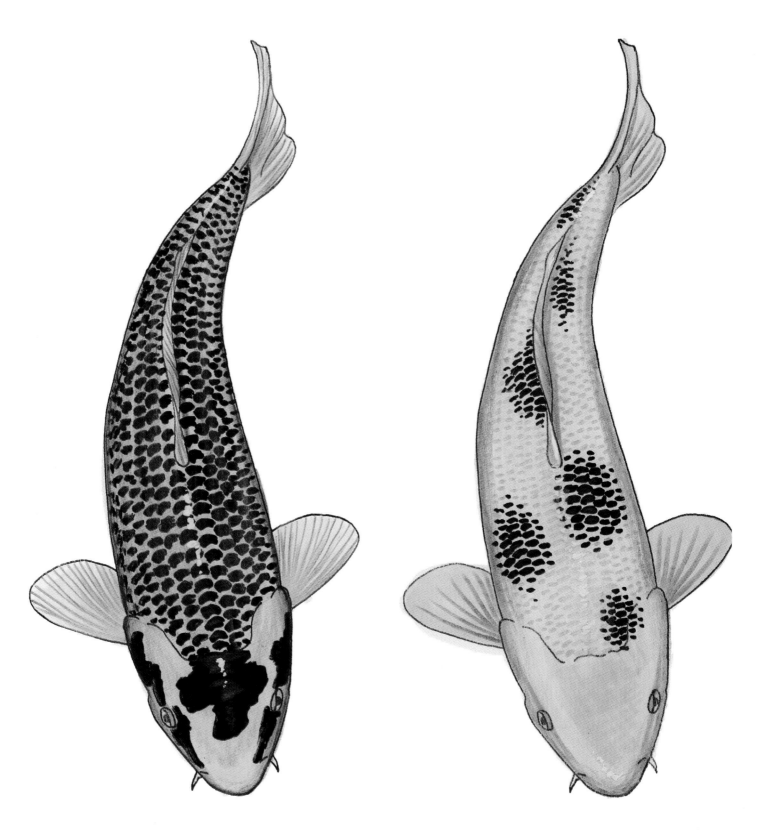

An idealized Kin Kabuto.   An idealized Tora Ogon, the Tiger Ogon.

Six splendid examples of Goshiki koi.

A champion (1994, Tokyo) Hikari Utsurimono.

simple to breed that the connoisseurs lost interest in them and they never are found in the winner's circle.

A good ogon is solidly colored in gold, sliver or light silver (platinum). It should not have any shading or scale of any other color. This is especially true of the belly scales since they indicate a pollution of the true strain and usually foreshadow mismarkings as the fish matures and grows.

Ogons seem to be sturdy fish with their very robust bodies enhanced by strong muscle development between the end of the dorsal fin and the tail. While ogons are extremely desirable as part of the school of koi in a given pond, they are boring if the pond ONLY has ogon.

Some of the more popular ogon are as follows:

The *fuji ogon* is named after Fujiyama (Mount Fuji) because this variety has an outstanding head which glistens in metallic splendor more than the rest of the body.

The *orenji ogon* is simply an orange ogon.

The *nezu ogon* is a metallic gray. These fish are not as lustrous as many of the other ogon.

The *yamabuki ogon* is the golden yellow ogon. *Yamabuki* means yellow in Japanese.

The *platinum ogon* was once called the *purachina*. Purachina means *pure china* referring to the white porcelain dishes that are even called *chinaware* in the English language.

The *kin* and *gin matsuba* ogon are the pine cone varieties. The kin (gold) and the gin (silver) ogon have dark centers to their scales giving them the appearance of a pine cone.

There are other names for other shades, but only those strains named are produced in commercial quantities.

HIKARI UTSURIMONO

The name *hikari utsurimono* comes from *hikari* which means *metal* and *utsuri* which means *homologous*. Mono means *single* or *one* but it refers to the utsurimono from which an ogon-cross with utsuri produced the present fish variety. Crosses with ogon and showa have also produced hikari utsurimono. These fish are very interesting because they are derived from the tri-colored utsurimono, which is a black fish with yellow, red and white patchwork. This is differentiated from the bekko

Six examples of Hikari Utsurimono. These are single colored, metallic koi.

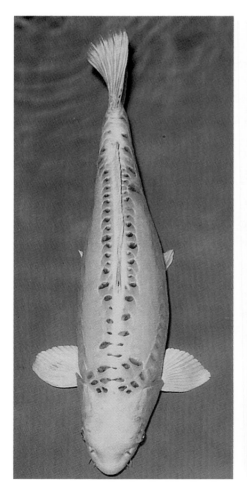

An idealized Kin Showa.

which is a white, yellow or red fish with black patchwork.

This is not a very popular fish because its colors are neither strong nor outstanding in size. The black looks gray; the red looks brown; and the metallic scales do not really glisten.

Showa are essentially black koi marked with red and white.

When showa are crossed with ogon, the showa become metallic and are called *kin showa* if they glisten with gold, or *gin showa* if they glisten with silver.

The *gin shiro* is a white (=silver) utsuri and its black pattern should follow the standards set for the shiro utsuri variety.

The *kin ki utsuri* is an ogon/ki utsuri cross. A fine specimen will glisten with shiny metallic gold. Good ones are especially rare but even good ones often fail to be recognized with prizes at major koi shows. A bit more popular is the *kin hi utsuri,* which is essentially a black and red fish with some luster. But like all the hikari-utsurimono, it is NOT a spectacular fish and is, therefore, hardly appreciated at competitions.

TANCHO

This is a very popular koi, especially with beginners. The main reason is that the fish is beautiful, simple and easy to recognize. Don't think that *recognition* is not an important characteristic!

Tancho is the name of the Japanese national bird. It has a solitary red marking on its head. The crane was revered because it resembled the Japanese national flag which is a red circle

A modern Chinese stamp showing a tancho bird. The red spot on the head is the characteristic that is so admired in koi.

An idealized Gin Shiro.   The Tancho Kohaku in an idealized drawing.

A Goshiki which looks like a Tancho but is not.   A champion Tancho.

Six champion Tancho, which may also be shown as Bekko and Kohaku.

Japanese are very proud of their *rising sun* and use it as ornamentation on fans, etc. This then makes it understandable that they admire the Tancho bird and the Tancho fish.

on a white background. Scientifically the crane is known as *Grus japonensis,* but in Japan it is merely tancho.

The tancho marking is only found on the head; it is only hi (pronounced *he*) red; and it must be isolated so it is recognizable. There are many recognized shapes to the tancho, but the perfect circle exactly straddling the center of the head is the one that wins all the prizes. The white of the body must be snow white to more perfectly set off the tancho.

The tancho is accepted on three varieties: the kohaku, the sanke and the showa. The standards for the three varieties should follow the basic standard for that variety, but it must also have a great tancho.

Great tanchos are intensely red with surrounding snow white. The tancho must be as circular as possible and must not cover the eyes.

KINGINRIN

The group of metallic scaled fishes which have a general luster are called *hikarimono*. When the luster is in each scale BUT NOT ALL SCALES, and the pattern of lustrous scales is

A champion B Ginrin.

attractive, then this koi is referred to as *kinginrin*. Fishes that have this pattern have a yellowish skin which causes some of the scales to glisten with gold, while others, especially on the the black and white color patches, glisten with silver. Thus these fish have both silver and gold metallic scales with varying densities in each scale group. These fish truly have a mother-of-pearl essence of color, but the Japanese see them as golden silver.

The kinginrin are exquisite fish. If you have a nice *kinginrin kohaku* in a pool with dark sides and bottom, you will never take your eyes off it! The fish will be outstanding and certainly be the prize of your collection.

The fish appeared in the fish farms of Yoshida in 1927 and were shown in 1929 when they were first sold. They are still very far from being perfected, however. Like with all fish, the basic pattern (like *kohaku*) must be excellent to begin with, then the kinginrin must be beautiful as well.

The judgment of these fishes keeps changing. In the 1995 All Japan Koi Show, there were two classes: *A-Ginrin* and *B Ginrin.*

There was no *kinginrin* at all, but every few years, as the kinginrin strain becomes more and more developed, additional classifications are established.

What is interesting about these freaks (yes, they are freaks of nature!), is that a given fish may have as many as six different kinds of scales. The kinds of scales are never proclaimed in judgment. The judges only care about the overall beauty of the fish. They are first concerned about the sparkling scales. Are there enough of them on the body of the fish to protect their inclusion in the kinginrin (or, in 1994 and on, in the *A Ginrin* or the *B Ginrin*)? The usual standard is 20 scales of kinginrin or the fish is not a kinginrin.

Three varieties of kinginrin are relatively common, namely the *kinginrin kohaku, kinginrin showa* and *kinginrin sanke.*

The *A-Ginrin* and the *B-Ginrin* can have any color variety in their class. The basis of differentiation is what they call the *tsubu-gin* or *pearl ginrin.* This *tsubu-gin* is a pearl-like growth in the center of the scale which makes it look like mother-of-pearl. These *tsubu-gin* form their own class. All other kinginrin are in the *B-Ginrin* classification, at least according to the 1994 ruling in Tokyo.

A champion A Ginrin.

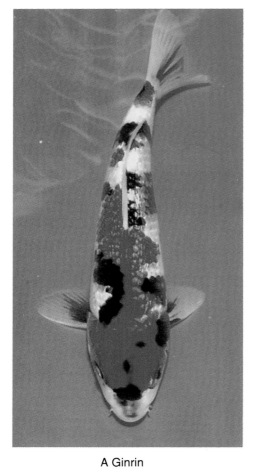

A Ginrin

B Ginrin

A Ginrin

A Ginrin

B Ginrin

B Ginrin

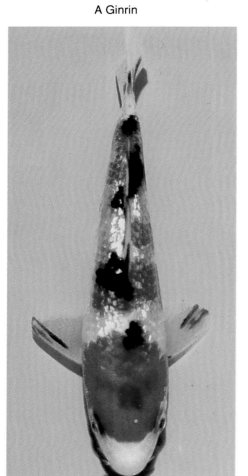

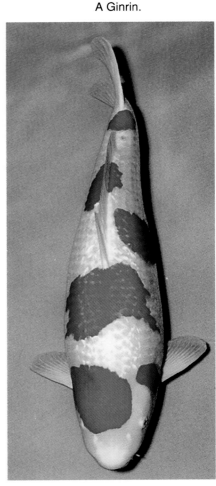

A Ginrin

A Ginrin

B Ginrin

B Ginrin

B Ginrin;

A Ginrin.

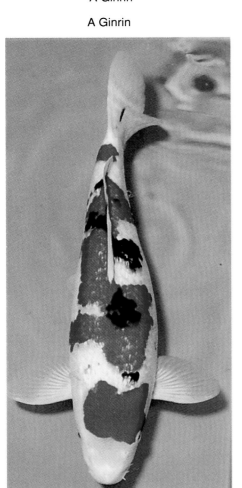

A magnificent painting owned by Tendo Koi Farm shows ideal nishikigoi. Israeli koi farmers are closely approaching ideals with their sophisticated genetic engineering.

METHODS FOR IMPROVEMENT OF JAPANESE ORNAMENTAL (KOI) CARP

DRS. SHMUEL ROTHBARD AND GIORA W. WOHLFARTH

This chapter was started in the summer of 1994, when one of my best friends and colleagues, Dr. Giora W. Wohlfarth, discussed with me our plans for further work on color inheritance in koi. On the same occasion we also decided to write an article for publication in *Tropical Fish Hobbyist* magazine, and by doing this we intended to express our appreciation to Dr. Herbert R. Axelrod for his deep interest in our work and for his continuous encouragement. Dr. Axelrod has been involved for many years in koi culture, and recently he visited Israel several times. His enthusiastic approach to koi culture in Israel and its commercial potential was cheering. In 1992 he initiated a one–week workshop on gynogenesis in koi for the MAG-NOY members, which was held at YAFIT Laboratory, Gan Shmuel Fish Breeding Center, Israel.

Dr. Wohlfarth, co-author of the article, died in an automobile accident in August, 1994. Giora graduated from Birmingham University, England, in 1951, and due to his meritorious scientific contributions was awarded a D.Sc. in 1992. He completed his Ph.D. in 1971 at the Hebrew University, Jerusalem, and worked as a fish geneticist and senior scientist in the Israeli Agricultural Research Organization. Giora was a very productive scientist, contributing much to the knowledge of fish genetics. His humor and insightful thinking enriched the lives of his friends and all those who knew and surrounded him. Personally, I miss him very much and hope to fulfill some of his ideas in writing this chapter that was projected and outlined by both of us.

We include a glossary of some of the genetic terms used. These may be of a help for hobbyist readers and may facilitate reading of the text.

THE WORLD COMMUNITY OF KOI KEEPERS AND KOI BREEDERS

One should distinguish between the enthusiastic koi keeper and the professional koi breeder. Koi hobbyists appreciate and admire

Top: The fully scaled wild carp. **Bottom:** The Taiwanese (upper) and Hong-Kong (lower) big-bellied carp.

the fish for their beauty, as if they were living jewels. They take pride in possessing a collection of fish with unique colors and excellent body shape and size. Some of the most experienced koi keepers present their fish in local or international shows where the fish are evaluated by professional judges. The exhibited fish are divided into 14 judgment categories according to color patterns. Each category is divided again into six size classes (in the world–famous All Japan Show, fish are divided more precisely into 15 different size classes).

This article first appeared in **Tropical Fish Hobbyist Magazine***, March, 1995, pages 224-242. Photos by the authors unless otherwise specified.*

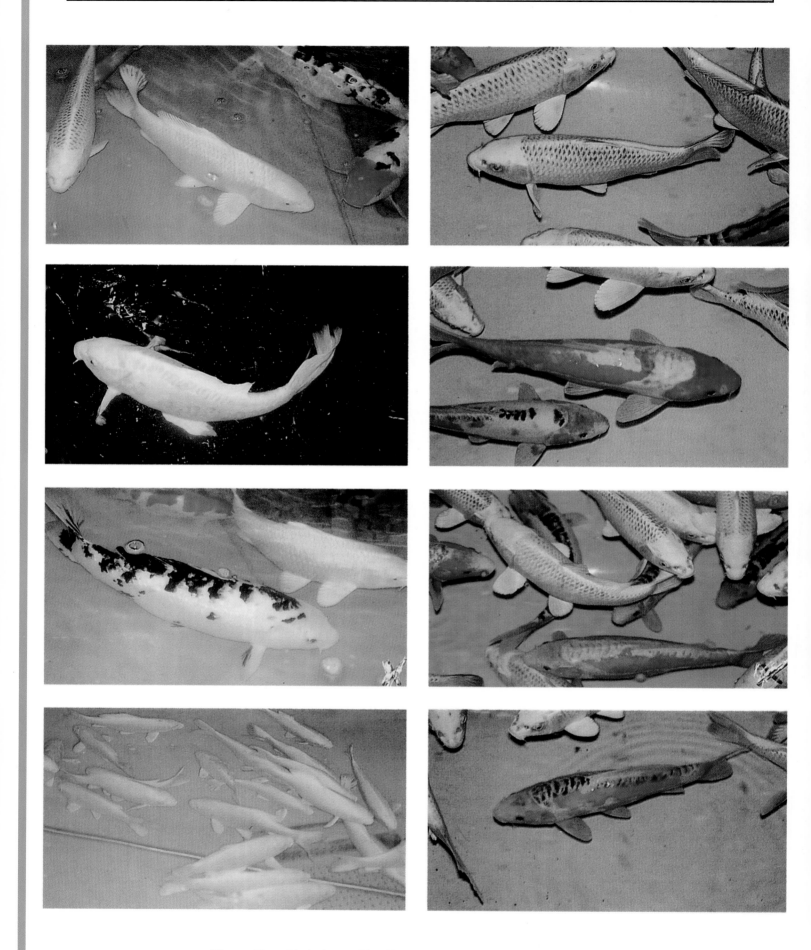

Views of Israeli koi taken at Mag Noy, Israel. Photos by Dr. Herbert R. Axelrod.

These are judged according to restrictive rules, traditionally established by Japanese koi keepers. Awards and trophies given for the best fish express appreciation and admiration by the public. The prized champion fish are valued at enormous prices. But there is no guarantee that a show winner, a champion koi, will transmit beauty to its offspring, and thus the potential to win a koi championship. **THESE ARE NOT TRUE-BREEDING FISH.**

In the category of koi breeders, we may include both small koi farmers who raise fish in two to four small ponds, as well as others who manage many ponds of sizes varying between 0.1 and 15 acres, producing fish on a large scale. The small family farms are well-known from many places in Japan, but perhaps the most famous are the koi farmers from Niigata Prefecture, where koi culture was initiated. Others, although not possessing the historical background of the Japanese koi growers, deliver most of the fish to the koi world market. Farms sometimes have hundreds of acres of water. The farms in Israel are large and belong to the MAG-NOY partnership, which produces koi and goldfish on a large scale.

Methods involved in the artificial propagation of koi are beyond the scope of this chapter. Popular as well as scientific information on breeding fishes (and particularly koi) is available in numerous handbooks, hatchery manuals, and scientific periodicals. People interested in the subject should consult these publications. (Most are published by T.F.H. Publications; many are written by Dr. Axelrod.)

THE GENETIC ANCESTOR OF NISHIKIGOI, THE COMMON CARP

The common carp, *Cyprinus carpio* Linnaeus, 1758 is perhaps the most popular teleost in the world. Its dissemination from Asia has encompassed hundreds of years. Its adaptation to various environmental conditions has resulted in numerous subspecies, strains, and genetic variants. One of these variants is the famous Japanese ornamental carp (*nishikigoi*), commonly known as *koi* (*koi* means "carp" in Japanese).

Carp are probably the only truly domesticated fish species and were characterized in ancient Roman chronicles (*Historia Animalium*

Top: The big-bellied carp cultivated in China. **Center:** The European mirror carp. **Bottom:** A white mutant carp.

by Aristotle and *Naturalis Historia* by Pliny) as well as in one of the first known fish culture manuals to be published (Fan-Li, 475 B.C.; cited by Hickling, 1971).

According to Kirpichnikov (1979), a very prominent Russian fish geneticist, carp were widely distributed within the huge continental area extending between central Europe (Don and Danube basins) and eastern Asia (China). The common carp was probably distributed west to Europe, east to China and Southeast Asia. This was the main cause that exposed the species to divergent processes of evolution and different domestication regimens. Consequently, it resulted in a large number of genetic strains and phenotypes. Ancient Christian monks living in cloisters of Central Europe, as well as Buddhist monks dwelling in the monasteries of eastern Asia, played an important role in the development of carp breeding techniques and management, since carp culture was closely related to religious traditions.

The ornamental (koi) carp may be regarded as a group of colorful variants of the common carp that was developed in Japan during the last two centuries. Contrary to a common belief, koi are not indigenous to Japan, although closely linked to their culture and tradition. According to an ancient Chinese handbook on breeding koi entitled *Yogyokyo* and written in 533 B.C. (McDowall, 1989), the koi and the common carp originated elsewhere in the central part of Asia and in eastern China. The koi, as color variants of the common carp, began to be developed as ornamental fish in Niigata Prefecture, Honshu Island, Japan, about 200 years ago. Thus, koi are much "younger" ornamental fish than goldfish, which have been cultivated in China for more than 1000 years (Zhong-ge, 1984).

Top: A "gold" mutant mirror carp. **Center:** A "gold" mutant big-bellied carp. **Bottom:** A "blue" carp variant.

COMMON CARP PIGMENTATION

Coloration in common carp is affected by the presence or absence, or relative proportions, of three types of chromatophores or cells carrying pigment: (1) *melanophores* are cells carrying the pigment melanin and are responsible for dark coloration; (2) *guanophores* carry guanine crystals that produce iridescence; (3) *xanthophores* carry yellow to reddish pigments. Absence of melanophores and xanthophores will result in white colora-

The cloned koi produced by the Israelis may be 100% identical in color and scalation. Photo by Dr. Herbert R. Axelrod.

Table 1. Coloration in Cross-Breeds of Nishikigoi Lines and Varieties*.

PARENTS	Kohaku	Tancho	Taisho sanke	Showa sanshoku	Bekko, Shiro- & Ki-	Asagi	Utsuri, Shiro- & Ki-	Ogon	C. carp Wild-type
Kohaku	Shiro-muji Aka-muji Kohaku (very seldom: Sanke, Tancho)				Taisho sanke	Aigoromo	Showa sanshoku		Wild-type
Tancho									
Taisho sanke						Goshiki Koromo			Wild-type
Showa sanshoku				Absence of Showa		Koromo		Kin/Gin Showa	Wild-type
Bekko, Shiro/Ki-	Taisho sanke								Wild-type
Asagi	Aigoromo		Goshiki Koromo	Koromo					Shusui
Utsuri, Shiro/Ki-	Showa sanshoku								Wild-type
Ogon			Kin/gin	Showa			Ogon	Kabuto var.	Kin/Gin
C. carp W.-type	Wild-type		Wild-type	Wild-type	Wild-type	Shusui	Wild-type	Kabuto Kin/Gin	C. carp W.-type

* Based on information extracted from either literature (see references indicated by *) or personal communication and experience.

The particular color variants indicated in the table appeared among the offspring in various cross-breeds in quite remarkable numbers; however, all populations included also many phenotypes of different and unexpected colors.

tion (*not* albino). The relative amounts of red and yellow pigments present in the xanthophores can be expressed as yellow, orange, or even red coloration. An over-abundance may create an all–black fish. Absence of guanophores can cause transparency. Other combinations are possible.

Mutants, including white, gold (mirror), gold (scaled), and blue phenotypes appear quite frequently among the domesticated common carp strains. Some of these have been investigated for their color inheritance (Probst, 1949; Moav and Wohlfarth, 1968; Katasonov, 1973, 1974, 1976, and 1978; Merla, 1982). The results do not confirm unequivocally whether the colors represent different genotypes or are phenotypic variants affected by environmental factors. However, bright carp colors are recessive; the normal (wild-type) coloration is dominant.

VIEWS AT HAZOREA, ISRAEL.
Photos by Dr. Herbert R. Axelrod.

Every variant of ornamental koi, when crossed with a homozygous wild-type carp, will yield exclusively wild-type–colored progeny. There is no evidence of co–dominance in crosses involving various color varieties.

Perhaps the first fish geneticist to report crossing koi with common carp was Katasonov (1978). He found that crosses between common carp and blue or orange koi, yield all wild-type offspring.

NISHIKIGOI COLORATION

Koi may possess a wide variety of colors: black, blue, red, orange, yellow, green, and white, or combinations of these. The only published investigations dealing with colors in koi involve the inheritance of single colors such as orange, blue, white, and "light" (Katasonov, 1978; Wohlfarth and Rothbard, 1991; Szweigman, et al., 1992). Thus, it is not yet possible to predict the color of progeny based solely on the parents' color. A wide variation of color patterns is produced among

VIEWS AT HAZOREA, ISRAEL

Aerating heavily stock ponds.

Hazorea from the air.

Birds are a constant menace.

Even young girls have to do physical work.

Huge silos holding koi feed.

Koi spawning grass.

Pre-shipment koi holding tanks.

A water snake hatching; they eat koi fry.

Photos by Dr. Herbert R. Axelrod

the progeny of commercial group spawns. Thus, even the top-quality individuals, prized at koi showings and admired by the koi-keepers for their body shape, scalation, and coloration, and selected from the most famous and appreciated "bloodlines" (a controversial term that does not have clear genetic meaning), are **NOT TRUE-BREEDING** fish. For instance, mating a single pair of excellent *kohaku* (snow-white–colored koi randomly covered with red *hi* markings) will not produce solely *kohaku* offspring. The empirical results of different crossbreeds (Table 1) were extracted from various popular aricles and some scientific studies. No pattern is evident, so their contribution to our understanding of color inheritance in koi is limited. Nevertheless, the mysticism surrounding coloration of koi and its inheritance, as sometimes expressed in popular literature, cannot be accepted as viable. Rather, we believe that this complicated subject is ruled by the laws of nature, which are as yet not sufficiently understood. We further believe that additional reliable information would enhance our understanding of koi color inheritance and benefit both koi-keepers and koi-breeders.

THE EXHAUSTING WORK OF CULLING

Traditionally, koi were cultured on small family farms by labor–intensive methods. These farmers were joyful if a few thousand fish, out of hundreds of thousands produced, could be grown and sold.

Great variation exists in colors and color patterns among individuals of the same spawn as well as among offspring of different spawns. Only some of these are regarded as being of commercial value. The traditional Japanese concept of selection is based on continually culling those fish considered unsuitable for the koi trade. This frustrating process is often carried out by well–paid professional cullers who travel from farm to farm and rapidly discard large numbers of young koi at a very small size. The effectiveness of this culling is unknown and thus controversial.

Culling koi is an unpleasant, time–consuming, and sometimes inefficient job, even for Japanese professionals. The process may become more efficient when after years of experience they make fewer errors in selecting good koi. They sort the subtly "better" fish as

Above and below: Sorting koi at Mag Noy.

early as possible from the almost identical background population. The most experienced teams can sort two–week–old fry, although the efficiency of selection at this early age cannot be unequivocally assumed. For example, some of the black patches (*sumi*), appear or disappear during the first or second year of a koi's life. Another problem involves the possibility of unexpected environmental influences on koi coloration. Genetics and environment interact to form the final colors in koi. This is perhaps the major constraint to the establishment of reliable koi lineages.

Koi fry are sorted according to body shapes, colors, and size categories. Tamadachi (a pseudonym of Dr. Axelrod) (1990) estimated that koi producers discard around 90% of koi during the 3-4 months of culling. He indicated that the first to be picked

Elaborate electronic controls run the Mag Noy Koi Farm.

A new type of electronic automatic koi feeder at Mag Noy.

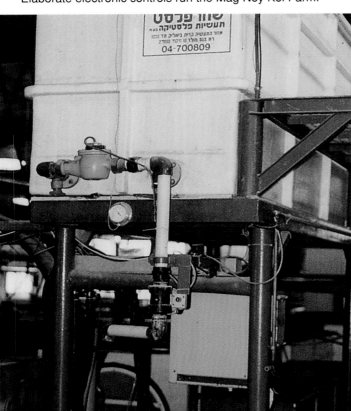

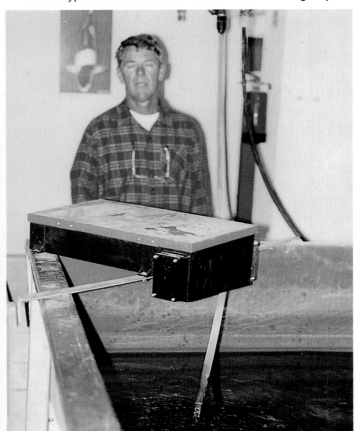

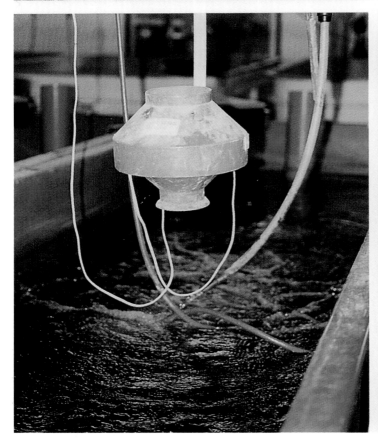

Old fashioned koi feeder at Mag Noy.

The movement and control of water is of prime importance at the Mag Noy Koi Farm in Israel.

Photos by Dr. Herbert R. Axelrod.

Table 2. Color segregation in offspring, progenies of single-pair matings between koi of various phenotypes.

Spawners		Segregation of phenotypes in offspring (%)						
Female	Male	Kohaku	Tricolor	Orange	Transp.	W.-type	S/bek.	Ogon
Kohaku	Kohaku	**7.1**	**64.3**	2.4	7.2		**19.0**	
Kohaku	Kohaku	**13.0**	**38.5**	6.2	29.2		**13.1**	
Kohaku	Sanke	**45.7**		28.4	23.5	2.4		
Kohaku	Sanke	**35.2**		15.7	49.1			
Kohaku	Showa	**43.5**		34.8	17.4	4.3		
Kohaku	Showa	**34.7**		35.3	26.7	3.3		
Kohaku	Ogon*			20.0	14.3			65.7
Kohaku	S.bek.	**22.0**			70.0	8.0		
Kohaku	Asagi	**45.5**			54.5			
Showa	S/uts.	**9.5**			66.7	23.8		
H/uts.	S/uts.	**26.8**	**29.3**		43.9			
Asagi	Matsuba	**6.2**	**3.1**	41.5	29.5		**19.7**	

- Eggs obtained from the same *italic* female spawner (*Kohaku*) were fertilized with sperm collected from four different males.
- Bold numbers indicate fish of commercial value.
- **Tricolor**–Due to small size of fry, it was impossible to identify whether the fish were Showa or Sanke; **W.-type**–Wild-type color; **S/bek.**–Shiro-bekko; **S/uts.**–Shiro-utsuri; **H.uts.**–Hi-utsuri; *****Ogon**–Ki-ogon.

---

are the **showasanke** at the age of 2-3 weeks, followed by 5-6-week-old **ogon** and then by 3-4-month-old **taishosanke** and **kohaku**. The result of such a restricted sorting is that less than 10% of the initial number of koi are retained to marketable size. The financial loss resulting from such an extreme selection process is substantial.

Koi production in Israel is integrated with the edible fish farming industry, carried out on cooperative kibbutz farms, which are substantially different from traditional Japanese family farms. Nevertheless, although professional cullers have not yet appeared, culling methods are quite similar.

It is believed that increased understanding of color inheritance in koi may save some of the repetitive, monotonous, and wasteful sortings (see photos by Fletcher, 1991), during which many fish are discarded simply because they do not fit our preconceived standards of beauty. This has a very important financial impact. Culling does save pond space, which is a limitation in every fish culture operation.

There are some exceptions. For instance, breeding mono-colored fish, such as the *ogon* varieties, usually results in higher rates of *ogon* offspring, presumably because the *ogon* are "more true-breeding" than multicolored koi varieties.

PREREQUISITES FOR A KOI BREEDING PROGRAM

Almost every professional koi breeder who is planning to produce koi will face a confusing array of questions:
- Which fish should be selected as broodstock?
- How is the color pattern of parents inherited by the offspring?
- What will be the colors and color patterns in progeny of fish carrying certain coloration when mated with fish that possess similar (or different) phenotypes?
- How are spawners selected for their breeding performance?
- Is it possible to repeat particular pairings and produce consecutive generations of selected quality offspring?

Much empirical and scientific work will be required to answer most of these burdensome questions. We are trying to share with the reader some beneficial ideas that can be realized and put into practice.

VIEWS AT MAG NOY KOI FARM IN ISRAEL.

Huge round tanks for koi.

Mrs. Axelrod with the Hazorea staff.

Water leveling apparatus inside koi tank.

Plastic holding tanks for koi fry.

Empty boxes in which koi are shipped.

All outdoor pools are covered to protect the fish from the birds.

Photos by Dr. Herbert R. Axelrod.

There are two considerations that should be incorporated into programs to improve koi. These are: 1) the capability to individually identify broodstock, and 2) adequate nursery facilities.

(1) Individual Markings

Broodstock must be identifiable with individually recognizable markings so as to establish a record of past performance. Tags are commercially manufactured and available (e.g., BIOSONICS, Seattle, Washington, USA, or TROVAN, SFM-Wachtersbach, Germany). Implantable glass tags that are magnetically coded are inserted into the dorsal musculature; these can be decoded , recorded, and stored by a portable reader. Some can be downloaded to a PC.

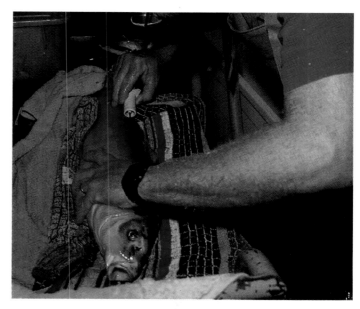

Above: Marking koi with magnetic glass tags. **Below:** Electronic reader of the magnetic glass tags.

(2) Nursery facility for group testings

A random sample of post-hatching larvae is taken from each population of fish produced by a single–pair mating. These must be separately reared until they reach the size/age that allows recognition of colors. Since each batch of fish tested requires a separate compartment, the number of units soon becomes the bottleneck of the method.

One method to raise multiple groups utilizes a set of cages. A fine mesh (500 μm mesh size) cage is used for the hatchlings and is then replaced with one having larger mesh after growth to fry size. About 200

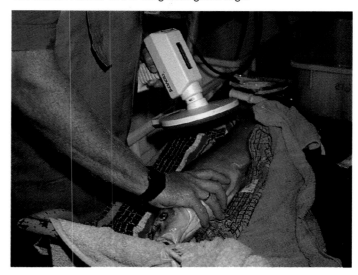

Table 3. Color Segregation in Offspring, Progenies of Single Koi Females of Various Phenotypes, and Sperm Pooled from Kohaku and Sanke Males.

Spawners		Segregation of phenotypes in offspring (%)			
Female	Males	Kohaku	Tricolor	Orange/Transp.	Shiro bekko
Sanke		**15.8**	**36.0**	40.6	**7.6**
Sake		**13.1**	**34.5**	40.7	**11.7**
Sanke	Kohaku	**31.8**	**21.0**	41.5	**5.7**
Sanke	&	**12.4**	**53.6**	21.6	**12.4**
Sanke	→ Sanke	**29.4**	**8.1**	62.5	
Hi-Uts.	(pooled	**19.1**	**25.1**	55.8	
Hi-Uts.	sperm)	**13.4**	**19.8**	45.9	**20.9**
Hi-Uts.		**5.3**	**21.9**	41.3	**31.5**
Sh-Bek*		**25.0**	**12.5**	41.7	**20.8**
Sh-Utsu.	Sh/Hi-Uts.	**13.3**		83.4	**3.3**

- Bold letters indicate fish of commercial values.
- **Hi-Uts.** - Hi-utsuri.

- **Sh-bek*** - Shiro-bekko fertilized with Kohaku & Sanke (gin-rin) sperm; the cross yielded 50% gin-rin progeny.
- **Sh-Utsu.** - Shiro-utsuri.

Above: An experimental cage farm for rearing groups of koi,
Below: A fine-mesh cage for rearing koi larvae.

fish/m^3 can be maintained for the several weeks required to reach a size of 2-4 inches. Overcrowded cages will result in retarded, less uniform growth, and finally increased mortality.

METHODS FOR KOI IMPROVEMENT

In farms where koi are produced on a very large scale, application of scientific methods is required. These should consider long–term planning with the objective of producing select progeny by choice of parents. This concept is already being practiced at some koi farms belonging to the MAG-NOY partnership, Israel. It includes investigation of color inheritance according to Mendelian principles, as well as production of genetic clones of koi (Rothbard, 1991 & 1994). The goal of such investigations is to increase the proportion of koi characterized by good quality of color and color pattern. Here we suggest three alterna-tive, though not mutually exclusive, methods that could be applied by professional koi breeders interested in improvement of their koi broodstocks:

1. Selection of single broodfish by continuous progeny-testing and examination of off-spring from the corresponding single-pair matings.
2. Study of single–color inheritance, by mating individual mono-colored fish, and testing the segregation of colors among the off-spring. This may help with understanding the more complex multi-color inheritance.
3. Producing clones (copies) of selected indi-viduals by chromosome-set manipulations.

COMMERCIAL PRODUCTION OF QUALITY KOI

The application of a program to use geneti-cally controlled color inheritance in koi seems difficult because it requires involved investiga-tion and a long-term commitment. It strongly depends on availability of scientific manpower and skilled technicians, as well as appropriate facilities. Most koi breeders cannot afford such an investment in time and money.

The selection of pairs for mating largely depends on the experienced koi breeder. Pairs of fish are induced to spawn on artificial mats or are stripped, following hormonal stimula-tion by injecting proper dosages of gonadotro-pins (GTH) or gonadotropin–releasing hor-mones (GnRH). In the case of stripping, the so-called "dry method" is applied. Eggs are mixed with sperm (3-5 ml sperm per liter of eggs) collected in advance, and incubated in flow-through hatching jars.

The interesting information shown in Tables 2 and 3 was kindly delivered by Mr. Z. Kulikovski of the MAG-NOY partnership, Israel. The aim of the trial, carried out by Mr. Kulikovski and the Koi Group of the Gan Shmuel Fish Breeding Center, was to learn whether certain combinations of broodfish yield significant proportions of fish that are of commercial value. Eggs were obtained from single females and fertilized with sperm either pooled from two males or collected from a single male. Random samples of post-hatch fry taken from each spawn were grown in separate cages until the fish reached a size permitting examina-tion of color.

Transparent, gray (wild-type or poor-colored), or orange fish were not considered as of marketable quality and were culled. Good assortments of koi, as evaluated by good quality of colors, included relatively high percentages of marketable fish (40-60%) (Tables 2 and 3). These were mostly obtained in progeny of *kohaku* (white/red colored) crossed with *kohaku*, or eggs stripped from *kohaku* and fertilized with pooled sperm collected from *kohaku* and *taishosanke* males. In some cases, one female was tested with different males to evaluate the potential of an individual spawner. Following this method, a commercial producer can establish a pool of koi broodstock that have been progeny–tested for production of a high proportion of salable fish.

MONO-COLORED KOI

Koi keepers and producers may possess intuitive or experiential knowledge that certain parental combinations are likely to yield relatively high proportions of fish of a given color or color patterns. Some are claimed to be true-breeding according to certain commercial advertisements. Such declarations should be considered to be unproven as a basis for breeding programs.

We initiated a long-term investigation on the heredity of body coloration in koi, starting with mono-colored koi. At first, two phenotypes, namely orange (*orenji*) and white (*shiro-ogon*) were chosen for the study. The investigation was next extended to include black koi (*karasu*). Some of the parent fish possessed pearl (*kin-gin-rin*) and other metalic scalation. Segregation of the scale phenotypes among crossbreeds indicated that there is a dominant-recessive relationship between these traits, the *kin-gin-rin* being dominant.

According to results of our investigation based on segregation of color morphs, orange and white are true-breeding variants. Orange is dominant to white. We performed single-pair matings within and between mono-colored fish that clearly showed that black is dominant to the light colors. We interpret the dominant-recessive relationships, as obtained from various crosses performed between and with these three color morphs, as follows:

Above: a 4mm mesh cage for rearing koi fry. **Below:** Synthetic brushes framed as spawning mats.

DOMINANCE = Black > Orange > White = RECESSIVE

Although in some cross-combinations fish appeared with extraordinary and unexpected colors, the inheritance of mono-colored koi is generally explained by simple Mendelian di-allele inheritance. Limited observations suggest that yellow (*yamabuki-ogon*) also may be a true-breeding variant that is recessive to the orange and black color phenotypes. These results may have some immediate practical application in the mass production of white (*shiro-ogon*), yellow (*yamabuki-ogon*), orange (*orenji-ogon*) and black (*karasugoi*) varieties.

COPYING (CLONING) OF NISHIKIGOI THROUGH GYNOGENESIS

Traditions and even mysticism abound among koi enthusiasts; however, it should be re-emphasized that color in koi is inherited according to strict genetic rules, as defined by the Augustinian monk Gregor Mendel (Mendel, 1865). We are trying to demonstrate that by following Mendel's theory through the manipulation of chromosome sets, it is possible to achieve genetic "copies" of parental fish. Traditionalists frequently say that if the heredity of coloration in koi were to be predictable *"it might reduce the pleasure of koi-lovers"* (Taniguchi, 1991). However, it is complicated to predict the impact of the commercial application of such technology.

In normally reproducing organisms, each of the two diploid parents contributes one-half (haploid) the number of chromosomes to the offspring. Fertilization results in the combination of the maternal and paternal chromosome-sets and generation of heterozygous diploid individuals. The reduced number of chromosomes in gametes is achieved through the complex cytological process of *meiosis*, which involves genetic recombination and crossing-over between homologous chromosomes. During meiotic division each primary spermatogonia produces four spermatozoa, half of them carrying the Y and half the X gonosomes. Each oogonum generates only one ovum; the other sets of chromosomes produced during the process, included in the first and the second polar bodies (1 & 2PB), are extruded.

Literally, *gynogenesis* means production of females (*gyno*=female; *genesis*=generation). In gynogenesis the paternal information carried by sperm is inactivated by exposing sperm to ionizing radiation with gamma-rays, X-rays, or UV. Sperm irradiated with appropriate

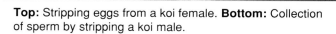

Top: Stripping eggs from a koi female. **Bottom:** Collection of sperm by stripping a koi male.

dosages remain motile, but the genetic information "packed" in the chromosomes is deactivated. The motile but genetically inactivated sperm can enter the egg and stimulate embryonic development without the contribution of paternal inheritance to the zygote. Penetration of a sperm into the egg and initiation of normal diploid embryonic development is termed *fertilization*. The term *insemination* is more appropriate when we use irradiated sperm to stimulate embryonic development of ova. If external intervention is not applied, the gynogenetic embryo will develop as a haploid *gynogenote* and will not survive beyond the yolk sac stage. Alternatively, diploidy can be restored and the gynogenote embryos will develop into totally or almost homozygous individuals. The degree of homozygosity of the gynogenotes is dependent on the timing to induce diploidy; in either "early" or "late" shock, each type of gynogenote will carry exclusively maternal inheritance. Since in carp (as well as in koi) the females are homogametic for sex determination (XX) and males are heterogametic (XY), all gynogenetic offspring will develop as females.

The dominance of wild-type color is advantageous in gynogenesis, where sperm of common carp are irradiated and inactivated, but remain motile and may stimulate embryonic development of koi eggs. The success of gynogenesis can be estimated in the hatch-out larvae, since the koi gynogenotes do not possess pigmentation and can be easily recognized and separated from the dark-pigmented (wild-type) larvae.

Diploidization of the activated (inseminated) haploid eggs is achieved by exposing them to either thermal (heat or cold) shock, hydrostatic pressure, or even chemical shock. There are several important factors that affect the efficiency of the shock to induce diploidization and thus survival of the gynogenote. These factors include, (a) type of shocking, (b) intensity of shock, (c) timing of shock initiation, and (d) duration of shock.

Gynogenesis, as reported for carp or for koi, was successfully induced with heat shock (40.0±0.5°C for 1.5–2.0 minutes), with a cold shock down to 1–2°C for 40-60 minutes), and with pressure shock (7000-8000 psi for 1.5–2.0 minutes). Age of shocking, termed also as *biological age* and identified by the Greek τ0 (tau zero), was estimated by a factor related to ambient temperature, which affected time intervals between two consecutive and synchronous embryonic cell divisions. Optimization of treatment parameters was developed with the aid of genetic color markers which were used to assure quality control. The dominance of wild-type color provided one useful visual marker.

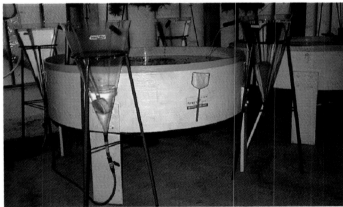

Top: Mixing sperm and eggs; the "dry method" of fertilization. **Bottom:** Conical incubators for koi eggs attached to a larvae tank.

Two methods for inducing gynogenesis are applied in fish culture:

(1) Heterozygous (2PB) gynogenesis

The second polar body (2PB), a product of the second meiotic division, carries one set of maternal chromosomes and is retained from extrusion by shocking the inseminated egg. The 2PB is extruded soon after the egg is activated and therefore retention of 2PB must be executed by application of an early shock. In this case, although the diploidized zygote would appear to have only maternal inheritance, the diploid gynogenote will be characterized by a certain heterozygosity. This is the result of some genetic recombination through crossing-over between chromosomes which occurs during meiosis. The rate of heterozygosity in a 2PB-gynogenote can be statistically estimated, since it depends on the distance between the locus where the crossing-over occurs and the centromere. Nevertheless, it is unpredictable and cannot be controlled.

(2) Homozygous (EM) gynogenesis

If the egg is activated by insemination and the 2PB is not retained but is extruded, the first mitotic cell division (*cytokinesis*) will still follow after a short time even though it is haploid. Each of the chromosomes will double itself in a process termed *endomitosis* (EM). Without external intervention the embryo will continue development as a haploid gynogenote and will not survive beyond the yolk stage. However, shocking the egg during the first mitotic nuclear division (*endomitosis*) and at the anaphase before the cell division (cytokinesis) has been completed, may result in a diploid gynogenote. These individuals will be completely homozygous at all loci. In other words, all traits in such an organism, besides being of maternal origin, will appear in a homozygous form. It should be emphasized that if common methods of inbreeding were to be used, such a homozygosity could not be achieved even by mating related individuals for more than 20 consecutive generations.

In an EM-gynogenote, all genes, even those that are responsible for negative or lethal traits, appear in a homozygous form. Thus, EM-gynogenotes suffer from inbreeding depression, have extremely low survival in early development, and also have high delayed mortality. However, the totally homozygous individuals that survive after such a strong selection have the potential to serve as ancestors of clones. Repeated reproduction of an EM-gynogenote will yield offspring that should be identical copies of their mother.

The lability of sex-differentiation in fishes also permits manipulation of phenotypic sexes through the use of hormones. It is a common and successful practice in fish culture (e.g., in *Tilapia*) to obtain male monosex cultures by feeding fry a diet that contains male hormones (testosterone or its synthetic derivatives). Some of the EM-gynogenotes can be sexually inverted into phenotypic males. Since these are carrying the same genotype as their non-sex-inverted sisters, they can be used for in-breeding. Propagation of sexually inverted EM-gynogenotes with their EM sisters will perpetually yield clones (genetic copies) of the maternal ancestor. In some fish species the method has already been successfully applied.

Koi hatchlings attached to the wall inside the incubator.

FUTURE PROSPECTS

Application of gynogenesis to koi breeding may appear as fantasy, and to a certain extent it is. However, some institutions in Japan and in Israel are involved in the bio-technology of koi, applying the technology of chromosome-set manipulations. These are aimed to obtain fish of desired colors and color patterns.

The traditional koi-lovers fear that the application of bio-technology to allow mass-production of high-quality koi will damage the koi industry. Others conclude that the requirements of such a sophisticated and long-term process will not result in a practical end. We will try to relate these two perspectives.

Color improvement of koi through gynogenesis has not yet been achieved. All reports published until the present are dealing with fragments of the planned investigation. In research carried out in the YAFIT Laboratory, we succeeded in producing broodstock that consist of females generated through EM-gynogenesis. These have reached sexual maturity, and in 1995 we will try the next step to produce the second filial generation (the F_2 generation) from each gynogenetic female. These presumably will be totally homozygous fish. Because of homozygosity of the female ancestor, the second generation of gynogenetic offspring can be produced with a "simpler" method, i.e., 2PB gynogenesis, which results in relatively higher survival of offspring. Finally, these progeny are expected to be genetic copies of the gynogenetic female.

Two constraints are associated with the application of gynogenesis:

(1)   Although the EM-gynogenotes are carrying exclusively maternal inheritance, the phenomena of crossing-over and genetic recombination that occur during meiosis result in fish with different phenotypic (and genotypic) expression, which do not fit our expectations in all circumstances (e.g., sisters of the same F_1 gynogenetic generation do not possess uniform coloration). The immediate implication of these findings is that only the second generation (F_2) of gynogenotes is expected to be cloned fish. Therefore, the female chosen as an ancestor for cloning should be carefully selected from the group of gynogenotes according to restricted criteria and desired characteristics.

(2)   Surprisingly, among the gynogenetic

offspring that theoretically should solely consist of females, there has been the appearance of some males. Komen, et al. (1992) investigated such a phenomenon in common carp. They concluded that the existence of a recessive mutation that represents a gene located on one of the autosomes affects the expected female sex-determination mechanism of the gynogenotes. The result is that a certain number of males carrying the homogametic (XX) sex-determination mechanism, similar to that of the females, can be found among the gynogenotes. In spite of those limitations, gynogenesis should be an effective tool for improvement of koi. Together with classic methods of selection and progeny-testing, it may provide conditions for better understanding of the mechanism controlling coloration in koi. A combination of methods, as suggested in this work, may help the commercial koi-breeder to increase the quality and thus the profitability of a fish operation.

ACKNOWLEDGMENTS

We wish to express our deep thanks to Professor W. L. Shelton (Zoology Department, Oklahoma University, Norman, OK, U.S.A.) for careful reading and revision of the manuscript.

Some photos were kindly provided by Dr. Gideon Hulata (Agricultural Research Organization, Volcani Center, Beth-Dagan, Israel).

GLOSSARY

The aim of this short appendix is to facilitate understanding of the genetic jargon used in the article.

Allele–One of two or more alternative forms of the same gene that can occur at a particular locus on homologous chromosomes.

Anaphase–The third stage of nuclear division during mitosis or meiosis, characterized by migration of chromosomes from spindle equator to spindle poles.

Autosomes–All chromosomes excluding sex chromosomes.

Centromere–Spindle attachment region; the part of the chromosome located on the equator of the spindle and controlling chromosome activity during cell division.

Chromosome–Nucleoprotein structure that contains DNA, carrying genes arranged in a linear order. Chromosomes are found in the nuclei of cells.

Clone–Genetically identical group of organisms, derived from one common ancestor; DNA sequences replicated through genetic engineering.

Codominant–Equal contribution to the phenotype expression of a heterozygote of both alleles found at the same locus.

Crossing over–A process occurring during meiosis in which parts of homologous chromosomes (DNA) are mutually exchanged.

Diploid–An individual (cell or an organism) carrying a double set of chromosomes, each inherited from a different parent.

Diploid gynogenote–A gynogenote possessing a double set of maternal–origin chromosomes.

Dominance–The ability of an allele to suppress expression of other alleles at the same locus. The dominant allele is expressed in a heterozygous individual.

Fertilization–The infusion of an egg and sperm that starts the embryonic development.

Gamete–A reproductive (sex) cell; a mature ovum or spermatozoid.

Gametogenesis–The formation of gametes (eggs and sperm).

Gene–A segment of DNA situated on a specific location (locus) on the chromosome, which can be transmitted to the descendants and effect the phenotype of an organism.

Genotype–Set of alleles in one or more loci in an organism. The entire set of genes carried by an organism.

Genotype-environment interaction–The interaction between genotype and environment that results in phenotypic expression of an individual or mean phenotype of the population.

Gonosome–Sex-chromosome carrying the sex-determinant (usually marked as X, Y, Z, or W.)

Gynogenesis–Production of progeny possessing exclusively maternal inheritance; production of gynogenotes (all genetic information of the offspring has maternal source).

Gynogenote–An organism produced through gynogenesis and carrying exclusively maternal inheritance.

Haploid–An individual cell or organism carrying a single set of homologous chromosomes.

Heterogametic–The status in which an organism has, as in sex-determination, two different sex-chromosomes (in koi the male is carrying XY and the female, which has homogametic sex, is carrying XX chromosomes).

Heterosis–Hybrid vigor. Increased phenotypic values of a hybrid as compared to the parents and usually caused by increasing heterozygosity.

Heterozygote–An organism or a cell carrying two different alleles at a given locus.

Homogametic–The condition in which the organism is carrying two copies of the same sex-chromosomes (as in the female koi, which has XX chromosomes).

Homologous chromosomes–Chromosomes carrying the same genes.

Homozygote–An individual or cell carrying two copies of the same allele at a given locus.

Inbreeding–The mating of related organisms (e.g., brother-sister, father-daughter, etc.). Repeated inbreeding results in inbreeding–depression.

Inbreeding-depression–A decrease of fitness (or vigor) due to increased homozygosity.

Locus–The position (location) where a specific gene is located.

Meiosis–A sequence of events involved in cell division that results in the reduction of the number of chromosomes, prior to generation of gametes: ova and sperm. In *spermatogenesis* from a single primary cell (spermatogonum), four single spermatozoa are generated. In the process of *oogenesis* sets of chromosomes are extruded from the cell in the form of two polar bodies, and each single primary cell (oogonum) results in one ovum.

Mendel's principles–(1) Every gamete carries only one allele from each pair in the parent organism (the principle of segregation); (2) Alleles at different loci assort independently during the process of gametogenesis (the principle of independent assortment).

Mitosis–Nucleus division during cell division that does not result in production of gametes with haploid number of chromosomes.

Phenotype–The detectable character of an individual as expressed by the interaction between its genotype and environment.

Recessive–An allele or trait expressed phenotypically only in a homozygote.

Recombination–Exchange of alleles between homologous chromosomes during meiotic crossing-over.

Segregation–The separation into different gametes and thence into different offspring.

Sex-chromosome (gonosome)–A chromosome carrying the sex determinants.

Trait–Any detectable (phenotypic) characterisitic of an organism.

Zygote–Primary diploid cell resulting from fertilization (fusion of sperm and egg).

LITERATURE CITED

Fletcher, N. 1991. Planned parenthood in the pond. *Practical Fishkeeping*, June 1991:94-97.

Hickling, F. C. 1971. *Fish Culture*. Faber & Faber, London. 371 pp.

Katasonov, V. Ya. 1973. Investigation of color in hybrids of common and ornamental (Japanese) carp. Communication I. Transmission of dominant color types. *Soviet Genetics*, 9:985-992.

Katasonov, V. Ya. 1974. Investigation of color in hybrids of common and ornamental carp. II. Pleiotropic effects of dominant color genes. *Soviet Genetics*, 10:1504-1512.

Katasonov, V. Ya. 1976. Lethal action of the light color gene in carp (*Cyprinis carpio* L.). *Soviet Genetics*, 12:514-516.

Katasonov, V. Ya. 1978. Color in hybrids of common and ornamental (Japanese) carp. III. Inheritance of blue and orange color types. *Soviet Genetics (Genetika)*, 14:1522-1528.

GYNOGENESIS IN KOI
REPRODUCTION

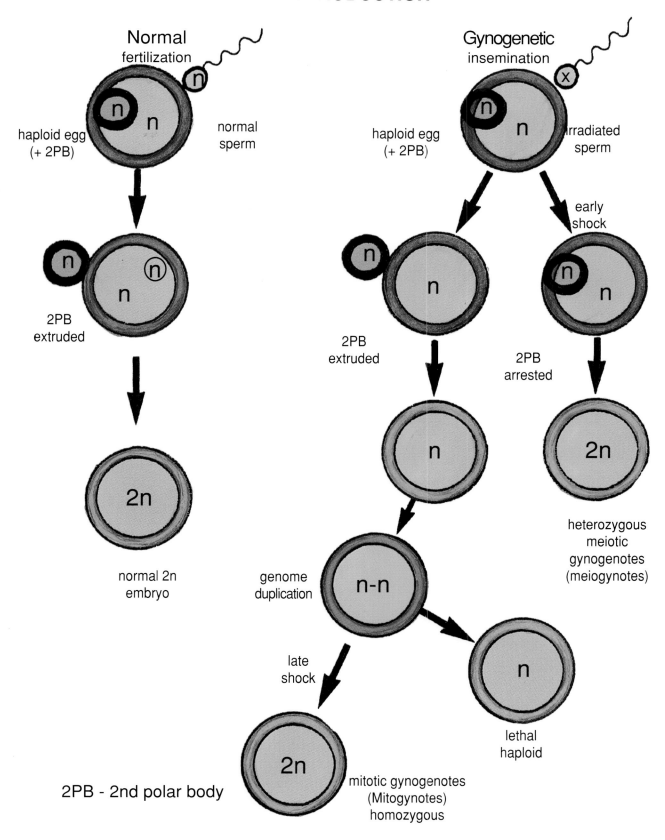

Schematic comparison of normal fertilization and gynogenesis.

Kirpichnikov, V. S. 1979. *Genetic Bases of Fish Selection.* (Translated by G. G. Gause). Springer Verlag, Berlin (1981). 410 pp.

Komen, J., P. de Boer, and C. J. J. Richter. 1992 Male sex reversal in gynogenetic XX females of common carp (*Cyprinus carpio* L.) by a recessive mutation in a sex-determining gene. *J. Heredity,* 83:431-434.

Kuroki, T. 1986. *Manual to Nishikigoi.* Shuji Fujita, Shin Nippon Kyhoiku Tosho Co., Ltd., Shimonoseki-city, Japan. 240 pp.

Kuroki, T. 1986. *Modern Nishikigoi, Basic Varieties and Unique Koi.* Shuji Fujita, Shin Nippon Kyhoiku Tosho Co., Ltd., Shimonoseki-city, Japan. 240 pp.

Matsui, Y. 1972. *Goldfish Guide.* T.F.H. Publications, Neptune, N.J. 250 pp.

McDowall, A. (ed.) 1989. *The Interpret Encyclopedia of Koi.* Salamander Books Ltd., London & New York. 208 pp.

Mendel, G. 1865. *Experiments in Plant Hybridization.* Reprinted in: J. A. Peters (ed.) 1959. *Classic Papers in Genetics.* Prentice Hall, Englewood Cliffs, N.J.

Merla, G. 1982. Farbvarianten und ihre Vererbung bei Wirtscharftsfischen. *Z. Binnenfish. DDR,* 29:155-158.

Moav, R. and G. W. Wohlfarth, 1968. Genetic improvement of yield in carp. *FAO Fish. Rep.,* 44(4):12-29.

Probst, E. 1949. Der blaulig Karpfen. *Allg. Fisch. Atg.,* 74:232-238.

Rothbard, S. 1991. Induction of endomitotic gynogenesis in the nishikigoi, Japanese ornamental carp. *Israeli J. Aquacult.-Bamidgeh,* 43:145-155.

Rothbard, S. 1994. Cloning of nishikigoi, Japanese ornamental (koi) carp. *Israeli J. Aquacult.-Bamidgeh,* 46:171-181.

Szweigman, D., S. Rothbard, and G. Wohlfarth, 1992. Further observations on the inheritance of color in koi. *Nichirin,* 5:37-41.

Taniguchi, N. 1991. New improvement method of nishikigoi. *Nichirin,* 5:20-29.

Tamadachi, M. 1990. *The Cult of the Koi.* T.F.H. Publications, Inc., Neptune, NJ. 288 pp.

Wohlfarth, G.W. and Rothbard, S., 1991. Preliminary investigations on color inheritance in Japanese ornamental carp (nishiki-goi). *Israeli J. Aquacult.-Bamidgeh,* 43:62-68.

Zhong-ge, Z. 1984. Goldfish. pp. 381-385 in: I. L. Mason (ed.). *Evolution of Domesticated Animals.* Longman, London & New York.

t395-89

A hydrostatic pressure cylinder for diploidization of fish eggs.

The Common Carp, *Cyprinus carpio:* Its wild origin, domestication in aquaculture, and selection as colored nishikigoi

Eugene K. Balon

Institute of Ichthyology and Department of Zoology,
University of Guelph, Guelph, Ontario NIG 2WI, Canada

SYNOPSIS

Paleogeographical, morphological, ecological, physiological, linguistic, archaeological and historical evidence is used to explain the origin and history of the domestication of the wild common carp. The closest wild ancestor of the common carp originated in the drainages of the Black, Caspian and Aral Seas and dispersed west as far as the Danube River and east into Siberia. The common carp today is represented by the uncertain east Asian subspecies *Cyprinus carpio haematopterus* and by the European *Cyprinus carpio carpio*. There is some reason to think that Romans were the first to culture carp collected from the Danube, and that the tradition of the "piscinae dulces" was continued in monasteries throughout the Middle Ages. We have much better documentation of carp culture in ponds of lay and clerical landowners in western Europe after the 11th century. Distribution of the common carp west of the Danube's piedmont zone was clearly brought about by humans, as was its introduction throughout the continents. Some domestication in China may have occurred independently of similar activities in Europe, but most of the modern-day activities with the common carp in far east Asia are restricted to the domesticated common carp imported from Europe, or at best to hybrids of local and imported strains. The xanthic (red) common carp seem to have first appeared in early cultures of Europe, China and Japan but reached their fame through recent artificial selection of multicolored aberrants in Niigata Prefecture of Japan. In monetary value, production of the colored carp — the Japanese "nishikigoi" — now exceeds the production of carp as human food. As "swimming flowers" nishikigoi delight modern people as much as the taste of carp

may have delighted the Romans and medieval folks at the beginning of carp domestication. The common carp is not only the most important domesticated fish but contributes over 1 million metric tons to world aquaculture. The surviving wild forms of the common carp are threatened or close to the fate of the aurochs, the ancestor of cattle, which became extinct in 1627.

PRELUDE

According to the latest statistics for 1992 available (FAO 1994, Tacon 1994) the common carp, *Cyprinus carpio*, contributed 1,022,887 metric tons (mt) to the total of 9,417,153 mt of aquaculture production of fishes around the world. Out of this, 125,893 mt were produced in European ponds, 706,119 mt in China and 87,000 mt in Indonesia, to select the highest few (see also Kestemont 1995).

In that same year (1992) all cultured carp species combined yielded 5,386,201 mt. The following figures are for the individual species: silver carp *Hypophthalmichthys molitrix* — 1,616,613 mt, grass carp *Ctenopharyngodon idellus* — 1,252,728 mt, each more than the common carp; bighead carp *Hypophthalmichthys nobilis* — 786,604 mt, mrigal carp *Cirrhinus mrigala* — 295,551 mt, goldfish *Carassius auratus*[1] — 259,198 mt, mud carp *Cirrhinus mulitorella* — 81,050 mt, the black carp *Mylopharyngodon piceus* — 52,287 mt, the milem carp *Osteochilus hasselti* — 9,870 mt, and the hovens carp *Leptobarbus hoeveni* — 9,413 mt. In all cases China contributed the largest amount.

Even though the accuracy of the above statistics might be doubtful, especially where

[1]In the FAO statistics goldfish is erroneously given as the crucian carp *C. carassius*. Crucian carp is not used in aquaculture and is quite rare (J. Holčík, personal communication).

Fig.1. The wild common carp from a spawning school of the Lesser Danube above Kolárovo (photograph by E.K. Balon, 1955).

China is concerned, the percentage of carp species in aquaculture production is considerable: all carp species together provided 57% of all fishes produced in aquaculture in 1992, 19% of which were common carp alone; thus common carp yielded twice as much as all the salmonids combined[2]. These values do not include the aquaculture production of nishikigoi, the most expensive fish in the world, which is merely a color aberrant of the common carp, selectively bred for ornamental purposes. Clearly, the common carp is the most widely cultured and domesticated fish in the world, and the dominant aquaculture product of Europe and Asia. Yet we know less about its origin than about the origin of other domesticated organisms.

In its wild state the common carp depends on floodplains for spawning, the rapidly disappearing habitat of its native rivers. Most of the wild populations of common carp are now extinct or threatened by introgression with escaped or stocked domesticated forms. Genetically pure wild forms may be extremely rare.

The worldwide economic importance of the common carp and the endangered condition of its wild populations are one reason why I am presenting this updated version of my essay on the origin and domestication of the common carp recently published in "The Carp" volume of Aquaculture (Balon 1995). Some additions, amendments and corrections have been made but large parts are reprinted verbatim. The present "revised edition" also gives me the opportunity to include more figures, many in color.

With this study I come full circle — the wild common carp became a focus of attention soon after I started my first permanent position after graduation, and I have again been asked to focus on it now, when close to retirement. This revised version will appear in the year of my retirement, shortly after my first supervisor, collaborator and friend, Ota Oliva, died. I did not realize all this when asked to revisit the topic once again by the organizers of "The Carp" symposium, and it is of little relevance to anybody but me. Impatient readers may wish to skip the rest of this Prelude.

One of the most conspicuous fish in

---

[2] Furthermore, while salmonid aquaculture is solely feed based, common carp production "is mainly under semi-intensive pond culture conditions with only a small proportion (2-3%) cultivated intensively (Tacon, 1993) using relatively low-cost artificial diets...." (Kaushik 1995, pp. 225-226).

commercial catches during my early work on the Slovak part of the Danube (1953 to 1967) was the wild common carp. Some fishermen even designed special boats (Mišík 1957) to capture the abundant spawning schools on the flooded areas of the river. These schools consisted of large, torpedo-shaped, fully scaled and gold colored carp (Fig. 1), and were so strikingly different from the pond carp I had known since childhood that the parallel to aurochs and domestic cattle came to my mind. Most of the wild common carp of spawning size were over 0.5 m long and had 3 to 5 kg wet mass; some females were 9 and some males up to 15 years old. As a consequence I designed and started a research program on many aspects of the biology of these wild common carp which had been ignored earlier. A series of papers from the Ichthyological Laboratory in Bratislava (Slovakia) I founded (Balon 1957, 1958a,b, 1967a,c, 1969, Balon & Mišík 1956, Mišík 1958, Tuča[3], Mišík & Tuãa 1965, Bastl, 1961, 1962) and from other institutes of that time in Poland and Bohemia (Rudziński 1961, Chytra et al. 1961) ensued. Subsequently, time has shown that this was the last opportunity for such studies, for towards the end of my 14 years of work on the Danube, these fish became rare and now are listed as endangered (Holčík 1989, 1995b).

None of these initial zoological studies were published in English: most appeared in Slovak, some in Czech or German. Only my first attempts to incorporate aspects of cultural history into the discussion on the domestication of the wild common carp were written in English (Balon 1969, 1974). The theory advanced at that time was later accepted by archaeologists (e.g. Rajtár 1990, 1992) and may have influenced the collection of fish bones ignored during earlier excavations of Roman settlements on the Danube (Carnuntum, Brigetio). Additional evidence can now, 25 years later, be presented in support of the Roman origin of carp domestication. The evidence for the Roman involvement, however, still remains weak. Recently Hoffmann (1994, 1995) even cast doubts on any such involvement of Romans for

lack of direct "historical" data. Nevertheless, Hoffmann (1994) supports the idea that the wild common carp had its origin in the Danube River, but he claims that according to historical sources uncovered by him, the introduction of the carp west of the Danube occurred much later, into secular as well as ecclesiastical ponds of medieval times (10 to 15th century).

While I acknowledge that evidence for common carp culture by the Romans and by the early religious orders is mostly circumstantial (e.g. Dubravius 1547, von Hohberg 1687 and even Walton 1676), Hoffmann's (1994) reliance on secular sources of the late Middle Ages mentioning carp explicitly may merely reflect more frequent production and preservation of such documents. Likewise, as fishes were little known then and literacy limited, the vernacular "carp" may often have referred to not only the common carp, and one should not uncritically trust such documents. Therefore, I see no reason to abandon the Roman and monastic involvement in the initial domestication of the common carp.

Another aspect which emerged during the 25 years since the publication of my first essay on the domestication of the wild carp is the artificial selection, breeding, popularity and commerce of the colored carp, initially in Japan and now also in other countries of the world. Carp domestication for food was expanded by aquaculture of nishikigoi, the colored carp also called "living jewels" — domestication of the "fancy carp" for pleasure only (Amano 1968, 1971). While these colored carp are the latest addition to the importance of common carp around the world, their origin is just as clouded as the information on the original involvement of the Romans, due to incomplete and inconsistent documentation and reporting (Axelrod 1973, 1988, Davies 1989, Tamadachi 1990). Maybe all the textbooks are wrong and it all happened differently than popularly believed!

---

[3] Tuča, V.1958. Studium genetickej (exterierovej) čistoty dunajskeho kapra (Study of the genetic purity of the Danubian carp). Final Report, Laboratory for Fishery Research, Bratislava (unpublished).

INTRODUCTION

Domestication of plants and animals is one of the most significant and fascinating aspects of human history. The questions of where and how organisms were first domesticated have occupied many scholars. Definitive answers are rarely produced (Zeuner 1963, Isaac 1970) because most of these domestications happened as early as the Neolithic (roughly 14,000 years ago). "In the study of domestication the scientist and the cultural historian join forces, each playing a role which the other discipline, by its very nature, cannot fill" (Isaac 1962).

Some plants and animals are kept, tamed and even bred in captivity with little change from their wild state. Most of these are continuously backcrossed with wild individuals and can escape or be returned to the wild without marked differences from their ancestral wild stock. These are not domesticated (Isaac 1962, 1970). In a truly domesticated organism,

(a) the individual is valued and kept for a specific purpose,

(b) its breeding is subject to human control,

   (c) its behavior is different from that of the wild ancestor, and

   (d) its morphology (including size, coloration) exhibits variation never seen in the wild,

   (e) some of which would not survive without human protection .

"During the late Mesolithic and early Neolithic periods when man was experimenting with the breeding of early domestic dogs and livestock animals it is probable that those animals that were easy to distinguish and markedly different from the wild species would be especially favoured ..." (Clutton-Brock 1981, p. 22). "There are many visible earmaks of domestication. One, however, must be stressed above all others, and that is the matter of *dependence*. All domesticated animals depend for their day-to-day survival upon their owners. The capacities of wild self-sufficiency having long since been substracted from them, they must depend upon whatever prosthetic devices their owners see fit to provide" (Livingston 1994, p. 14).

With these arguments in mind we can now

Fig. 2. Aurochsen depicted by various artists: a - by Heberstain, 1549; b - this figure is based on a painting which Hamilton Smith found in a shop in Augsburg, of the last living aurochs; c - bull of *Bos primigenius* of the Upper Paleolithic as depicted in the cave of Lascaux, France (all from Zauner 1963).

return to the initial association of the carp domestication with that of cattle. While domesticated at a much earlier date then the common carp, the "present-day types of domestic cattle, zoologists believe, are all derived from one ancestral strain, *Bos primigenius*, or the wild urus[4], an animal which survived in Europe until the late Middle Ages (the last remaining specimen died in 1627). *Bos namadicus*, whose relics are found in Asia[5] and *Bos opisthonomous* found in North Africa are assumed today to be *Bos primigenius*. The urus formerly ranged over a vast area of Eurasia, from

Fig. 3. Plate 16 from volume 1 of *Illustrations of Japanese aquatic plants and animals* (Ishikawa et al. 1931) attests that by 1931 at least some colored carps were known in Japan beside goldfish. Suspiciously absent are any of the modern "nishikigoi" which puts in doubt the popularly claimed at least a century older selection of the first "fancy carps": the depicted fish are labelled "koi" carp (left top), "sytsui" colored leather carp (top right), "higoi" red carp (center right) and "kohakugoi" colored carp (bottom right). The remaining two are goldfish.

the Pacific to the Atlantic" (Isaac 1970, p.81). However, "zoology, indeed, has little to say about the social conditions of domestication, and for clarification of this problem we must rely on the hypotheses of the culture historians. In the absence of conclusive evidence, they have constructed their theory on the origin and process of domestication of cattle largely on the basis of deductive reasoning (...)" (Isaac 1962, p. 195).

Hahn (1896), for example, "relates the taming of the wild ox to lunar cults of the people from the Hoeing Era of the Upper Stone Age. The moon with its regularly changing phases was the symbol of fertility, and the crescent-shaped horns of the ox became the hallmark of the lunar goddess, who, at specific times, demanded consecrated animals as a sacrifice. In the beginning, oxen from the wild were still captured for this purpose, but soon people changed to keeping the captured animals in pens. Thus, they eventually formed the first herds of cattle in the holy groves of the goddess. Since only certain organs of the animal were burnt during ceremony, the participants ate the meat [see another parallel in Harris 1977], and many peoples may have come to consider the cattle a useful supplier of meat. The use of sacred animals to pull a plough was at first also a ritual act. But as the plough lost its sacred value, cattle became more of a work animal. The utilization of the milk came thousands of years later" (Wünschmann 1972, p. 371).

While the captured aurochsen (Fig. 2) were kept in corrals as a ready supply for

---

[4] I prefer the name of **aurochs** to urus or wild oxen for the ancestor of cattle, but left the latter two in original citaitons.

[5] *Bos primigenius namadicus* has been recognized from Pleistocene fossil records. It is possible that this form was the ancestor of the humped zebu cattle of India which later spread to Africa and Asia (Clutton-Bock 1981, p. 64).

sacrifices, free to reproduce and protected from predators, individuals of different forms and colors started to appear. Their establishment within the herd was possibly accelerated by selection of the best aurochs-like types for sacrifice. According to archaeological evidence, this early domestication occurred in the ancient agricultural societies of the Near East, but was preceded by the domestication of the gray wolf, *Canis lupus*, at several other places.

Not all domestications can be interpreted as a consequence of rational decisions by humans who recognized the potential benefits of bringing the animal under their control (Galton 1865). The gray wolf, for example, was undoubtedly the first animal which started to change about 12,000 years ago into races of domestic dogs by cohabitation with humans (Clutton-Brock 1981). The first changes were caused by the new environment associated with living among people and less, or not at all, by a deliberate human manipulation (Frank 1987, Morey 1994). The economic importance of cattle was also recognized gradually and the first traits of domestication developed naturally through the association with humans. Conscious artificial selection by people nearly always started when the potential of domestication was recognized. Therefore, each domestication process can be identified as having two phases of varying length: **association** with humans causing natural evolutionary changes and **artificial selection**, an aspect of human cultural history. During domestication of the wild carp, the phase of association may go back to Romans but artificial selection may have started only after the 13th century. Extremely rapid artificial selection is evident in the recent creation of nishikigoi in which the spontaneous occurrence of color aberrations (Fig. 3) was followed by organized artificial selection (see later).

The wolf persists in its wild form despite a multitude of domesticated derivatives ranging from large to miniature forms, and feral sidelines (e.g. dingo). The same applies to the red jungle fowl, *Gallus gallus* of Thailand, the ancestor of the domestic chicken (Raethel 1972). The aurochs did not make it, however, and cattle became orphaned without a living ancestor (Fig. 4a). The common carp is or will soon be another such orphan. His fate receives much less attention than the similarly endangered Przewalski's horse (Fig. 4b,c).

While the gray wolf, sheep, goat, guanaco, pig and the aurochs are the oldest economically important animals to be domesticated, followed by the red jungle fowl, the wild cat, *Felis silvestris libyca*, Przewalski's wild horse, *Equus przewalskii* (e.g. Volf 1975), and a multitude of other animals, the wild common carp may be one of the youngest, but it competes for that distinction with the rabbit, *Oryctolagus cuniculus*. The origin of domestication of both carp (Balon 1966, 1967a,c, 1969, 1974) and the rabbit (e.g. Angermann 1975, Clutton-Brock 1981, Robinson 1984) has been traced, ultimately, to the Romans.

Before reviewing and expanding my original hypothesis of the first common carp domestication by Romans and the medieval Europeans, I will consider distribution, morphology and life-history of the wild carp in the area from which the initial specimens were, most likely, taken for domestication.

THE WILD COMMON CARP

The identity of the preglacial remnants of the common carp, *Cyprinus carpio*, in western Europe (Ruetimeyer 1860, Zaunick 1925) is doubtful (Forel 1906, Steffens 1980) and was never confirmed. The ancestral form with a greater number of pharyngeal teeth, akin to *C. carpio anatolicus* Hankó, 1924, probably evolved in the area of the Caspian Sea at the end of the Pliocene. Some fossil forms from Hungary had more numerous pharyngeal teeth, much like *C. c. anatolicus* (see Hankó 1932). During the various glacial periods of the Pleistocene, the carp's range shrank dramatically. Modern common carp, *Cyprinus carpio*, evolved from the Caspian Sea ancestor and spread again into basins of the Black and Aral Seas (Berg 1948, 1964). Under conditions of the postglacial thermal optimum some descendants spread as far as the Danube and, possibly, into eastern mainland Asia; the natural occurrence of the extant common carp in Japan, however, is dubious because the Japanese archipelago was last connected to mainland Asia during some of the Pleistocene glacial episodes (e.g. Fujita 1973, Ikebe 1978), long before the possible arrival of the modern common carp (Ishikawa et al. 1931). While teeth of fossil *Cyprinus* were present in Japanese Pliocene deposits, the "difference in shape of the teeth between the fossil and living forms gives suggestion [sic] that the fossil *Cyprinus* is a different species from *Cyprinus carpio*" (Nakajima 1986, p. 505).

Cyprinus carpio appeared in the Danube River only about 8,000 to 10,000 years ago (Borzenko 1926, Hankó 1932, Bǎnǎrescu 1960). Therefore, it is unlikely that the carp occurred naturally in waters of central and western Europe outside the Danube River at the beginning of the Christian era. Ausonius (A.D. 310 - 393; 1933) did not mention carp in the fauna of the Rhine and Mosel Rivers. Likewise, none of the known archaeological remains of carp in Europe before the Middle Ages are from sites west of the Danube (Hoffmann 1994a). All later records of sporadic occurrence of carp in west European rivers may be explained by individuals having escaped from ponds [see Bloch's (1782) claims above and Hoffmann 1994a].

According to "ancient stories and myths", the Great Schütt Island (origin of most of the specimens described in the next sections) was surrounded by a "great number of golden carp (*Cyprinus auratus*) that enabled even the poorest people to make a living; yes, there were times when the fishermen gave them away as gifts" (translated from Khin 1930). We saw and sampled the great spawning schools still there in 1955-1956 (Balon & Mišík 1956) and were aware of their continued existence until the early 1970s. Why, then, did Jordan & Evermann (1896-1900, 1902), Thieneman (1950), Maar (1960), Vooren (1972), and so many others believe that the carp reached Rome from China? Plainly because, once claimed[6], it was copied from one "authority" to the next (e.g. Leonhardt 1906, Tamura 1961, Hickling 1962, Steffens 1967, Borgese 1980).

[6] For example, Gilbert White (1720-1793) in a letter published 1786 about goldfish then introduced to England, stated that *"Gold* and *silver fishes,* though originally natives of China and Japan, yet are become so well reconciled to our climate as to thrive and multiply very fast in our ponds and stews. Linnaeus ranks this species of fish under the genus of *cypiinus,* or carp, and call it *cyprinus auratus"* (Massingham 1985, p. 214).

a

b

c

Fig. 4. Recent intergeneric crosses between cattle, the domesticated aurochs *Bos primigenius taurus,* and the European *Bison bonasus* yield a heavy hybrid (a) but no substitute for the forever lost wild **aurochs**. An attempt to revive by reverse breeding one of the ancestors of the domesticated horse extinct in the central European forests of Middle Ages, the forest tarpan, *Equus przewalskii silvaticus,* were only partially successful (b) (photographs by E.K. Balon at the Białowieża Forest, Poland 1993). The main horse ancestor, Przewalski's wild horse of the Mongolian plains, *Equus przewalskii przewalskii* (c), is now extinct in the wild and survives only in zoological gardens (photograph by E.K. Balon in the Prague zoo, the main breeding center of the remaining wild horses, 1991).

It is possible that the domestication of wild carp in China began independently from Europe and, if so, then probably involved the east Asian subspecies *Cyprinus carpio haematopterus*, if such is taxonomically valid. The latest, anonymous Chinese study [the following quotations are from the Russian translation (Anon. 1961)] on pond culture stated that "thanks to the creative efforts of the Chinese people for many generations, breeding of the carp in this country has proceeded successfully for more than 2,000 years. From China the breeding of this fish spread all over the world (...) to Europe and later to America, Australia, and Africa" [sic]. [Readers of medieval travelers' accounts, i.e. of Marco Polo, will doubt also the likelihood of the common carp coming alive across Central Asia or the Indian Ocean; all these accounts are of later date than the documented presence of carp in western Europe (Richard Hoffmann, personal communication).] The sources usually given are similar to these compiled by Borgese (1980, p. 16): "In China, aquaculture is rooted in antiquity. A treatise called *Fish Breeding*, the 'Classic of Fish Culture', ascribed to Fan Li and dated 475 B.C., illustrates the spawning of captive carp and indicates that fish farming was widely practiced in China at that time. *Kwai Sin Chak Shik*, a book written during the Sung Dynasty in A.D. 1243, describes how carp fry were transported in bamboo baskets — much the way they are transported and traded today. The fry were collected in rivers and reared in ponds; this is recorded in *A Complete Book of Agriculture*, written in A.D. 1639". But if the fish "fry were collected in rivers" it is doubtful whether they were the common carp, *Cyprinus carpio*, which is not a riverine pelagic spawner. They were more likely the young of other carps, such as the grass carp *Ctenopharyngodon idellus*, silver carp *Hypophthalmichthys molitrix*, bighead carp *H. nobilis*, and black carp *Mylopharyngodon piceus*, which are true riverine pelagic spawners and cannot be bred in ponds or rice paddy conditions. I am dubious as to whether the collective vernacular name "carp" in these documents did refer to *Cyprinus carpio* (e.g. Hervey 1950, but see Hensel 1980).

There is much evidence that in China the common carp was never truly domesticated, but stocked at most, in a semi-domesticated condition with other fishes (Wohlfarth 1984). As China was virtually inaccessible until a century ago, would it be possible for the common carp to have been brought from there in the first years of the Gregorian calendar or the beginning of the Middle Ages? While I am willing to admit, hesitantly, the possibility of independent domestication of the wild common carp, *C. carpio haematopterus*, in China, there is good evidence that the European pond carp was introduced in some regions of eastern Asia (Ishikawa et al. 1931, Buschkiel 1933, Fernando 1971) and so at best introgressed stocks of domesticated European and Asian subspecies of carp may actually be present (Wohlfarth 1984). This hypothesis needs to be critically examined (Fig. 5). Amano (1971, p. 23) vaguely asserts that "Central Asia is the original home of the carp. It is said to have been transferred eastward to China and Japan, and westward into the whole area of Europe by way of Greece and Rome". In a recent book on nishikigoi (koi), Tamadachi[7] (1990, p. 13) even writes that "the original stock that was to produce the many beautiful koi that can be seen today can be traced back to the wild carp exported from Eurasia [sic] to the Far Eastern countries some 2,000 years ago". Would this not be poetic justice after such a long time of misinterpretation?

Therefore, while there is evidence of introductions of domesticated common carp from Europe to Asia (and of course America, Australia and Africa), introductions in the reverse direction are not documented until quite recently (mainly as nishikigoi). Consequently, the Danubian wild common carp may be the purest form and, among extant fishes, the best parallel to the aurochs.

As will be documented later, the true wild form of common carp is a powerful, elongated and torpedo-shaped animal with large, regular scales and a golden (yellow-brown) color (Fig. 1). The dorsal contours of its head and body continue in

[7] Found out to be a frivolous pseudonym for Herbert Axelrod.

one smooth curve. A scaled carp was illustrated by Bloch (1782, fig. 16) together with another domesticated "line mirror carp", the smooth dorsal contour clearly an artist's simplification of the area where a notch should occur. Nevertheless, Bloch states that "Das Vaterland des Karpfen ist ohnstreitig in den südlicheren Theilen

more years ago, when there were no carps in England, as may seem to be affirmed by Sir Richard Baker, in whose *Chronicle* you may find these verses:

Hops and turkey, carps and beer,
Came into England all in a year."

Burton & Burton (1968, p.384), however, claim that "Emma Phipson, in *The*

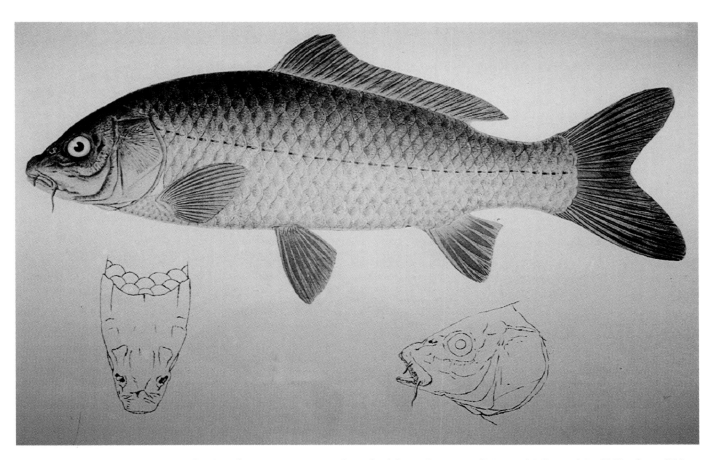

Fig. 5. The Asian common carp *Cyprinus haematopterus* was described from the area of Nagasaki (Japan) in 1850 where 200 or so years earlier the first colonies of Portuguese and Dutch were established. The common carp culture was by then widespread in the European homelands of these colonists and it is, therefore, possible that carp was imported by them to Japan (see also Fig. 34) (from Siebold 1850).

Europens zu suchen (...) in den nördlichen Ländern hingegen ist er durch die Versetzung gemein geworden. So brachte ihn Maschal im Jahre 1514 nach England" (p. 93). The chapter in Izaak Walton (1676, after the 1988 Bloomsbury Books edition with modernized spelling, p. 145) on carp starts "The Carp is the queen of rivers; a stately, a good, and a very subtle fish; that was not at first bred, nor hath been long in England, but is now naturalized. It is said they were brought hither by one Mr Mascal, a gentleman that then lived at Plumstead, in Sussex ... (...) there was a time, about a hundred or a few

Animal-Lore of Shakespeare's Time (1883) speaks of Leonard Mascall, a Sussex gentleman, who has had the credit for importing the carp into England about the year 1514. She also points out that in the Privy Purse Expenses of Elizabeth of York, 1502, mention is made of a reward paid for the present of carp". As the carp is the "coarse" fish most sought by freshwater anglers in modern Britain, the following paragraph from Zeuner (1963, pp. 480-481) seems also worthwhile quoting: "Hahn (1896) paid attention to the question of its [the carp's] introduction into the British Isles. The rhyme that

Turkey, carps, hops, pickerell and beer,
came into England all in one year,
by which year is meant 1514, is nonsense throughout. The turkey arrived later, and the other items earlier. As to the carp, Dame Juliana Barnes mentions it in the *Book of St Albans*, printed in 1468 as one of the first English books. From her words it is evident that the fish was not very popular...". However, the latter collection of four treatises on gentle pursuits, in existence since ca. 1400, was not authored by the Julyans Barnes (or Juliana Berners). It was published at St Albans in 1486, and the "treatyse" on fishing was added in 1496 for the edition of Wynkyn de Worde (Ousby 1992). How can a biologist make sense of such contradictory historical evidence (e.g. Hoffmann 1994a)!

A feral form of the common carp is depicted in the Baron Carl von Meidinger's "Icones Piscium Austriae" (1785-1794), for it has the typical notch at the dorsum between the end of the head and the beginning of the back (Fig. 6). The enormous variation in forms, illustrated and described later, for example, by Heckel & Kner (1858), Hermann (1887), Antipa (1909) and even recently by Pintér (1989), can reflect various states of reversal from the domesticated pond form to the feral form. In addition to the common Danube carp *Cyprinus carpio* akin to Bloch's scaled form, Heckel & Kner (1858) also described from the Danube the deep-bodied *C. acuminatus* and *C. hungaricus*, of which only the latter has the shape typical of the wild carp (Fig. 7). In contrast, Antipa (1909) described and illustrated from the Danube delta a wild carp-like *C. carpio* forma *typica*, a feral-like form *C. carpio* var. *gibbosus*, and again wild carp-like *C. carpio* var. *hungaricus* and *C. carpio* var. *oblongus*, but presents an illustration of the pharyngeal bones from Heckel & Kner (1858, fig. 25) which belong to *C. hungaricus*. Antipa's last plate represents a wild carp-like *Cyprinus carpio* var. *imperator*, more greenish with silver in scale centers and red in fins rather than gold, at least in my copy of the book (Fig. 8).

It is time to put some order into this confusion. Both the scientific nomenclature and the natural distribution of the wild carp need to be clarified.

LINGUISTIC THESIS IN SUPPORT OF THE DANUBIAN WESTERN-MOST DISTRIBUTION

The natural occurrence of the wild carp in Europe is restricted to the stretch in the Danube downstream of the river's piedmont zone (Balon 1964, 1967c, 1968, Balon et al. 1986). The mistaken belief that the carp's natural distribution went beyond this area can be finally put to rest by a linguistic argument, first raised by Leonhardt (1906), which asserts that local names used for the carp in different areas can tell much about the natural and cultural distribution of that fish. Much misinterpretation could have been avoided had later linguists (e.g. Leder 1968, Kolomyets 1983) followed similar reasoning and not overlooked Leonhardt's book.

The scientific binominal name assigned by Linnaeus to the common carp, *Cyprinus carpio*, has two different older cultural origins. What has become the generic name of carp is from Greek — *kyprinos* or *kyprianos* — the name used by Aristotle (384-322 B.C.; 1862). This name was probably derived from "Kypris" (Lat. *Cypria*), a secondary name of the goddess of love, Aphrodite — perhaps because the high fertility of carp and noisy mass spawning in shallows was known even then. Later the name was latinized to *cyprinus*, probably by Pliny the Elder.

What has become the specific name for common carp comes from what Leonhardt (1906) hypothesized was its vernacular name among Celtic-speaking humans who, before the Roman conquest of the area, dominated what are now the eastern Austrian and Slovak-Hungarian shores of the Danube River. From an original *karpo* or *karfo* the name came into Latin as something like *carpa* and then gradually changed to the present *carpio*.

Large schools of spawning carp in the westernmost floodplain of the Danube, the margins of which were inhabited by Celts beyond the middle of the first century A.D. (Mócsy 1974), were a conspicuous occurrence (Fig. 22b). As far upstream the mighty Danube as above the confluence with the Morava (March) River, where the Celts built their Devín (Divinium, Dowina, Theben, Dévény) fort on the northern shore and the Romans the fortress and town Carnuntum on the southern shore, the Latin and Dacian material culture was often found mixed

(Pelikan 1960). As this was also the major crossing point of the river by the Amber Road, traffic in both directions must have been frequent. Some Celts, and later the Romans, were displaced, although most were assimilated, from this area by invading German tribes. The name of carp, if not the fish, likely went with them to the west.

Everywhere to the west and north the fish is named from the root "carp": *Karpfen* in German, *carpa* in Italian, *carpe* in French, *carpa* in Spanish and Portuguese, *carp* in English, *karper* in Dutch, *karpe* in Danish, *kapor* in Slovak, *kapr* in Czech, and *karp* in Polish. Some of these vernaculars could have learned the

word from central European Celtic speakers, others more likely acquired it through either Latin or some Germanic dialect.

Downstream from its westernmost natural distribution in the Danube (i.e. along its endemic range) the carp is called *ponty* in Hungarian, *sharan* in Serbian, *saran* in Bulgarian, *crap, ciortocrap, saran, ciortan, ciuciu, ciuciulean, ciuciulicã, olocari* or *ulucari* in Rumanian, *sazan baligi* or *husgun* in Turkish, *šaran* in Croatian, *sharan* or *podrojek* in Ukrainian, *sazan* in Russian[8] (on the Volga River and elsewhere, see Berg 1948), and *kalynshyr* in Kirgizia. The names are local in the entire endemic area of distribution. As no local names of carp were present west, north and south of the piedmont zone of the Danube, the natural occurrence of this fish beyond that zone is highly unlikely. This corresponds with

[8] *Carp* in Russian is used only for the domesticated form, *sazan* for the wild form.

Fig. 6. A typical wild common carp and a feral form (below) from the Danube delta (after Antipa 1909).

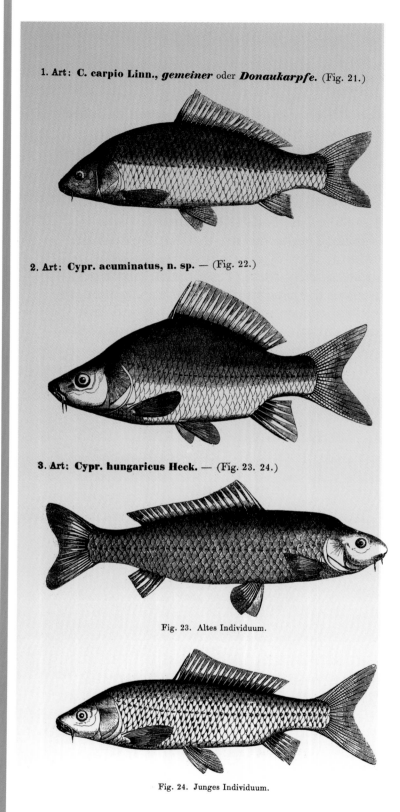

1. Art: **C. carpio** Linn., *gemeiner* oder ***Donaukarpfe.*** (Fig. 21.)

2. Art: **Cypr. acuminatus, n. sp.** — (Fig. 22.)

3. Art: **Cypr. hungaricus Heck.** — (Fig. 23. 24.)

Fig. 23. Altes Individuum.

Fig. 24. Junges Individuum.

Fig. 7. Carp forms from the Danube River described by Heckel & Kner (1858).

the inventory of the earliest archaeological remains of the common carp given by Hoffmann (1994a) which all come from the Danube and Black Sea drainages.

HOW MANY WILD FORMS OF COMMON CARP ARE THERE, IF ANY?

Kirpitchnikov (1967) claimed that there are at least four subspecies of wild carp — the European and Transcaucasian *Cyprinus carpio carpio*, the Middle East *C. carpio aralensis,* east Asian *C. carpio haematopterus*, and the south Chinese and Vietnamese *C. carpio viridiviolaceus*. Kirpitchnikov did not present any evidence to support his view but he basically revived some of the lower taxa which had been lumped by Berg (1964). Others, for example Wu (1977), list numerous (at least 13) species and subspecies from China, each no more than a domesticated to feral intermediate described separately by various authors between 1803 and 1977 (J. Holčík, personal communication). Mišík's (1958) data still remain the only respectable source, and so until molecular biologists confirm or revise his conclusions I will summarize them here again (Balon 1974).

Linnaeus (1758) described only one species of the common carp from Europe, *Cyprinus carpio*. He probably based his description on carp from pond cultures; however, as the origin of such carp was clearly traced to the Danubian wild common carp, we may safely declare the wild carp from the Danube River to be the forma typica (Fig. 9a), the aurochs-like equivalent for the common domesticated carp.

There are three distinct groups of the wild common carp: (1) The European common carp, represented by the western-most populations in the piedmont zone of the Danube River and designated as the representative form; (2) the east Asian common carp from Siberia; and (3) the wild common carp "from the Aral Sea and from other central Asian regions which in some respect appear more closely related to the European form, in others seem to be closer to the east Asian wild carp, and which at the same time are mutually substantially different" (translated from Mišík 1958, p. 106).

The differentiation of the wild common

Fig. 8. Wild common carp *Cyprinus carpio* var. *imperator* described by Antipa (1909) from the Danube River delta.

carp in the region of western central Asia was influenced by an earlier geological age. If western central Asia was indeed the center of origin for the modern common carp, descendants of this original form had a longer time to evolve in isolation than the common carp that had dispersed eastward and westward in the last postglacial period. Even though populations integrated later, more morphs may exist in the western part of central Asia than elsewhere.

However, today we can at best identify only two subspecies: the European common carp *C. carpio carpio* formed from the western dispersant, and Asian common carp *C. carpio haematopterus* from the eastern dispersant of the wild carp. According to Svetovidov (1933) these subspecies may be distinguished mainly by the number of gill rakers. This has been confirmed by Mišík (1958); *C. c. haematopterus* has fewer gill rakers (x = 27) than *C. c. carpio* (x = 32), but their ranges overlap from 24 to 31 and 29 to 36, respectively. A similar pattern was noticed for several other meristic characters, such as the number of the dorsal fin rays, in which the overlap is even greater (Berg 1964). A similar phenomenon was observed, for example, in the bitterling *Rhodeus sericeus*, and led Holčík & Jedlička (1994) to suggest that we dispense with such vague subspecific taxa altogether. As we do not even know if the holotype of *C. haematopterus* from Nagasaki (Fig. 5) was not a feral escapee of European domesticated common carp imported by the Dutch

colonists, the subspecific status for common carp is not justified (see later).

While there may be many altricial and precocial common carp forms within each population and geographical area of distribution (Balon 1989, 1990, Balon & Goto 1989), there is only one species with a continental natural range in Eurasia. Feral common carp, *Cyprinus carpio*, descendants of earlier escapees or introductions (Lelek 1987), are currently confusing the picture and I see no reason for any subspecific distinction.

MORPHOMETRY AND MORPHOLOGY OF THE WILD COMMON CARP

By sheer luck of being in the right place at the right time, Mišík and I were privileged to sample the last remnants of the European wild common carp at its westernmost natural occurrence in the Danube River. We believed that these fish could be the descendants of the much larger wild carp schools that the Celts and Romans encountered near the same area almost two millennia earlier. We thought that if the first captive wild common carp were taken from the westernmost floodplain of the River Danube, detailed studies would be of significance.

So while the age, growth and early ontogeny studies were in progress (Balon 1957, 1958a) Mišík (1958), my technician at that time and a talented statistician, embarked on a morphometric and taxonomic revision. From all the specimens, now deposited at the Slovak National Museum in Bratislava, 87 were se-

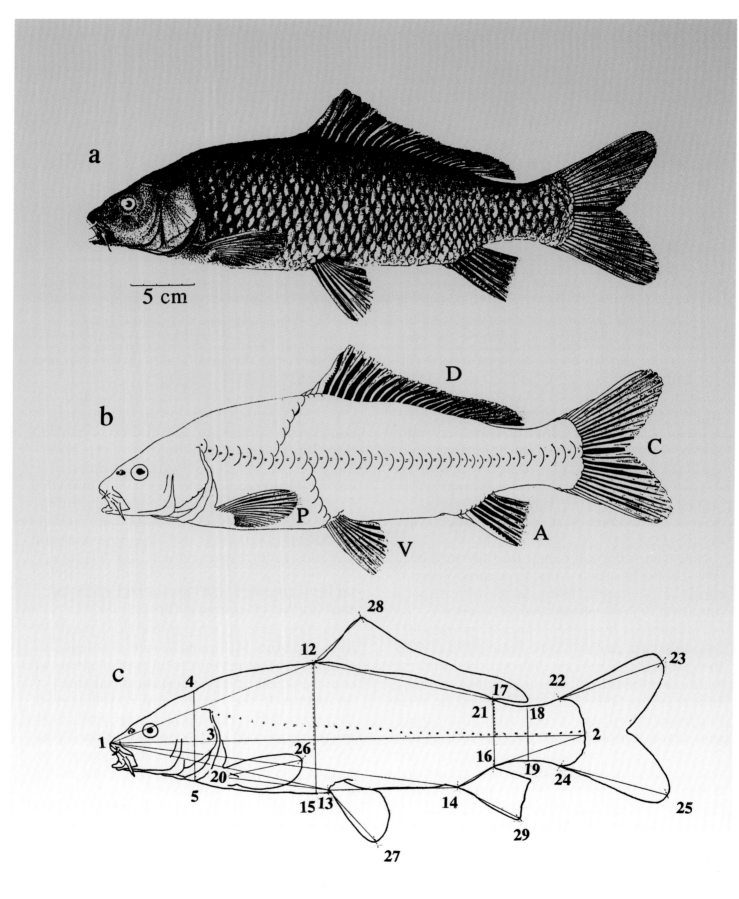

Fig. 9. a - The wild common carp from the Danube River at Medved'ovo, caught 21.5. 1954; b - scheme for counting the meristic characters; c - scheme for mensural characters.

lected as wild carp closest to the type designated as form *hungaricus* (Fig. 10). All specimens were collected in the Slovak part of the Danube and Lesser Danube between May 1954 and May 1956, inclusive.

The wild common carp has an elongated and torpedo-shaped body. The transition between the head and body dorsum is nearly straight, without the clear notch (depression) typical for domesticated or feral carp (Fig. 11). Scales are regular, large and their caudal edges are marked by dark pigment, giving the body a mesh-like appearance (Fig. 1, 9a). The coloration is brown to dark brown on the dorsum, dark golden at the sides and light golden with an orange tinge on the ventral part. The leading spines of the anal fin are yellow-orange, as is the part around the anus. Other fins are dark brown. The lateral line runs through the middle of the sides, and is complete, but barely visible (Fig. 9b).

The meristic characters (Fig. 9b) can be summarized as follows: (a) number of spines and rays in the dorsal fin (II) III-IV 18-21 (22), most frequently 19-20; (b) number of spines and rays in the anal fin (II) III 4-5, most frequently 5 [in both fins the last spine is a large bone strongly serrated along its posterior edge]; (c) number of rays in the caudal fin IV-VIII 16-18 IV-VIII, most frequently V-VII 17 V-VI; (d) number of rays in pectoral fins I (14) 15-18 (19), most frequently I 15-17; (e) number of rays in pelvic fins II 7-9, most frequently II 8 (no significant difference in numbers of lepidotrichia between females and males); (f) number of scales in the lateral line (34-35) 36-39 (40), most frequently 37-39 (no difference between left or right side or between sexes); (g) number of scales above and below lateral line 5-7/5-7, most frequently 6/6; (h) number of gill rakers (outside / inside: 22-28 / 29-34 (36), most frequently 23-27 / 30-34 (no difference between sexes, the inside number is always larger, Fig. 12a); (i) pharyngeal teeth moliform with clear grooves on the crushing edges, in three rows 1.1.3 - 3.1.1 (Fig. 12b); and (j) number of vertebrae constant 38, like the most frequent number of scales in the lateral line. There were no significant differences in these meristic characters from those given by Heckel & Kner (1858), Siebold (1863), Hermann(1887) and Antipa (1909).

The mensural characters (Fig. 9c) of the Danube wild common carp are presented in Table 1. The females were larger than the males (498.5 ±11.17 vs. 447.5 ±6.95 mm SL). Of the 87 specimens investigated 57 were males and 30 females (Fig. 10). Head length of the wild carp from the Danube River is slightly less than $\frac{1}{4}$ of SL. Females have, on average, longer heads than males. The average length of the front barbels is about half that of the rear barbels. Both barbel pairs are longer than in the Russian wild carp (Berg 1964), but Mišík (1958) noted a substantial variation and a clustering of the barbels into long and short barbel morphs. The interorbital width (= width of forehead) is about half the head

Fig. 10. Two wild common carp from a spawning school of Lesser Danube above Kolárovo caught 7.6. 1955. See scars after key scales removal for the age and growth study (Balon 1957). From the collection of the Slovak National Museum, Bratislava. Scale 5 cm (photographs by K. Hensel).

depth. Females have a broader forehead than males. Mature prespawning females have more rounded bellies and therefore a larger pre-anal distance. The most variable character is, of course, the body depth. This character was used in the past by Heckel (1836) and Heckel & Kner (1858) to distinguish among the three forms: *Cyprinus carpio* whose body depth equals $1/3$ of body length, *C. acuminatus* whose depth fits 2.5 to 2.75 times in length, and *C. hungaricus* whose depth fits 3.5 to 4 times in length. Antipa (1909) declared Heckel's species as varieties and distinguished new var. *oblongus* with depth 3.75 to 4.2 times in length. In the meantime, Kessler (1856) described a wild carp from the Dnepr as var. *gibbosus* with depth 2.5 to 2.8 times in length. Other authors kept describing still more morphs until Berg (1964) lumped these into three main morphs: *typica* with depth 33% of length, *hungaricus* with depth 25 to 28% of length, and *elatus* with depth 36 to 40% of length. The domesticated common carp is reported to have body depth 31 to 39% of length (e.g. Brylińska 1986).

While the wild carp studied were mostly within the morphometric range of *hungaricus*, some specimens fell into the range for *typica*. Since body depth reflects condition, sex, and possibly the lotic or lentic environment, the use of this character to distinguish even morphs is unwarranted. On the other hand, large body depth is a clear sign of domestication and probably reflects both the pond's lacustrine conditions and conscious selection; therefore, deep bodied forms of carp — *elatus*, *gibbosus, acuminatus* — if they occur with low bodied wild forms, must be of domesticated origin prior to change into the feral form.

The typical torpedo-like, riverine wild common carp has a conspicuously wide body, much wider than most other cyprinids. In addition, maturation of ovaries in the wild carp is reflected less in body depth than in body width, which in contrast to many other cyprinids, facilitates retention of the torpedo-like body form at all times, possibly as a prerequisite for overcoming strong currents to reach inundated areas for spawning at high water levels.

The length of all fins and of the posterior barbels is slightly larger in males than in females. These and other differences are very

small; they are noticeable only statistically and are probably not of practical significance for distinguishing the sexes. The greater body width of the females at spawning time is the only clearly distinguishable mensural character of sexual dimorphism. In addition, males can be recognized during that time by their release of "milt" in response to the slightest abdominal pressure.

Shortly before and during spawning, males can be safely distinguished by breeding tubercles, which appear as very small granules on the scales above and, more frequently, below the lateral line, on the caudal peduncle and on the head, especially on the anterior parts of opercles, preopercles and under the eyes. Tubercles occur even along the insides of the first rays of the pectoral and pelvic fins, and along the unbranched rays of the dorsal, anal and caudal fins. Breeding tubercles are present also in some females, but only on the head. No females have them on scales or on fins.

The chromosome number of the common carp is 100 (2n) (Ojima & Hitotsumachi 1967) and the species is pseudo-tetraploid (Horváth & Orbán 1995), in contrast to many related diploid cyprinids (Ohno et al. 1967). Ráb (1994) considers the common carp to have ancestral polyploidy of 100 chromosomes with no karyotypic difference between *C. c. carpio* from the Danube and *C. c. haematopterus* from the Amur River.

LIFE HISTORY AND ECOLOGY OF THE WILD COMMON CARP

The wild common carp was a portional spawner. Each female released two or three portions of eggs within a 10 to 14 day interval. The spawning commenced at about 17° C when large schools of carp entered flooded grassflats within the inundated areas of the river. Meadows, freshly flooded to 25-50 cm, were the preferred substrate at all times. Mating groups of one female and several males (but several females per one male were also observed) circled ferociously, often disturbing the surface or with dorsal parts out of the water. The released eggs adhered to grass blades. Spawning was interrupted when the water temperature fell below 16° C.

In 1955 wild common carp spawned in large numbers on the meadows above Kolárovo. The first spawning occurred on the 6th and 7th of May. Because of receding water and low temperatures, spawning was interrupted and resumed again on the 5th to the 7th of June when high water returned and temperatures rose to 18° C .

During this time, deep-bodied domesticated carp with various scale patterns were present in the vicinity (Fig. 13), but were rarely seen or caught together with the spawning school of wild carp. Single specimens of the domesticated form, when landed as a bycatch, were either immature or not in spawning condition. This led us to believe that the wild carp retained its genetic purity through reproductive allochrony (see also Lelek 1987), and possibly

through behavioral isolation from the stocked pond carp (akin to the species recognition concept, Paterson 1985). By seining spawning schools of carp together with associated fish species it was established that the main predator on carp eggs was *Chondrostoma nasus* (Mišík 1957).

When we subsequently witnessed similar turbulent matings of wild carp groups on other freshly flooded meadows along the Lesser and main Danube's inundation areas, by then already grossly restricted by flood dikes, it became obvious to me that the original floodplain of this piedmont zone of the Danube (e.g. Mákkai 1985) must have been clearly dominated by this fish during Celtic and

Fig. 11. The common carp was first introduced in Canada from imports of the European domesticated carp (McCrimmon 1968) and became established early in this century as feral forms (note for feral carp the typical notch at the head dorsum, marked by arrowhead) in some areas of the Great Lakes and the St. Lawrence River: a - the scaled feral form is most common, b - the mirror aberrant less so; both forms from St. Lawrence at Valleyfield, Quebec (original drawings by Paul Vecsei).

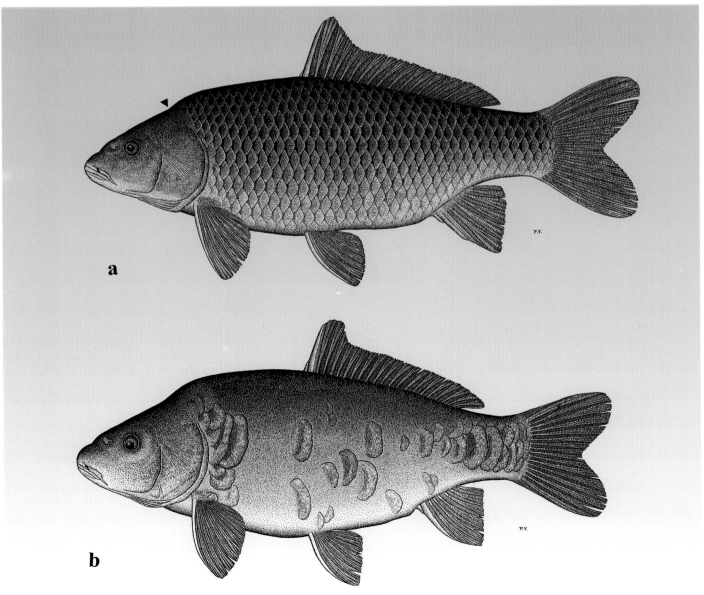

Table 1. Mensural characters of wild carp from the Danube River.

Measurement[1]	Character	Mean	Range
1-2	*in % of standard length*	(359-635 mm)	
1-3	head length	24.2	22.7-26.7
1-6	snout length	9.3	7.6-10.8
A-B	front barbel length	1.7	0.9-2.5
C-D	rear barbel length	3.6	2.2-5.4
6-11	orbit diameter	3.3	2.9-3.9
7-9	interorbital width	10.2	8.9-11.7
11-3	postorbital head length	12.2	11.2-13.8
4-5	head depth	20.5	18.5-23.4
1-12	predorsal distance	44.6	42.1-48.1
1-13	prepelvic distance	44.7	42.1-47.3
1-14	pre-anal distance	73.5	70.8-77.0
12-15	body depth	27.7	24.6-30.9
12-26	body width	17.2	13.8-22.0
16-2	caudal peduncle length	20.3	18.1-23.2
18-19	minimum body depth	12.4	11.1-13.6
20-13	pectoral origin to pelvic base	23.0	20.7-26.4
13-14	pelvic base to anal base	29.9	27.5-33.1
12-21	base length of dorsal fin	40.5	35.8-44.9
14-16	base length of anal fin	8.9	7.3-10.4
22-23	caudal fin upper lobe length	24.1	21.2-27.4
24-25	caudal fin lower lobe length	24.2	20.8-26.9
20-26	longest pectoral ray length	18.7	15.6-20.9
13-27	longest pelvic ray length	17.0	14.7-19.9
12-28	longest dorsal fin ray length	16.6	14.0-18.8
14-29	longest anal fin ray length	16.0	14.3-17.5
1-3	*in % of head length*		
1-6	snout length	38.7	32.6-41.3
A-B	front barbel length	7.2	4.1-10.8
C-D	rear barbel length	15.2	9.5-22.6
10	internasal width	22.8	19.9-26.3
6-11	orbit diameter	14.3	12.0-17.3
7-9	interorbital width	42.5	38.4-46.1
11-3	postorbital head length	50.6	47.5-54.5
4-5	head depth	84.5	78.0-94.3
4	head width	62.6	55.3-73.0
2-16	*in % of caudal peduncle length*		
16-17	caudal peduncle depth	71.9	63.9-83.3
17	caudal peduncle width	40.7	32.6-50.8
18-19	minimum body depth	61.3	52.7-69.9

[1] See numbers in Figure 9c.

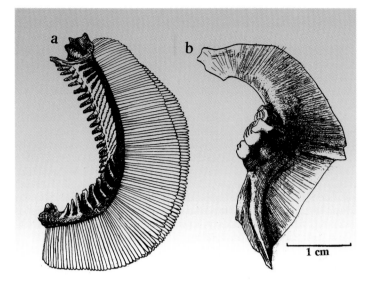

Fig. 12. a - The first gill arch from the right side of a wild common carp. b - Pharyngeal bone and teeth of a wild common carp (from Mišík 1958).

Fig. 13. Juraj Holčík with a scaled feral common carp caught in the Danube River near Rusovce (photograph by E.K. Balon, 1962).

Roman times. Subsequent further enlargement and expansion of the embankments, pollution and overfishing eliminated nearly all of the spawning schools of wild carp from this area (e.g. Chmelár 1993). Holčík (1995b) recently noted: "The wild carp was commercially harvested four decades ago and its distribution in Slovakia covered the Danube and also the lower segments of all large tributaries including the rivers Morava, Váh, Hron, Ipel and also Tisa. At present, however, its distribution is restricted to the minor part of the main channel of the Danube. Only single specimens are occasionally cought. Among 1536 fish taken, tagged and released in the Danube at Gabčikovo in 1993, only 5 (0.3%) were carp but only one still displayed the typical characters of the wild form! (...) The extinction of (...) the wild carp is expected within a decade ...". The Gabčikovo disaster (Balon 1967c, Holčík et al. 1981, 1995a, Hraško 1993) changed this entire area (replacing the vestiges of the original floodplains by concrete waterways) so that the smallest sturgeon, *Acipenser ruthenus*, a river channel spawner and formerly a rare fish in this area, replaced the carp and is now caught in numbers and sizes

never before seen (Fig. 14).

The Volga River wild common carp (Kryzhanovsky 1949) *C. carpio carpio* and the Amur River wild carp (Kryzhanovsky et al. 1951) *C. c. haematopterus* seem to spawn in much the same manner as the Danube wild carp. Spawning on aquatic vegetation or other substrate in permanent waters, while sometimes mentioned, was not documented and so may be another artefact of domestication. Consequently, according to its reproductive style, the wild carp can be classified as a nonguarding, open substratum egg scattering, obligatory plant spawner, within the system of reproductive guilds (Balon 1975, 1981, 1990).

The common carp has indirect ontogeny, with a larval period inserted between the embryo and juvenile periods (Flegler-Balon 1989). The activated eggs have a yellowish tint (Fig. 16), are 1.5 to 1.8 mm in diameter, with a yolk diameter of 1.2 mm. The outer egg envelope is adhesive and sticks to grass blades, preventing the eggs from falling onto the anoxic bottom (Kryzhanovsky 1949). At about 20 to 23° C most embryos hatch in 3 days. Embryonic respiratory vessels, like the ducts of Cuvier, the inferior caudal vein,

Fig. 14. Large catches of *Acipenser ruthenus* are now common in the main Danube River channel, like here at river kilometer 1730 (Čenkov): a - over 100 were captured on 9. 6. 1993 at about 23:30 h, from which, b - Karol Hensel displays the largest specimen ever seen by us (photographs by E.K. Balon).

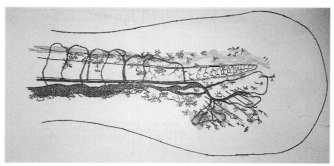

Fig. 15. Blood circulation and pigmentation in the caudal fin of a wild common carp larva over 9 days old and 8.7 mm long (from Balon 1958a).

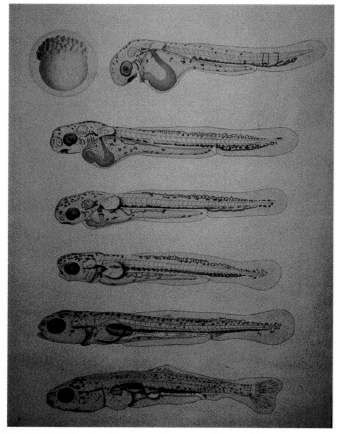

Fig. 16. Early developmental stages of the wild common carp from the Volga River (after Kryzhanovsky 1949), made into a color poster which hangs in the hall at the Moscow State University (photograph by E.K. Balon).

Fig. 17. Free embryo of the wild common carp from the Danube after hatching 5.9 mm long and 3 days 9 h old. Note the carotenoid pigment on the head dorsum (from Balon 1958a).

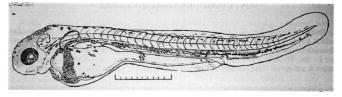

segmental capillary loops in the dorsal finfold, capillaries in the caudal fin (Fig. 15), and the extension of the subintestinal vein on the yolk dorsum, are well developed at an early time (Fig. 16) and can compensate for any oxygen deficit on the spawning grounds. Free embryos hang in a vertical position (Fig. 17) on the grass blades for about 2 days after hatching (Balon 1958a).

At the beginning of the larval period more than 5 days after activation, the posterior part of the swimbladder is filled, the larva swims horizontally and starts to ingest external food. The gills begin to take over as the main respiratory organs. Neuromasts along the sides of the body and on the head develop cupulae that elongate under low prey density (Fig. 18), enhancing their motion-detecting function (Balon 1958a, 1960). In the later half of the larval period the anterior chamber of the swimbladder is filled, gut folds and coils develop, the unpaired fins differentiate, the pelvic fin buds appear, and a dense melanophore network covers the entire body.

There seem to be differences between the early ontogenies of the wild common carp from the Danube, Volga and Amur rivers (Fig. 19). The developmental studies, however, were carried out under different rearing conditions and with different resolutions of observers. Therefore, a reliable interpretation of the variation is not possible at the present time. Illustrations of the observed early ontogenies are presented here for the benefit of future researchers, because these differences in early development, if corroborated, might turn out to be responsible for the phenotypic differences among the adult *C. carpio carpio, C. carpio haematopterus*, and the domesticated forms (Balon 1983, 1984, 1988, 1993).

Unlike most other fishes (Balon 1959, Sire & Arnulf 1990) the scales of the wild common carp develop from the anterior center of the body side, as shown in Figure 20 (Balon 1958b). The common carp larvae, from the beginning of exogenous feeding to the beginning of the juvenile period, feed mainly on plankton. Larger common carp are able to crush shells of mollusks, or eat seeds, and may be considered omnivores.

Age, determined from the annuli on key scales and back-calculated growth, were studied on samples from the spawning schools of the wild common carp in the Lesser Danube near Kolárovo (Balon 1957). Males in this spawning stock belonged to age groups 3 to 15, mostly in the age group 5. Females were represented by age groups 5 to 9, most of them in age group 7 (Table 2). The F_1 progeny of wild common carp reared in nearby ponds grew more slowly in the first two years but in the next two years they grew faster than the wild common carp under natural conditions (Table 3). It was possible to dwarf the progeny of the wild common carp by food deprivation, details of which are given in an earlier study (Balon 1974).

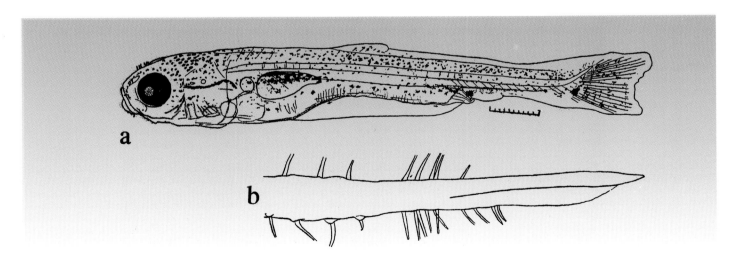

Fig. 18. a - Wild common carp larva from the Danube 25 days and 15 h old reared under conditions of food deprivation with longer than normal cupulae on the head. b - Cupulae on the caudal peduncle of the same individual from above (from Balon 1958a).

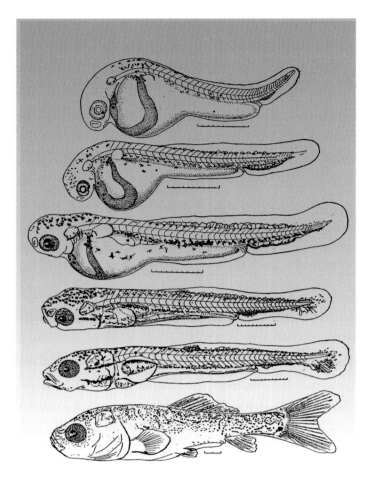

Fig. 19. Some stages of the early ontogeny of the wild common carp *C. carpio haematopterus* from the Amur River (from Kryzhanovsky et al. 1951).

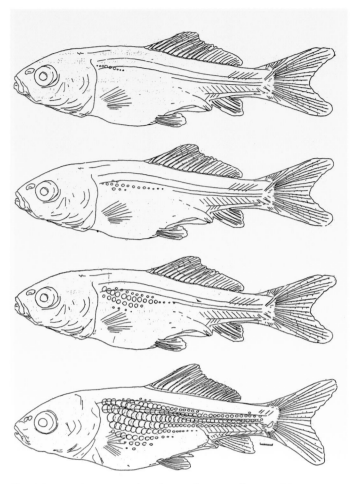

Fig. 20. Development of scales in the Danubian wild common carp on juveniles from 15 to 25 mm long and 20 to 25 days old (from Balon 1958b).

Table 2. Back-calculated mean standard lengths (SL) for males and females of the wild carp from the spawning stock in the Lesser Danube above Kolárovo.

Year of spawning	Age group	Mean SL at time of capture	Back-calculated mean SL at the end of each growth season														
			l_1	l_2	l_3	l_4	l_5	l_6	l_7	l_8	l_9	l_{10}	l_{11}	l_{12}	l_{13}	l_{14}	l_{15}
1952	III males	422	154	382	410												
1951	IV	400	158	298	360	391											
1950	V	428	149	298	354	391	414										
1948	VII	459	135	228	304	363	398	425	448								
1947	VIII	462	142	196	296	358	391	426	445								
1945	X	548	180	203	246	436	450	472	504	522	541						
1944	XI	478	150	230	283	302	341	375	410	440	460	470					
1940	XV	598	148	235	278	335	361	410	422	467	485	501	521	536	550	568	583
			152	259	316	368	392	422	446	476	495	501	521	536	550	568	583
1950	V females	418	120	321	366	390	411										
1949	VI	458	137	228	325	416	430	450									
1948	VII	491	136	276	343	385	422	453	475								
1947	VIII	483	150	271	379	404	456	450	468	478							
1946	IX	527	169	231	323	384	421	452	491	509	526						
			142	265	347	396	424	451	478	493	526						

ARGUMENTS FOR THE ROMAN ORIGIN OF DOMESTICATION

Two significant historical events coincided and contributed to the fact that wild carp became, for the first time, an object of captive rearing. In the last years B.C. and the first and second century A.D., an extraordinary luxury, even excess, of food consumption and the associated importation of foreign foods developed among the Romans (Friedländer 1936). In the first years A.D., the Roman empire broke through the barrier of the Alps as a northern boundary and "extended [its] power right up to the Danube many miles further north" (Sitwell 1981, p. 113).

Establishing the province of Pannonia right up to the Danube River, the empire faced directly the formidable forces of Celts and Germans on the opposite shores and had to establish, faster than elsewhere, a strong military presence. "In the second century, the comparatively short stretch of river between Vienna and Budapest, about 150 miles long, required no less than four legions to guard it — X Gemina at Vienna itself, XIV Gemina Martia Victrix (...) at Carnuntum, I Adiutrix at a place called Brigetio (...), and II Adiutrix at Aquincum (modern Budapest). By contrast, all Roman Britain in the second century required only three legions; Roman North Africa managed with a single one" (Sitwell 1981, p. 120). In addition to the four legions stationed in Pannonia two more legions, IIII Flavia at Singidunum and VII Claudia at Viminacium, guarded the province of Moesia Superior further east (Mócsy 1974).

To paraphrase further from Sitwell's synthesis, these at least 20,000 fighting legionnaires were accompanied by supporting troops, wives, mistresses, children, slaves and tradesmen to a total of over 100,000 Romans, in addition to "indigenous communities (*civitates*) [which] came under the military control of a high-ranking officer (...) from a neighbouring Roman unit. (...) there was at least one auxiliary unit for every two civitates" (Mócsy 1974, p. 49). These together formed a human population large enough to establish a carp-eating tradition, if wild carp was, as I believe, at least seasonally the most abundant and easy to catch fish in the area. The influence of this youngest province and its army was so strong that "instead of Rome controlling the Danube frontier, it would be nearer the truth to say that men from that frontier controlled Rome" (Sitwell 1981, p. 122).

Movements of legionnaires, troops, auxiliary units and civilians from Pannonia across or around the Alps to Poetovio, Emona via northeastern Italia to Rome (Fig. 21) required the construction of relatively good roads (see

Table 3. Growth values of the Danubian wild carp from natural habitat, ponds and aquarium rearing under food deprivation.

Origin	Values	Growth season															
		0	1	2	3	4	5	6	7	8	9	10	11	12	13	14	15
Spawning stock (from Balon 1957)	SL (in mm)		147	262	331	382	408	436	462	484	495	501	521	536	550	568	583
	Wet mass (in g)		56	322	742	1155	1472	1815	2150	2495	2590	2780	3110	3320	3630	4010	4400
	Absolute increments (in mm)	147	115	69	51	26	28	26	22	23	26	6	20	15	14	15	
First generation in ponds (from Bastl 1962)	SL (in mm)		86	237	348	393												
	Wet mass (in g)		19	343	1078	1408												
	Absolute increments (in mm)	86	153	109	45													
First generation under food deprivation (from Balon 1974)	SL (in mm)		53	112	134	144	146	146	146									
	Wet mass (in g)		4	30	53	62	64	64	64									
	Absolute increments (in mm)	53	59	22	10	2	0	0										

also fig. 59 in Mócsy 1974), one of which ended as the Roman branch of the Amber Road at Carnuntum — the most important legionary fortress and town — and crossed the Danube north into the Celt, German and Sarmatian territory towards the Baltic Sea as a footpath. Legionary fortresses and Roman towns were established at the edge of the largest floodplain area within the piedmont zone of the Danube: castra and colonia Carnuntum upstream and castella Gerulata (today's Rusovce) downstream of the Morava (Marus) River entry into the Danube at the upper end of the floodplain. Castellas Ad Flexum, Quadrata, Arrabona and Ad Statuas before the larger castra and colonia Brigetio (todays Szöny) at the Váh (Duria) River entry opposite the castella Celamantia (near today's village Iža) at the floodplain's downstream end. This floodplain area was utilized as the westernmost spawning grounds of the wild common carp, *Cyprinus carpio* (Fig. 22a, b). Another series of forts followed before the next castra and colonia Aquincum (Visy 1985) even further downstream.

LUCULLAN DEMANDS OF PATRICIAN LIFE STYLE AND THE PISCINAE

As early as the first century B.C., Cicero's teacher of gastronomy, Sergius Orata, had devised special salt water reservoirs, separated from the sea, where he stored oysters and fishes for the kitchen. This may have been little more than a copy of a 500 m^2 pond constructed by Carthaginian prisoners-of-war at Agrigentum, Sicily, which because of costly maintenance had been filled in by the first century B.C. (Zeuner 1963). Soon these reservoirs, called *piscinae*, became extremely fashionable, for they ensured a permanent supply of a variety of fresh fishes independent of weather conditions and fishing success. The importance of such a supply grew with the development of luxurious eating habits.

According to Pliny the Elder (A.D. 24-79; 1958-1962) fish rearing in piscinae was adopted by Lucinius Muraena, who began storing freshwater fishes. The patricians liked this manner of keeping their fishes and soon competed in establishing such piscinae, often spending enormous sums of money on them. Consul Lucullus (75 B.C.), whose reputation as a gourmet was well known, dug through a hill near Naples to bring water to his ponds, which

were reputedly more costly than his villa.

Although the original idea of the piscinae was to store fish for gastronomic purposes, later on, rearing fish often turned to simply watching them or even to rearing fish as pets. According to Pliny (see Zeuner 1963, p. 479) "Antonia, the daughter of Drusus, had such a pet which was adorned with golden ear-rings, and people travelled to her country house at Baiae to admire this beautiful creature. Marcus Crassus, too, owned a murena [eel] which wore ear-rings and a bejewelled neck-lace; it obeyed the call of the great triumvir and fed from the hand. When it died he wept bitterly over it and had it buried." Hortensius, who was known for the love of his fishes, and was accused by Cicero of neglecting politics because of his fishes, became as famous as Lucullus.

The Romans preferred sea fishes, as Varro (116-27 B.C.; 1912) and later Columella (A.D. ~50; 1941-1968) emphasized; freshwater ponds (dulces) were apparently considered inferior and plebeian, but documented prejudice is at least proof of the existence of freshwater ponds (see Zeepvat 1988). More importantly, this involvement could expand the desire to transport and stock wild common carp from the Danube into piscinae beyond the patrician legionnaires to plebeian troops, merchants and artisans.

Did the Romans merely keep the fish in piscinae or did they breed them occasionally? Wohlfarth (1984, p. 376) claims that "there is no record of the Romans using fish spawned in captivity for farming", and therefore the Roman activities cannot be "regarded as the beginning of the domestication of carp in Europe". Zeuner (1963, p. 479), on the other hand, believes that "it is indeed probable that murenas were bred, for imperial Rome required quantities that could hardly be obtained by fishing. (...) They also had freshwater ponds, one of which was found in Roman Trier (west Germany) in 1892. In addition, natural lakes and ponds were used for breeding of freshwater fish by the Romans ...".

The first part of Zeuner's belief does not convince me; if his "murenas" were European eels, *Anguilla anguilla*, these will not spawn in piscinae and their larvae (leptocephali) will not survive in such reservoirs (Bauchot & Saldanha 1986). It is, however, possible that glass eels or elvers entered naturally or were

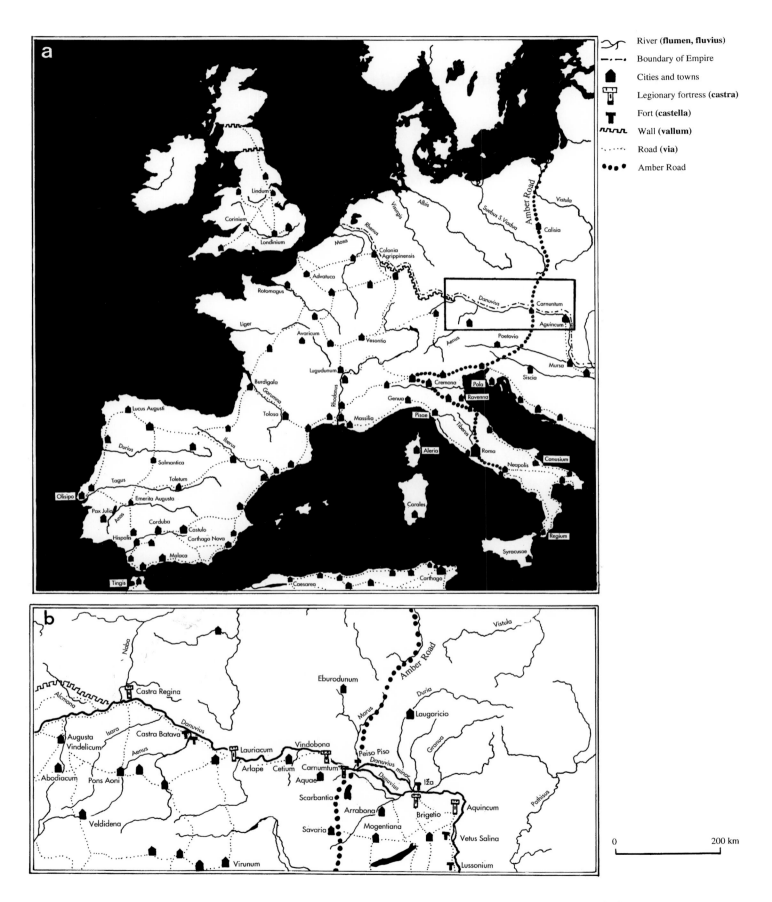

Fig. 21. a - Map of the main Roman roads and settlements in the western half of the empire with the Amber road. b - The Danube frontier (according to Sitwell 1981, modified).

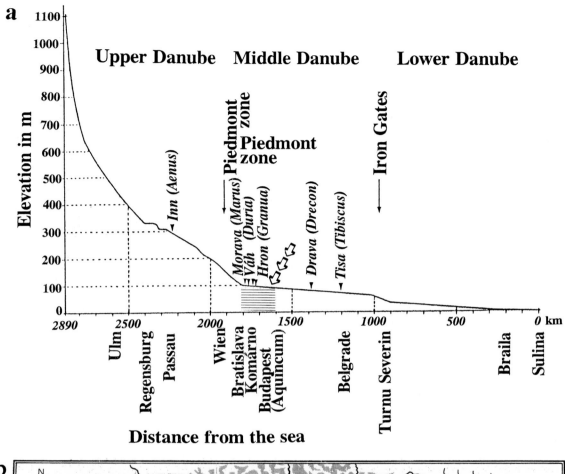

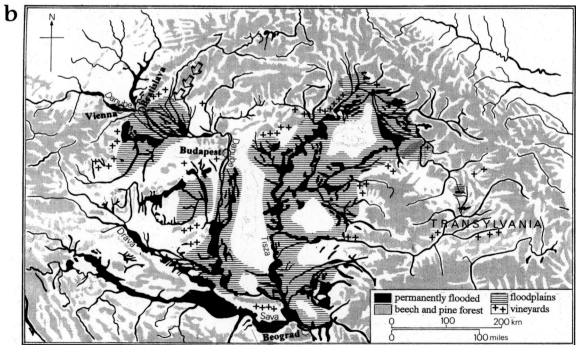

Fig. 22. a - Gradient diagram of the Danube River with the piedmont zone (westernmost floodplain) highlighted by horizontal lines and triple arrows, and the main tributary entries by triangles. b - The middle Danube from the fourteenth to the seventeenth century with permanent and intermittent (floodplains) waters; the westernmost floodplain is marked by triple arrows (after Mákkai 1985).

controlled breeding of common carp in ponds to be the 13th century as given in the first note on such activity in Albertus Magnus. The second condition of domestication [i.e. (b) breeding subject to human control], the only one documented last, could have been fulfilled since ancient Roman times without leaving a written or pictorial record. Perhaps one will be excavated or found in the future.

It was only about 100 years ago that Dubisch brought Danube wild carp to the upper Vistula River for hybridization with the local form of domestic carp (Morcinek 1909). In 1957 I repeated Dubisch's project by transferring 1,000 yearling Danube wild carp (Fig. 24) to the experimental ponds at Ochaby (Rudziński 1961). However, like the experiments on the Danube (Bastl[10], 1962), studies at Ochaby proved that wild common carp are better suited for stocking into natural fluvial habitats than are the domesticated forms of common carp (Leszczyńska & Biniakowski 1967).

PITFALLS OF DOMESTICATION, THE RABBIT PARALLEL, AND THE EMERGENCE OF NISHIKIGOI

The beautiful, golden creature, as the wild carp is or was, became severely changed under domestication. Its torpedo-like body became laterally compressed and hunchbacked. Its regular geometry of scales changed often to severe irregularities, scale reductions or even complete nakedness. Its golden color often changed into blueish hue (Fig. 25). However, even the most marked deformity induced or selected for under domestication, disappears when the artificial selection is relaxed and after release into a natural habitat. Under such conditions the original wild common carp form reappears, at least superficially, and a fully-scaled, elongated, feral carp might fool any unprepared observer (Fig. 11, 13). If we ignore its weak physiology (Steffens 1964) and overlook the notch behind the head (Mišík 1958) we might be led to believe that the wild common carp can be reborn. In the River Rhine Lelek (1987) identified a feral common carp which was very close in appearance to its wild ancestor and which maintained reproductive allochrony from the domesticated forms. This feral form spawned earlier and at lower temperatures than the domesticated forms, and behaved much like the wild form from the Danube. However, the mensural characters of these common carp from the Rhine, published elsewhere (Köhler & Lelek 1992, table 19), clearly identify it as feral, especially with respect to the body depth and relative head size.

In nearly all domesticated organisms it has been noted that reversal to the true wild ancestor is **not** possible. "Domestication changed the life of the beast, the character of the animal, and its anatomy and physiology" (Epstein 1972, p.91). When left to become feral domesticated cattle are known to remain in poor condition and never revert to a form similar to that of the strong, wild, ancestral aurochs, *Bos primigenius* (Talbot et al. 1965, Taylor 1970, 1972).

The domestication of goldfish, *Carassius auratus*, was started this time indeed in China and for entirely different reasons (Chen 1956). Buddhism requires a believer to perform, as an act of self-purification, one good deed per day. Ultimately, "ponds of mercy" were established near the temples so that aquatic creatures could be released into them as part of such a good deed. The occasional appearance of red aberrants in catches of a wild goldfish was a rare occurrence. These fish were espe-

---

[11] See the meaning of "aberratio" and "monstrositas" in Berg (1962, p.7)

cially chosen for such a release in the belief that freeing a very rare creature will be a better deed than the release of an abundant, normally colored form. Concentrated in ponds of mercy, the aberrant individuals started to interbreed and to produce more of their kind. When finally the wealthy started to keep such goldfish in jade vessels and breed them, not only color aberrants but also shape monstrosities began to appear. Goldfish with trailing fins, bulging eyes and bodies, various fish "hunchbacks", became desired objects for breeding. Nonetheless, if such "domesticated" goldfish are released into natural habitats few will survive the assault of predators and their progeny typically revert to normally shaped and colored, wild-like goldfish (Balon 1962, 1963).

I have found no record of domesticated carp with changed scalation, body shape or color prior to the 16th century. We cannot, however, exclude that such aberrant or monstrous[11] forms appeared under the protection of the earliest pond rearing, perhaps in Roman times or later in the monastery or secular ponds.

THE DOMESTICATED COMMON CARP IN MODERN AQUACULTURE

Using wild adults selected according to specially devised criteria (Mišík & Tuča 1965), juveniles from the same progeny were used to evaluate the extent of changes following initial domestication in southern (Bastl[10]) and northern (Rudziński 1961) ponds in Slovakia and Poland, respectively. Food deprivation did bring forth distinct changes in body proportions (Fig. 26) and even in some meristic counts (Balon 1958a). Pharyngeal tooth counts and arrangement, however, turned out to be the most unusual. Among three groups (wild common carp, domesticated common carp and food-deprived common carp) the food-deprived fish had the highest number of irregular teeth per individual, while the wild common carp had the fewest irregularities (Steffens 1964, Balon 1974).

The size of the gape of the mouth, a character that Rudziński (1961) and Steffens (1964) used so successfully to distinguish wild and domesticated carps, was considerably smaller in the food-deprived, dwarfed fish than in the domesticated or wild common carp (Table 4). Rudziński

and Steffens considered the enlargement of the mouth in domesticated animals to be related to changes in feeding habits, and also as a probable result of artificial selection. Domesticated common carp, selected to utilize supplementary food added to ponds, grew better in ponds when man-made food was added (see also Sibbing 1988).

The number of coils in the intestine in the food-deprived, dwarfed common carp varied from 4 to 7 (Table 4). Adult domesticated carp had, on average, six coils per intestine (Klust 1939); hence not all food-deprived fish developed fewer coils. Rudziński (1961) found, and Steffens (1964) confirmed, that the intestine of wild common carp was generally 15 to 25% shorter

Fig. 25. Typical deep bodied domesticated common carp from ponds in southern Bohemia: the blue leather carp (above) and the scattered mirror carp (photograph by E.K. Balon).

than that of domesticated carp; the ratio of gut length to wet body mass is 2.2 in domesticated, 3.0 in wild, and 8.3 in the food-deprived carp. Rudziński and Steffens also found that the body of the domesticated carp, which is nearly always much deeper than that of the torpedo-shaped wild carp, appears to have more flesh, but the calculated ratio of muscle in both the wild and domesticated carp is the same. Disregarding changes in body proportions, dressed weight of individual domesticated carp does not increase, even though its faster growth rate produces more absolute meat in a given period of time. Both the above authors noted that the wild common carp has both chambers of the swimmbladder of similar size, whereas the domesticated common carp has the anterior chamber greatly enlarged and the posterior much smaller. The faster growth of domesticated common carp can probably be correlated with the larger mouth and longer intestine acquired by the domesticated form for utilization of complementary foods.

The greater strength, mobility, and viability of the wild common carp are emphasized also by some physiological characteristics (Steffens 1964). The wild common carp has 18 to 19% more erythrocytes and haemoglobin than does the domesticated carp. Blood sugar level is 16 to 26% higher. The wild common carp has a much lower water content in muscles and liver than does the domesticated common carp. Furthermore, the wild carp has a greater fat content in individual organs, more glycogen in the liver, and more vitamin A in the eyes, intestine, and liver. Consequently, the taste of the wild carp is considered "better" because it is perceived to be juicier (the same applies to the wild versus domesticated rabbit). The wild common carp is more mobile, stronger, and nimbler because its muscles are better vascularized and do not fatigue as quickly as do those of the domesticated carp. Therefore, the wild common carp is, or was, also better able to overcome river currents.

The ecomorphological features in early ontogeny of the domesticated common carp seem similar to the wild form (Fig. 15-19). Compara-

Fig. 26. Seven-year-old wild carp reared under food deprivation, 15 cm long (photograph by E.K. Balon).

tive study under the same conditions and by the same observers, however, was not done. Eggs of the domesticated common carp seem to have more yolk in proportion to cytoplasm (Kiselev 1980), but the opposite relationship may be assumed (Fig. 27, 28, 29) from the data by Peňáz (1995). The domesticated forms reared in Czech ponds at least since the 16th century became, as other domesticated animals, more paedomorphic and, consequently, more altricial than the Russian pond carp which were probably domesticated much later. The Czech carp, much longer under domestication, have comparatively less yolk in their eggs (cf. Fig. 27 vs. 29). Similar correlations were observed in the wild and hatchery strains of some salmonids (Balon 1980). Hence, the domesticate is less vulnerable and more able

Table 4. Mouth-gape and intestine length indices for the wild carp, domesticated carp and food deprived (dwarf) wild carp: o l^{-1} = 10 x mouth gape (in cm^2) per standard length (in cm), o w^{-1} = 10 x mouth gape (in cm^2) per weight (in g), o lc^{-1} = 10 x mouth gape (in cm^2) per length of head (in cm); gut l^{-1} = length of intestine (in cm) per 1 cm of standard length, gut w^{-1} = length of intestine (in cm) per 10 g of wet mass.

Index	o l^{-1}	o w^{-1}	o lc^{-1}	gut l^{-1}	gut w^{-1}
Wild carp (after Rudziński 1961, Steffens 1964)	1.14				
supplementary diet	1.09	0.10	4.46	2.11	3.02
natural diet	1.24	0.08	5.27		
Domesticated carp (after the same authors as above)	1.91				
supplementary diet	2.00	0.08	8.12	2.64	2.25
natural diet	2.30	0.08	8.12		
Food deprived wild carp (after Balon 1974)	0.40	0.18	1.30	1.17	8.33

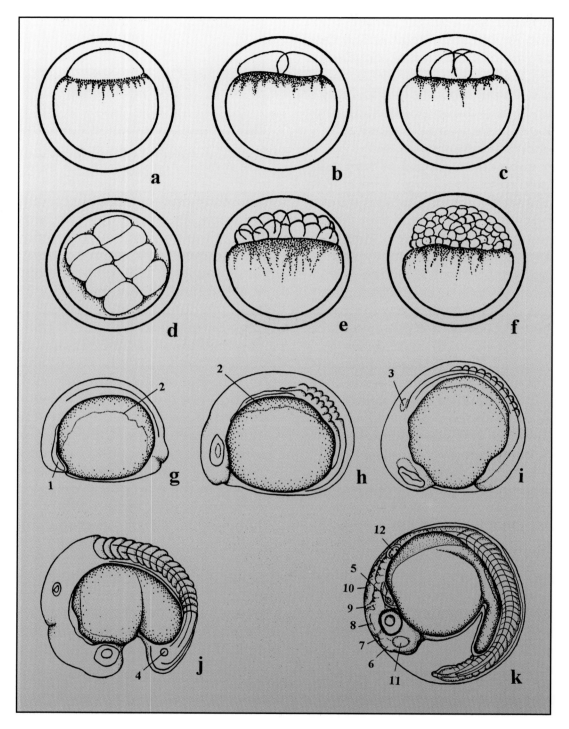

Fig. 27. Early embryonic development of the domesticated common carp: a - blastodisc fully formed, viewed from the side (at 26° C, 40-50 min after activation); b - two blastomeres after the first cleavage (1 h); c - four blastomeres (1 h 20 min); d - eight blastomeres from above (1 h 40 min); e - 32 blastomeres (2 h 20 min); f - 128 blastomeres (about 3 h); g - early embryo body (about 10 h); h - optic vesicles and first somites (13 h); i - more somites and otic placodes (15 h); j - eye lenses, otic vesicles and Kupfer's vesicle (18 - 20 h); k - tail free from the yolksac (1 d 6-8 h). 1 = the head mesoderm, 2 = flanks of the embryo, 3 = otic placode, 4 = Kupfer's vesicle, 5 = heart, 6 = forebrain, 7 = epiphyse, 8 = mesocephalon, 9 = cerebellum anlage, 10 = medula oblongata, 11 = nasal placode, 12 = otic vesicle with otoliths (from Makeyeva 1992).

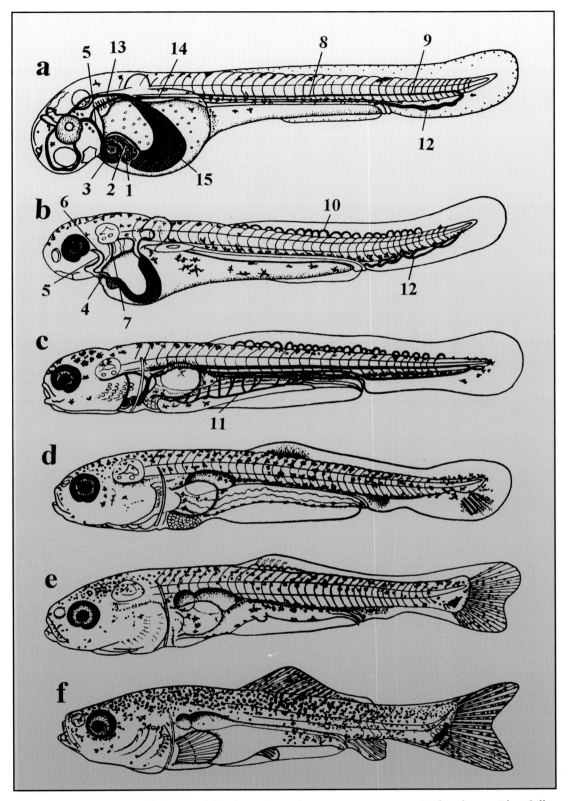

Fig. 28. Late embryos and larvae of the domesticated common carp: a - excised embryo with a fully developed circulation (1 d 10 h); b - embryo at hatching with a swimbladder anlage and first branchial circulation (2 d 5 h); c - finfold larva at first exogenous feeding (4-5 d); d - early finformed larva (6 d); e - finrays in unpaired fins, pelvic anlagen and anterior chamber of the swimbladder (8 - 9 d); f - rays in paired fins (12 - 14 d). 1 = sinus venosus, 2 = atrium, 3 = ventricle, 4 = ventral aorta, 5 = mandibular and 6 = hyoid arches, 7 = gill cover, 8 = dorsal aorta, 9 = caudal artery, 10 = segmental vessels, 11 = subintestinal vitelline vein, 12 = inferior caudal vein, 13 = anterior and 14 = posterior cardinal veins, 15 = enlarged duct of Cuvier (from Makeyeva 1992).

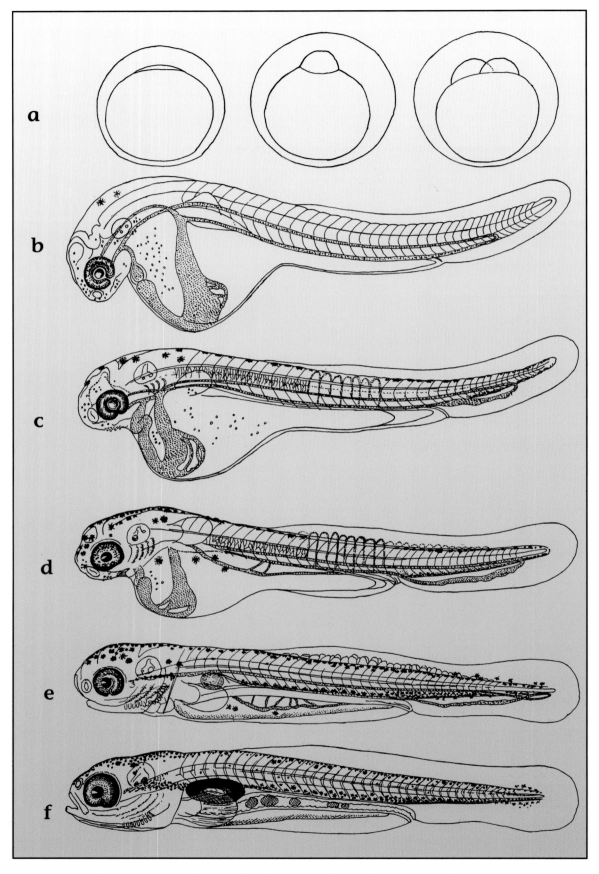

Fig. 29. Cleavage eggs, embryos and early larva of the Czech domesticated carp: a - bipolar differentiation to first cleavage (40 min +), b - excised embryo with a fully developed blood circulation and hatching gland cells (1 d 20 h, 3.3 mm TL), c - embryo at hatching (2 d, 3.7 mm TL), d - free embryo (2 d 10 h, 4.8 mm TL), e - advanced free embryo (3 d 3 h, 5.7 mm TL), and f - finfold larva at the beginning of exogenous feeding (4 d 10 h, 6.6 mm TL) (after Peňáz 1995).

Fig. 30. Rendering of the two most typical forms of the domesticated common carp in European aquaculture — the line mirror carp (above) and the leather or naked carp (drawings by B. Czarkowski from Brylińska 1986).

to cope with unpredictable environmental perturbations than their wild ancestor, a highly specialized, precocial form which depends on predictable floods (Balon 1988, 1989, 1990, Bruton 1989).

The wild common carp was first transferred by humans into the Rhine River drainage (Hoffmann 1995) west of the native Danube. Therefore, the Rhine River feral form of *Cyprinus carpio* is so similar to its wild Danubian ancestor (Lelek 1987). Domesticates which escaped and turned into feral forms much later became further removed from the physique and life style of the wild ancestral form. The different duration of artificial selection in aquaculture and the different times spent as feral forms may explain the variety of forms recorded (pp. 11, 16, and below) and should be the subject of future investigations beyond the orthodox "genetics".

The consequences of domestication ultimately led to the creation of standardized breeds maintained by constant artificial selection (Kirpichnikov 1981, Jhingram & Pullin 1985). In the centers of the common carp pond culture — the Czech Republic, Germany, Poland, Austria, Hungary and France — deep bodied (31 to 39% of SL), scaled to naked and fast growing phenotypes are maintained in carefully managed spawning, growing and overwintering ponds. The Fish Culture Research Institute at Szarvas, Hungary, maintains 30 morphs of the domesticated common carp and a stock of questionable Tisza River and Amur River wild morphs, from which another 140 hybrid forms were developed and tested (Gorda et al. 1995). In spite of some mapping of their biochemical polymorphism (e.g. Valenta et al. 1976, Csizmadia et al. 1995) it is inevitable that genetic purity under their pond system is nearly impossible to maintain and is affecting stocks in adjacent natural waters as well as pond cultures everywhere. In common production cultures, however, much fewer local morphs exist.

Brylińska (1986), for example, divides the domesticated common carp into four basic forms. The scales are controlled by a pair of alleles — scalelessness by N and n (*nudus*) and scalation by S and s (*squama*):

(i) **scaled carp**, homozygous SSnn or heterozygous Ssnn, with regular imbricating scales over entire body, much like the ancestral wild common carp;

(ii) **line carp**, heterozygous SSnN or SsNn, with a regular single row of scales along the

center of its sides, elsewhere none or only several scales;

(iii) **mirror carp**, recessive homozygous ssnn with rows of large scales along dorsum, along gill openings and some at the base of caudal fin. Three varieties are recognized; a - *scaled mirror carp* with three rows of scales along sides, b - *line mirror carp* with interrupted rows of scales along the lateral line and scattered scales in groups or singly elsewhere (Fig. 30 top), and c - *scattered mirror carp* with little scales along body contours;

(iv) **leather** or **naked carp**, heterozygous ssnN, with no scales (Fig. 30 lower), and sometimes colored blue (Fig. 25).

The coloured carp, nishikigoi, were artificially selected aberratios from some of the domesticated or feral forms. "Genetically engineered" forms may soon follow the "goldfish-like" monstrositas currently appearing on the market (see below).

THE COMMON CARP AND THE RABBIT

In general, the history of domestication of the old world rabbit, *Oryctolagus cuniculus*, and the wild common carp is similar, and may be of some interest as another support for the origin of common carp domestication. Fossil finds have shown that the old world rabbit was widely distributed throughout western Europe (including the British Isles) before the ice ages, but died out in most of that area during glacial times, remaining in post-glacial times only in Spain and northwest Africa (Angermann 1975). Varro (116-27 B.C.; 1912) wrote that Romans brought rabbits from Spain and bred them in special enclosures called *leporaria* to ensure a fresh supply of meat at all times. Unborn rabbits excised from pregnant females were prepared as a special dish called *laurices*.

In the Middle Ages rabbits were a popular fare in west European monasteries, and laurices were eaten even during fasting periods. It was in the paved leporaria and corridors of the monasteries that the rabbits began giving birth to their young above ground instead of in burrows. The young became accustomed to people and thus the species gradually became domesticated. Color aberrants appeared in abundance. "One major consequence of domestication of the wild rabbit", writes Angermann (1975, p.441), "has been a reduction in the sensitivity of the animal's vision, hearing, and taste. The do-

Fig. 31. Nishikigoi in the Japanese garden of a restaurant near Todai-ji in Kyoto (top), in pools of the old temple Myotsu-ji near Obama-shi at the Sea of Japan (center), and in the public Osawa-no-ike pond (left) near the Daikaku-ji temple, the Imperial Palace of Saga (photographs by E.K. Balon, 1994).

mestic rabbit's brain weighs twenty-two percent less and its heart weighs 37.5 percent less than those of a wild rabbit if both rabbits are the same size. Nachtsheim states, 'the stomach and caecum in the wild animal have greater absorption ability, and the small and large intestines are 50 cm longer in the wild rabbit'." When the domesticated rabbit goes feral it reverts to the body shape and coloration of the wild ancestor.

While breeding of rabbits must have occurred in the Roman leporaria, no written record of this exists. Domesticated rabbits were bred commonly in the French monasteries, although "the first descriptions of domestic breeds of rabbits come from the 16th Century" (Angermann op.cit.). In the middle of the 16th century, several color and size varieties of the domesticated rabbit were known. An albino rabbit is shown in Titian's "Madonna" (1530) at the Louvre (Valcanover 1960).

Around 550 B.C., the Chinese philosopher Confucius (1898) suggested to poor farmers that they keep some rodents similar to rabbits (Volf 1965). Unlike the misinformation on the origin of the common carp domestication, the origin of the domesticated rabbit was never assumed to be in China.

BEAUTY FROM THE BEAST

When I wrote, over 25 years ago, the first version of this essay on the origin and domestication of the wild common carp, little was known in the west on the selective breeding of domesticated carp for other purposes than for food, especially for traditional sabbath or Christmas dishes. Meanwhile, a new trend in common carp domestication long popular in Japan has gained popularity elsewhere around the world — the artificial selection of colored carp for recreation and pleasure (Amano 1968,1971, Axelrod 1973). These common carps called nishikigoi[12] are bred, selected and auctioned for use as pets in small garden pools but now also adorn historic ponds of ancient temples and many public waterbodies (Fig. 31). Fanciful color patterns and later, scale formations, to be viewed from above, are

selected for, with as little distortion as possible to the torpedo-shaped body.

The colored carps, nishikigoi, living jewels or simply **koi**, as they are known today, are color aberrations of the common carp. They are selectively bred, repeatedly culled to retain only the desired color patterns, and tamed as pets. I doubt that koi originated directly from the wild common carp, but rather from feral common carp and some domesticated pond common carp. However, the origin of colored common carp is also shrouded in the mists of antiquity, and speculations abound how far back its first appearances go. This is appropriately reflected in the beginning of Tamadachi's[7] (1990, p.8) book: "Once upon a time, long, long ago, there lived in the murky slow moving waters of Eurasia a very ordinary fish indeed — little did he know that one day, just like an ugly duckling, he would become very beautiful ...". But I do not entirely agree with Tamadachi because neither is the water of the Danube slow-moving nor do I consider the golden wild common carp "ordinary", let alone an "ugly duckling". In comparison to the domesticated common carp "ordinary" may be more acceptable and, of course, the carefully bred and selected koi are much more spectacular, retaining the torpedo-shaped body form of the feral common carp, and exhibiting vivid colorations of white, red, black, yellow, blue, gold, silver and brown spots and backgrounds in almost any combination, even with various scale patterns (Fig. 32). The beauty of the wild common carp was reinstated now in color, not unlike that of rabbit or cattle some time ago. Nonetheless, Tamadachi (1990) repeats only what Amano (1968, 1971) claimed all along.

Surely, red aberrants of common carp must have occasionally occurred in pond cultures since Roman times, but in China these were often confused with the goldfish (Chen 1956). The confusion is increased if merely the ancient artworks are presented for evidence. There the artist may add barbels to goldfish, which has none, and paint or carve "koi" without barbels, the carp's important character to distinguish it from goldfish. Hence, most Japanese specialists (e.g. Amano 1968, Kataoka 1989, Kuroki 1990) agree that there is little evidence for colored carp to have existed before 1800 in Japan, but some others still speculate whether they might have ap-

---

[12] "Nishiki" is an expensive white, red and black cloth (brocade) with golden and silver fibers, used for high class (e.g. shogun's wife) obi and kimono (see the parallel to "dolly varden" (Balon 1980). "Goi" is a derivation of "koi", which means carp.

peared earlier in China (Axelrod 1973, 1988, Davies 1989, Tamadachi 1990). It may as well be that the first colored common carp were selected from the imports of German pond carp (doitsu nishikigoi) which, of course, makes them direct descendants of the domestication in Europe. In this case some German imports would have to reach Japan before the usually given 1904 because the first successful white and red "kôhaku" were claimed to be crossbred between 1818 and 1843 (Amano 1968). Again, one recorded import supports the possibility of other similar imports before or after, with no written record left (Kataoka 1989). More importantly, various artefacts from the time (17th century) of the Dutch colony in Nagasaki depict common carp (Fig. 34), which later became abundant in adjacent waters. The European common carp might have been imported by the Dutch, as obviously did happen in the middle of the 19th century in Indonesia (Sumantadinata 1995). Paradoxically, Siebold (1850, sensu stricto Temminck & Schlegel) described the east Asian *C. haematopterus* from Nagasaki several generations (over 200 years) after the first Portuguese, Dutch and German settlers arrived there. It cannot be entirely excluded, therefore, that the Nagasaki common carp is but a feral progeny of earlier European imports (Fig. 5, 35), later adopted for paddy field and pond culture also elsewhere in Japan. The presence of the feral common carp, often considered to be the native wild common carp, is supported by the photographs of two large adult fish from Czuzenji-ko (lake) in the Tochigi Prefecture with a distinct notch at the neck dorsum (Kawanabe & Mizuno 1989, p. 337), the feral carp feature (Mišík 1958). The Chinese origin is, therefore, forced and highly unlikely even for Japan. McDowall (1990), for example, makes no distinction between "European carp" and colored koi introduced to New Zealand recently, and he may be right.

In Niigata Prefecture, the area between Nagaoka and Ojiya cities, about 280 km west of Tokyo close to the Sea of Japan (Fig. 33, 36), common carp was traditionally reared for food in small terrace ponds alternating with rice paddies. The area is known to be regularly under 6 or so meters of snow for most of the winter (Fig. 37) and these unusual conditions may have contributed to a more

frequent occurrence of color aberrations in common carp culture here then elsewhere. In other words, the high incidence of color aberrants here may be related to melatonin production in the prolonged life in darkness under the cover of deep snow. Not so long ago this mountaineous area had few roads and local farmers were stranded for many winter months. Combined with boredom and/or a quest for beauty it is generally assumed that about 160 years or so ago, colored aberrants of the common carp began to be selected and crossbred here (Kuroki 1990). In the absence of any evidence to support these early beginnings, it all probably happened much later (see Fig. 3). With time and demand, the progeny of these first color varieties started to be severely culled, leaving only the best colored (nowadays 1 out of 10,000 or more) for future breeding. The birth place of nishikigoi is today considered to be the united (1956) Yamakoshi Village (Fig. 38), where "87 per cent of the 906 families [are] being fancy carp producers" (Amano 1971, p. 37).

As in the goldfish, the first color aberrant was most likely red (higoi). Further selection and crossbreeding produced not only new color patterns but also new colors. Around 1904, the domesticated mirror carp, imported from Germany, was included in the breeding and new variety was added to the scaled and colored *hara-aka* or *hoo-aka*, by combining scale patterns with the color variations in the "doitsu nishikigoi". In about 1930, koi farmers produced the "kuchibeni koi"[13] which had red lips. "These are disliked today because red-lips have become associated with the lipstick worn by those ladies of the oldest profession!" (Tamadachi 1990, p.22)[14]. In the early 1920s, feral common carp with golden scales (possibly descendants of escaped Nagasaki imports) were used to cross with koi to produce the true golden ogon (Fig. 32). Today, the Japanese recognise approximately 15 basic color aberrants (Table 5), each with

---

[13] Kuchibeni means lipstick.

[14] Of course, what other interpretation can we expect from Michugo Tamadachi?

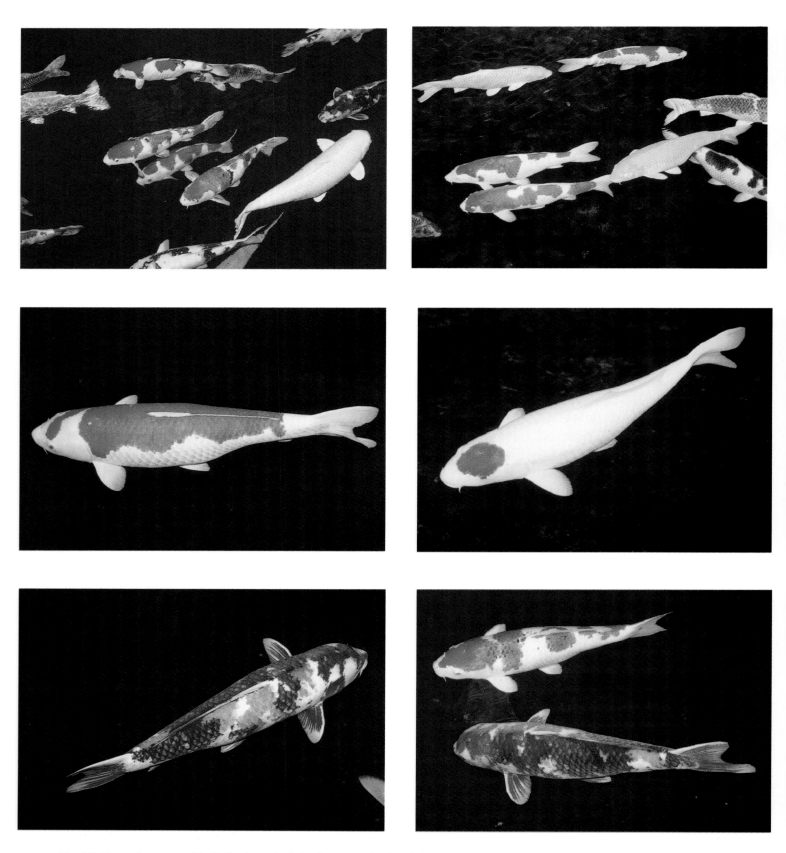

Fig. 32. From the covered hall display of adult, show standard nishikigoi at the *Nishiki-goi-no-sato* (municipal koi display park) of Ojiya city: among the colorful groups swimming nearby (top) one could single out "sandan kôhaku" (center left), "tancho-kôhaku" (center right), "showa-sanshoku" (bottom left), and another "showa-sanshoku" with "kuchibeni-kôhaku". The white in the top group must have been "platinum-ogon" and the yellow "yamabuki- ogon" (photographs by E.K. Balon, 24. 5. 1994).

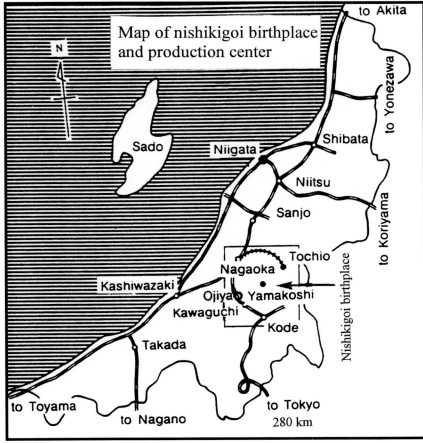

Fig. 33. Map of the Niigata area with framed nishikigoi birthplace and production center (after Kuroki 1990).

Fig. 34. Common carp on the artefacts of early Dutch colonists at the Nagasaki Municipal Museum (photographs by E.K. Balon, 1994).

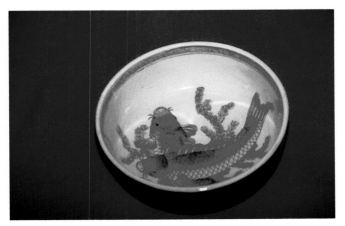

many varieties [see Kuroki 1990 , the Tetra Encyclopedia of Koi, pp.126-127 (as under Phipps 1989), and the current catalogue and Nishiki Goi monthly magazine].

Intensive selection and production of colored carps started only after the Second World War, probably in the 1950s, and was related to the growing living standards of people in Japan and in the West. More and more people could afford garden ponds, and in Japan — where land is more precious than elsewhere and Buddism

favors love of animals — garden pools utilized fully for decoration with "swimming flowers", were the logical progression in the development of the miniature garden. Already at the beginning of international nishikigoi popularity, Amano (1968, p.36) wrote "that the number produced in a year is ten million, amounting to 1,000,000,000 yen worth".

Even by careful crossbreeding, the resultant colors of the offspring are impossible to predict (Kataoka 1989). The prog-

Table 5. Classification of nishikigoi according to their color patterns (compiled from various sources).

Kôhaku	White nishikigoi with different red patterns superimposed. The most popular nishikigoi in Japan.
Taisho-sanke	Kôhaku to which black splashes are added. All three colors to be very deep. Black streaks on paired fins permissible.
Showa-sanshoku	A black nishikigoi with white and red imposed. The black pattern should wrap all around the body.
Bekko	On the basic color of white, yellow, orange or red small black blotches are dispersed.
Utsurimono	A black nishikigoi with yellow, red or white blotches.
Asagi	Pale blue nishikigoi with scales edged in white. Red ventrum preferred.
Shusui	Blue with some red and yellow on the head and ventrum and with mirror scalation, i.e. asagi with doitsu scalation.
Koromo	Nishikigoi with silver or blue cast over red and white areas or white with red markings under darker pattern.
Kawarimono	Black fish with white fin edges, blue bodied fish with white scale edges and red fin bases, single non-metallic color and any other unusual color variety which does not fit elsewhere.
Tancho	Kôhaku, sanke and showa with the red limited to a circular marking on the forehead.
Hikarimono (ogon)	Single colored metallic nishikigoi, like the white 'platinum ogon' or the yellow 'yamaboki ogon'.
Hikarimoyo-mono	Metallic white nishikigoi with red, black or yellow superimposed.
Hikari-utsurimono	Metallic black nishikigoi with white, red or yellow blotches.
Goshiki	Five-colored nishikigoi with white, black, red, yellow and blue combined. Often judged under kawarimono.
Doitsu	Any variety other than shusui with mirror carp scalation.

REFERENCES CITED

Amano, M. 1968. Colourful "live jewels". General survey of fancy carp. Kajima Shoten Publishing Co., Tokyo. 205 pp.

Amano, M. 1971. Fancy carp, the beauty of Japan. Kajima Shoten Publishing Co., Tokyo. 158 pp.

Andreška, J. 1984. Development of fish-pond culture in Bohemia. pp. 77-89. *In*: B. Gunda (ed.) The Fishing Culture of the World, Akadémiai Kiadó, Budapest.

Angermann, R. 1975. Hares, rabbits, and pikas. pp. 419-462. *In*: B. Grzimek (ed.) Animal Life Encyclopedia, Volume 12, Van Nostrand Reinhold Company, New York,

Anon. 1961. Pond fisheries. Izd. Selskochoz. lit., Moscow. (In Russian).

Anon. 1993. Lost your heart to koi? Tropical Fish Hobbyist 41(6): 174.

Anon. 1994. Aquaculture production 1986-1992. FAO Fisheries Circular 815, Rev. 6, FAO, Rome. 216 pp.

Antipa, G. 1909. Fauna ichtiologica a Romániei. Crol Göbl, Bucureşti. 294 pp. + 31 plates.

Aristotle, 1862. History of animals, in ten books. H.G. Bohn, London. 326 pp.

Ausonius, D.M. 1933. The Mosella. Translated into English verse by E.H. Blakeney. Eyre & Spottiswoode, London. 74 pp.

Axelrod, H.R. 1973. Koi of the world. Japanese Colored Carp. T.F.H. Publications, Neptune City. 239 pp.

Axelrod, H.R. 1988. Koi varieties. Japanese colored carp - nishikigoi. T.F.H. Publications, Neptune City. 144 pp.

Balon, E.K. 1957. Vek a rast neresového stáda dunajského kapra - sazana (*Cyprinus carpio* morpha *hungaricus* Heck.) z Malého Dunaja nad Kolárovom (Age and growth of the spawning school of the Danubian wild carp). Pol'nohospodárstvo (Bratislava) 4: 961-986.

Balon, E.K. 1858a. Vývoj dunajského kapra (*Cyprinus carpio carpio* L.) v priebehu predlarválnej fázy a larválnej periódy (Development of the Danubian carp during the prelarval and larval period). Biologické práce (Bratislava) 4 (6): 5-54.

Balon, E.K. 1958b. Die Entwicklung der Beschuppung des Donau-Wildkarpfen. Zool. Anz. 160: 68-73.

Balon, E.K. 1959. Die Beschuppungsentwicklung der Texas-Cichlide (*Herichthys cyanoguttatus* Baird et Girard). Zool. Anz. 163: 82-89.

Balon, E.K. 1960. Die Entwicklung der Fische bei ungünstigen Nahrungsbedingungen. Acta Hydrobiologica 2: 125-131.

Balon, E.K. 1962. Ökologische Bemerkungen über die Standorten der Donaufische mit einer Beschreibung des Fundes des *Carassius auratus gibelio* (Bloch, 1783) und *Alburnoides bipunctatus* (Bloch, 1782). Věst. čs. spol. zool. 26: 333-352.

Balon, E.K. 1963. K nálezu karase stříbřitého eurasijského (Discovery of the giebel). Živa (Prague) 11: 205-206.

Balon, E.K. 1964. Verzeichnis und ökologische Charakteristik der Fische der Donau. Hydrobiologia 24: 441-451.

Balon, E.K. 1966. Od dunajského kapra k vianočnému (From the Danubian wild carp to the Christmas carp). Polovníctvo a rybárstvo (Bratislava) 18 (12): 26-27.

Balon, E.K. 1967a. O pôvode kapra (On the origin of carp). Vesmír (Prague) 46: 344-347.

Balon, E.K., 1967b. Zaujímavosti o ustriciach (Curiosities about oysters). Svet vedy (Bratislava) 14: 296-299.

Balon, E.K. 1967c. Vývoj ichtyofauny Dunaja, jej súčasný stav a pokus o prognózu ďalších zmien po výstavbe vodných diel (Evolution of the Danube ichthyofauna, its recent state and an attempt to predict further changes after the construction of the planned water diversion schemes). Biologické práce (Bratislava) 13: 1-121.

Balon, E.K. 1968. Urgeschichte der Donau-Ichthyofauna (vor dem Einfluß seitens des Menschen). Arch. Hydrobiol. (Suppl. Donauforschung 3) 34: 204-227.

Balon, E.K. 1969. Studies on the wild carp *Cyprinus carpio carpio* Linnaeus, 1758. I. New opinions concerning the origin of the carp. Práce Laboratória rybárstva 2: 99-120.

Balon, E.K. 1974. Domestication of the carp *Cyprinus carpio* L. Royal Ontario Mus. Life Sci. Misc. Publ., Toronto. 37 pp.

Balon, E.K. 1975. Reproductive guilds of fishes: a proposal and definition. J. Fish. Res. Board Can. 32: 821-864.

Balon, E.K. (ed.) 1980. Charrs: salmonid fishes of the genus *Salvelinus*. Perspectives in Vertebrate Science 1, Dr W. Junk Publishers, The Hague. 928 pp.

Balon, E.K. 1981. Additions and amendments to the classification of reproductive styles in fishes. Env. Biol. Fish. 6: 377-390.

Balon, E.K. 1983. Epigenetic mechanisms: reflections on evolutionary processes. Can. J. Fish. Aquat. Sci. 40: 2045-2058.

Balon, E.K. 1984. Life histories of Arctic charrs: an epigenetic explanation of their invading ability and evolution. pp. 109-141. *In*: L. Johnson & B. Burns (ed.) Biology of the Arctic Charr: Proceedings of the International Symposium on Arctic Charr, University of Manitoba Press, Winnipeg.

Balon, E.K. 1988. Tao of life: universality of dichotomy in biology. 2. The epigenetic mechanisms. Rivista di Biologia/Biology Forum 81: 339-380.

Balon, E.K. 1989. The epigenetic mechanisms of bifurcation and alternative life-history styles. pp. 467-501. *In*: M.N. Bruton (ed.) Alternative Life-History Styles of Animals, Perspectives in Vertebrate Science 6, Kluwer Academic Publishers, Dordrecht.

Balon, E.K. 1990. Epigenesis of an epigeneticist: the development of some alternative concepts on the early ontogeny and evolution of fishes. Guelph Ichthyol. Rev. 1: 1-42.

Balon, E.K., 1993. Dynamics of biodiversity and mechanisms of change: a plea for balanced attention to form creation and extinction. Biological Conservation 66: 5-16.

Balon, E.K. 1995. Origin and domestication of the wild carp, *Cyprinus carpio*: from Roman gourmets to the swimming flowers. Aquaculture 129: 3-48.

Balon, E.K. & A. Goto. 1989. Styles in reproduction and early ontogeny. pp. 1-47. *In*: A. Goto & K. Maekawa (ed.) Reproductive Behavior in Fishes: Styles and Strategies, Tokai University Press, Tokyo. (In Japanese)

Balon, E.K. & V. Mišík. 1956. Zoznam nových dokladov o výskyte niektorých málo známych alebo nových druhov rýb na Slovensku (New data on the occurrence of some less known or new fish species in Slovakia). Biológia (Bratislava) 11: 168-176.

Balon, E.K., S.S. Crawford & A. Lelek. 1986. Fish communities of the upper Danube (Germany, Austria) prior to the new Rhein-Main-Donau connection. Env. Biol. Fish. 15: 243-271.

Bănărescu, P. 1960. Einige Fragen zur Herkunft und Verbreitung der Süsswasserfischfauna der europäisch-mediterranen Unterregion. Arch. Hydrobiol. 57: 16-134.

Bănărescu, P. 1964. Pisces - Osteichthyes. (Peşti Ganoizi şi Osoşi). Fauna Republicii Populare Romîne, Vol. 13, Editura Acad. R.P.R., Bucureşti. 962 pp.

Bastl, I., 1962. Rast divého dunajského kapra (*Cyprinus carpio carpio* (L.)) v rybnikoch na Kamennom mlyne (Growth of the wild Danubian carp in ponds). Biológia (Bratislava) 12: 757-770.

Bauchot, M.-L. & L. Saldanha. 1986. Congridae. pp. 567-574. *In*: P.J.P. Whitehead, M.-L. Bauchot, J.-C. Hureau, J. Nielsen & E. Tortonese (ed.) Fishes of the North-eastern Atlantic and Mediterranean, Volume 1, UNESCO, Paris.

Berg, L.S. 1948. Names of fishes and the ethnic relationships of Slavs. Sovetskaya etnografia 2: 33-35. (In Russian)

Berg, L.S. 1962. Freshwater fishes of the U.S.S.R. and adjacent countries, Vol. 1. Israel Program for Scientific Translations, Jerusalem. 505 pp.

Berg, L.S. 1964. Freshwater fishes of the U.S.S.R. and adjacent countries, Vol. 2. Israel Program for Scientific Translations, Jerusalem. 496 pp.

Bloch, M.E. 1782. Oeconomische Naturgeschichte der Fische Deutschlands (mit Sieben und Dreissig Kupfertafeln nach Originalen). Hesse, Berlin. 234 pp. [reprinted 1993 by Herbert R. Axelrod for the American Museum of Natural History]

Borgese, E.M. 1980. Seafarm. The story of aquaculture. Harry N. Abrams Publishers, New York. 236 pp.

Borzenko, M.P. 1926. Data on the biology of the wild common carp (*Cyprinus carpio* Linné). Izv. Bakin. Ikhtiol. Lab. 2(1): 5-132. (In Russian)

Bruton, M.N. (ed). 1989. Alternative life-history styles of animals. Perspectives in Vertebrate Science, Volume 6, Kluwer Academic Publishers, Dordrecht. 617 pp.

Brylińska, M. (ed.) 1986. Ryby słodkowodne Polski (Freshwater fishes of Poland). Państwowe Wydawnictwo Naukowe, Warszawa. 429 pp.

Burton, M. & R. Burton (ed.) 1968. Purnell's encyclopedia of animal life, Vol. 1. Purnell and Sons, Paulton. 448 pp.

Buschkiel, A.L. 1933. Teichwirtschaftliche Erfahrungen mit Karpfen in den Tropen. Z. Fisch. 31.

Cassiodorus, F.M.A. 1626. M. Aurelij Cassiodori Senatoris v.c. opera omnia quae extant, ex fide manuscr. auctiora & locupletiora, ... P. & I. Chouet, Aureliae Allobrogorum. 1622 pp.

Chen, S.C. 1956. A history of the domestication and the factors of the varietal formation of the common goldfish, *Carassius auratus*. Scientia Sinica 5:287-321. [first published in Chinese, 1954, in Acta Zoologica Sinica 6: 89-116]

Chmelár, V. 1993. Dunaj historický a dnešný. Dunajské úpravy (The historical and contemporary Danube. The Danubian modifications). Vydavatel'stvo Electa, Žilina. 71 pp.

Chmielewski, S. 1965. From the history of fresh-water fisheries in Poland. pp. 5-13. *In*: Fresh-water Fisheries of Poland, Hydrobiological Committee Polish Acad. Sci., Kraków.

Chytra, F., V. Krupauer & J. Picha. 1961. Růst dunajského kapra v rybnících v průběhu prvnich tří roků (Growth of the Danubian carp in ponds during the first three years). Prace ČSAZV Vyskumného ústavu rybářskeho ve Vodňanech 1: 73-91.

Clutton-Brock, J. 1981. Domesticated animals from early times. British Museum (Natural History) and W. Heineman, London. 208 pp.

Columella. 1941-1968. De re rustica. *In*: E.S. Forster & E.H. Heffner (ed.) On Agriculture, 3 volumes, Loeb Classical Library, Cambridge.

Confucius, 1898. Ssu Shu (The Four Books). Man Yu Tong, Hong Kong. 617 pp.

Csizmadia, C., Z. Jeney, I. Szerencsés & S. Gorda. 1995. Transferrin polymorphism of some races in a live gene bank of common carp. Aquaculture 129: 193-198.

Davies, M. 1989. The history of nishikigoi. pp. 10-13. *In*: The Tetra Encyclopedia of Koi, Tetra Press, Morris Plains.

Dubravius, J. 1547. De piscinis ad Antonium Fuggerum. pp. 11- 45. *In*: A. Schmidtová (ed.) Sborník filologický ČSAV, Praha.

Epstein, H. 1972. Domestication features in animals as functions. pp. 91-101. *In*: R.L. Smith (ed.) The Ecology of Man: An Ecosystem Approach, Harper and Row, New York.

Fernando, C.H. 1971. The role of introduced fish in fish production in Ceylon's freshwaters. pp. 295-310. *In*: E. Duffey & A.S. Watt (ed.) The Scientific Management of Animal and Plant Communities for Conservation, Blackwell Scientific Publishers, Oxford.

Flegler-Balon, C. 1989. Direct and indirect development in fishes — examples of alternative life-history styles. pp. 71-100. *In*: M.N. Bruton (ed.) Alternative Life-History Styles of Animals, Kluwer Academic Publishers, Dordrecht.

Forel, F.A., 1906. La pêche du Léman. Arch. Sci. Phys. Nat., Genève 22: 188-189.

Frank, H. (ed.) 1987. Man and wolf. Advances, issues, and problems in captive wolf research. Perspectives in Vertebrate Science 4, Dr W. Junk Publishers, Dordrecht. 439 pp.

Friedländer, L.1936. Roman life and manners under the early empire. George Routledge & Sons, London. 365 pp.

Fujita, Y. 1973. Formation of the Japanese island arcs, Green Tuff movement. Tsukiji-Shokan, Tokyo. 257 pp. (In Japanese)

Galton, F. 1865. The first steps towards the domestication of animals. Trans. Ethnolog. Soc. London N.S. 3: 122-138.

Geikie, A. 1912. The love of nature among the Romans during the later decades of the Republic and the first century of the Empire. John Murray, London. 394 pp.

Gorda, S., J. Bakos, J. Liska & C. Kakuk. 1995. Live gene bank of common carp strains at the Fish Culture Research Institute, Szarvas. Aquaculture 129: 199-202.

Górzyński, S. 1964. Przegląd historii rybactwa w dawnej Polsce (Overview of the history of fishery in the ancient Poland). Państwowe Wyd. Rol. Leś., Warszawa.

Hahn, E.1896. Die Haustiere und ihre Beziehungen zur Wirtschaft des Menschen. Leipzig. 581 pp.

Hankó B. 1932. Ursprung und Verbreitung der Fischfauna Ungarns. Arch. Hydrobiol. 23: 520-556.

Harris, M. 1977. Cannibals and kings. Random House, New York. 239 pp.

Heckel, J.J. 1836. Über einige neue, oder nicht gehörig unterschiedene Cyprinen, nebst einer systematischen Darstellung der europäischen Gattungen dieser Gruppe. Ann. Wien. Mus. Nat. 1: 219-234.

Heckel, J. & R. Kner. 1858. Die Süsswasserfische der östreichischen Monarchie, mit Rücksicht auf die angränzenden Länder. Verlag von Wilhelm Engelmann, Leipzig. 388 pp.

Hensel, K. 1980. Národné mená niektorých alochtónnych druhov rýb Československa (National names of some alochtonous species of Czechoslovak fishes). Kultúra slova 22: 152-161.

Hermann, O. 1887. A Magyar halászat könyve, 2 volumes. K.M. Természettudományi Társulat, Budapest. 860 pp.

Hervey, G. 1950. The goldfish of China in the XVIII century. The China Society, London. 66 pp.

Hickling, C.F. 1962. Fish culture. Faber and Faber, London. 295 pp.

Hoffmann, R.C. 1985. Fishponds. pp. 73-74. In: J.R. Strayer (ed.) Dictionary of the Middle Ages, Charles Scribner's Sons, New York.

Hoffmann, R.C. 1994a. Remains and verbal evidence of carp (Cyprinus carpio) in medieval Europe. pp. 139-150. In: W. Van Neer (ed.) Fish Exploitation in the Past, Proceedings of the 7th Meeting of the ICAZ Fish Remains Working Group, Ann. Mus. Royal l'Afrique Centrale, Sci. Zool. 274, Tervuren.

Hoffmann, R.C. 1994b. Mediaeval Cistercian fisheries natural and artificial. pp. 401-414. In: L. Pressouyre (ed.) L'espace cistercien, Comité des travaux historiques et scientifiques, Paris.

Hoffmann, R.C. 1995. Environmental change and the rise of the common carp culture in medieval Europe. Guelph Ichthyol. Rev. 3: 57-85.

Hohberg, W.H. von, 1687. Georgica Curiosa oder Adeliches Land und Feld Leben, Vol. 2. Michael & Johann Friederich Endters Seel. Erben, Nürnberg.

Holčík, J. 1989. Návrh červeného zoznamu ohrozených kruhoústych a rýb Slovenska (Proposal for threatened cyclostomes and fishes of Slovakia). Pamiatky a príroda 20: 26-28.

Holčík, J. 1995a. Rybárstvo pred a po prehradení slovenského úseku Dunaja (Fishery before and after the damming of the Slovak section of the Danube). pp. 144-152. In: A. Svobodová & M.J. Lisický (ed.) Výsledky a skúsenosti z monitorovania bioty územia ovplyvneného vodným dielom Gabčíkovo, Ústav zoológie a ekosozológie SAV, Bratislava.

Holčík, J. 1995b. Vanishing freshwater fish species of Slovakia. Aquatic Sciences (in press)

Holčík, J., I. Bastl, M. Ertl & M. Vranovský. 1981. Hydrobiology and ichthyology of the Czechoslovak Danube in relation to predicted changes after the construction of the Gabčíkovo-Nagymaros river barrage system. Práce laboratória rybárstva a hydrobiológie 3: 19-158.

Holčík, J. & L. Jedlička. 1994. Geographical variation of some taxonomically important characters in fishes: the case of the bitterling Rhodeus sericeus. Env. Biol. Fish. 41: 147-170.

Horváth, L. & L. Orbán. 1995. Genome and gene manipulation in the common carp. Aquaculture 129: 157-181.

Hraško, V. 1993. The Gabčíkovo project — saving the Danube's inland delta. Vodohospodárska výstavba, Bratislava. 32 pp.

Ikebe, N. 1978. Bio- and chronostratigraphy of Japanese Neogene, with remarks on paleogeography. Prof. Nobuo Okebe Mem. Vol.:13-34. (In Japanese)

Isaac, E. 1962. On the domestication of cattle. Science 137: 195-204.

Isaac, E. 1970. Geography of domestication. Prentice-Hall, Englewood Cliffs. 132 pp.

Ishikawa, C., K. Okamura, S. Tanaka, A. Terao, H. Marukawa, T. Higurashi & H. Senô (ed.) 1931. Illustrations of Japanese aquatic plants and animals, Vol. 1. Fisheries Society of Japan, Tokyo. 50 plates. (In Japanese)

Jhingran, V.G. & R.S.V. Pullin. 1985. A hatchery manual for the common, Chinese and Indian major carps. ICLARM Stud. Rev. 11, Manila. 191 pp.

Johnson, M.C. 1954. Preliminary experiments on fish culture in brackish-water ponds. Progr. Fish-Cult. 16: 131-133.

Jordan, D.S. & B.W. Evermann. 1896-1900. The fishes of North and Middle America. Bull. U.S. Nat. Mus. 47: 1-3313.

Jordan, D.S. & B.W. Evermann. 1902. American food and game fishes. A popular account of all the species found in America north of the equator, with keys for ready identification, life histories and methods of capture. Doubleday, New York. 573 pp.

Kataoka, M., 1989. Nishikigoi dangi (short stories). Published by Takayoshi Kataoka, Kumagayashi. 76 pp. (In Japanese)

Kaushik, S.J. 1995. Nutrient requirements supply and utilization in the context of carp culture. Aquaculture 129: 225-241.

Kawanabe, H. & N. Mizuno. 1989. Freshwater fishes of Japan. Yama-kei Publishers, Tokyo. 720 pp.

Kazantcheyev, E.N. 1981. Fishes of the Caspian Sea. Legkaya i pishtchevaya promyslennost, Moscow. 167 pp.

Kessler, K. T. 1856. Zur Ichthyologie des südwestlichen Russlands. Bull. Soc. Nat., Moscow 29: 335-393.

Kestemont, P. 1995. Different systems of carp production and their impacts on the environment. Aquaculture 129: 347-372.

Khin, A. 1930. Vyzy na Veľkom Žitnom ostrove a ich lovenie (Hausen at the Great Schütt Island and their fishing). Čas. Mus. slov. spol. 22: 110-112.

Kirpichnikov, V.S. 1967. Homologous inherited variation and evolution of the wild carp (*Cyprinus carpio* L.) . Genetica 3(2): 34-47. (In Russian)

Kirpichnikov, V.S. 1981. Genetic bases of fish selection. Springer-Verlag, Berlin. 410 pp.

Kiselev, I.V. 1980. The biological basis of fertilization and incubation of fish eggs. Naukova Dumka Press, Kiev. 296 pp. (In Russian)

Klust, G. 1939. Über Entwicklung, Bau und Funktion des Darmes beim Karpfen (*Cyprinus carpio* L.). Int. Revue Ges. Hydrobiol. Hydrogr. 39: 498-536.

Koch, W. 1925. Die Geschichte der Binnenfischerei von Mitteleuropa. *In*: R. Demoll & H.N. Maier (ed.) Handbuch der Binnenfischerei Mitteleuropas, Vol. 4a. E. Schweizerbart'sche Verlagsbuch., Stuttgart.

Köhler, C. & A. Lelek. 1992. Die Fischfauna des Rheins: Analyse der Artengemeinschaften sowie Daten zur Morphometrie und Meristic der vorkommenden Arten. Courier Forsch.-Inst. Senckenberg 148: 53-153.

Kolomyets, V.T. 1983. Origin of all Slavic names of fishes. *In*: The 9th International Meeting of Slavologs, Naukova Dumka Press, Kiev. (In Russian)

Kryzhanovsky, S. G. 1949. Eco-morphology of development in carps, loaches and catfishes (Cyprinoidei i Siluroidei). Trudy Inst. Morphologii Zhivotnych 1: 5-332. (In Russian)

Kryzhanovsky, S.G., A.I. Smirnov & S.G. Soin. 1951. Data on the development of Amur River fishes. Trudy Amurskoy Ichtiologitcheskoy Ekspedicii 1945-1949 gg., Vol. 2. Izdatelstvo Moskovskogo Obshtchestva Ispytateley Prirody, Moskva. 222 pp. (In Russian)

Kuroki, T. 1990. Manual to nishikigoi. Shuji Fujita Press, Shimonoseki-city. 272 pp.

Leder, I. 1968. Russische Fischnamen. Veröffentlichungen der Abteilung für Slavische Sprachen und Literaturen des Osteuropa-Institute an der Freien Universität Berlin 36: 112-118.

Lefever, R. 1993. The continuing saga of the butterfly koi. Tropical Fish Hobbyist 41(8): 94-102.

Lelek, A. 1987. Notes on the reproductive ecology of the feral form of the common carp, *Cyprinus carpio carpio*, in the Rhine River. Proc. V Congr. europ. Ichthyol., Stockholm: 169-173.

Leonhardt, E. 1906. Der Karpfen. Geschichte, Naturgeschichte und wirtschaftliche Bedeutung unseres wichtigsten Zuchtfisches. J. Neumann, Neudamm. 104 pp.

Leszczyńska, W. & L. Biniakowski.1967. Chów sazana w ośrodku zarybieniowym PZW Otorowo (The husbandry of the wild carp in the stocking center Otorowo). Gospodarka Rybna 19(2): 19-20.

Livingston, J.A. 1994. Rogue primate. An exploration of human domestication. Key Porters Books, Toronto. 229 pp.

Fig. 39. This "sweetheart koi" from Israel, a variety of "shusui" with a red heart on its left side, was reported earlier in the *Tropical Fish Hobbyist* magazine [1993, 41(6): 174].

This study is dedicated to the memory of Ota Oliva, Professor at Charles University in Prague who over 40 years ago pointed me in the direction of fishes, and to the memory of professional fishermen on the Slovak shores of the Danube River who 35 years ago assisted the young biologist in his first major field work.

In 1991, during my first visit to the free Czechoslovakia, Ota Oliva and I went to see the Elbe River pool "Poltruba", the site of my thesis on methods of ageing and growth in fishes (photograph by C. Flegler-Balon).

The late Gabi Tóth and his typical Danube fishing boat fetching us at the shore in Šturovo. In the background is the Esztergom cathedral on the Hungarian side (photograph by E.K. Balon, 1963).

Maar, A. 1960. The introduction of carp in Africa south of the Sahara. pp. 204-210. *In*: Third Symposium on Hydrobiology and Inland Fisheries Problems of Major Lakes, CCTA, Lusaka.

Magnus, Albertus (Saint, Bishop of Ratisbon) 1861. De Animalibus libri xxvi. Beiträge zur Geschichte der Philosophie des Mittelalters, Vol. 15, 16, Münster. 1664 pp.

Makeyeva, A.P. 1992. Embryology of fishes. Moscow University Press, Moscow. 216 pp. (In Russian)

Mákkai, L. 1985. Economic landscapes: historical Hungary from the fourteenth to the seventeenth century. pp. 24-35. In: A. Mączak, H. Samsonowicz & P. Burke (ed.) East-Central Europe in Transition From the Fourteenth to the Seventeenth Century, Cambridge University Press, Cambridge.

Mark, M. 1966. Carp breeding in drainage water. Bamidgeh 18: 51-54.

Massingham, H.J. (ed.) 1985. The essential Gilbert White of Selbourne. David R. Godine Publisher, Boston. 361 pp.

McCrimmon, H.R. 1968. Carp in Canada. Bull. Fish. Res. Board Can. 165. 93 pp.

McDowall, R.M. 1990. New Zealand freshwater fishes. Heinemann Reed, Auckland. 553 pp.

Meidinger, C., von, 1785-1794. Icones piscium Austriae indigenorum, quos collegit, vivisque coloribus expresos edidit C. Baro de Meidinger, Vindobonae. plate 41.

Mišík, V. 1957. Technika lovu rýb záťahovou sieťou na Malom Dunaji pri Kolárove (Fishing technique with seine at the Lasser Danube near Kolárovo). Poľnohospodárstvo 4: 135-165.

Mišík, V. 1958. Biometrika dunajského kapra (*Cyprinus carpio carpio* L.) z dunajského systému na Slovensku (Biometry of the Danubian carp of Slovakia). Biologické práce (Bratislava) 4(6): 55-125.

Mišík, V. & V. Tuča. 1965. Posudzovanie exteriéru dunajského kapra so zretelom na výber plemenného materiálu (Recognition of the shape of Danubian carp for breeding selection). Poľnohospodárstvo 11: 35-44.

Mócsy, A. 1974. Pannonia and Upper Moesia. A history of the middle Danube provinces of the Roman Empire. Routledge & Kegan Paul, London. 453 pp.

Morcinek, P. 1909. Geschichte des Dubischverfahrens. Land- und Forstwirtschaftliche Gesellschaft, Troppau.

Morey, D.F. 1994. The early evolution of the domestic dog. American Scientist 82: 336-347.

Nakajima, T. 1986. Pliocene cyprinid pharyngeal teeth from Japan and east Asia Neogene cyprinid zoogeography. pp. 502-513. *In*: T. Uyeno, R. Arai, T. Taniuchi & K. Matsuura (ed.) Indo-Pacific Fish Biology, Proceedings of the Second International Conference on IndoPacific Fishes, Ichthyological Society of Japan, Tokyo.

Ohno, S., J. Muramoto, L. Christian & N.B. Atkin. 1967. Diploid-tetraploid relationship among old-world members of the fish family Cyprinidae. Chromosoma 23: 1-9.

Ojima, Y. & S. Hitotsumachi. 1967. Cytogenetic studies in lower vertebrates. IV. A note on the chromosomes of the carp (*Cyprinus carpio*) in comparison with those of the funa and the goldfish (*Carassius auratus*). Japan. J. Genetics 42: 163-167.

Ousby, I. 1992. The Cambridge guide to literature in English. Cambridge University Press, Cambridge. 1110 pp.

Paterson, H.E.H. 1985. The recognition concept of species. pp. 21-29. *In*: E.S. Vrba (ed.) Species and Speciation, Transvaal Museum Monograph 4, Pretoria.

Pelikan, O. 1960. Slovensko a Rímske Impérium (Slovakia and the Roman Empire). Slovenské vydavateľstvo Krasnej literatúry, Bratislava. 348 pp.

Peňáz, M. 1995. Rozmnožováni (Reproduction). pp. 231-246. *In*: V. Baruš & O. Oliva (ed.) Mihulovci *Petromyzones* a Ryby *Osteichthyes*, (Fauna Čs a SR, vol. 28(1), Academia, Praha.

Perlbach, M. 1881-1882. Pommerellisches Urkundenbuch, 2 vol. Westpreussischer Geschichtsverein, Danzig.

Phipps, K. 1989. Koi varieties. pp. 122-201. *In*: The Tetra Encyclopedia of Koi, Tetra Press, Morris Plains.

Piekosiński, F. (ed.) 1896. Rachunki dworu króla Władysława Jagiełły i królowej Jadwigi z lat 1388 do 1420 (Accounts of the court of king Władysław Jagiełło and queen Jadwiga from years 1388 to 1420). Monumenta medii aevi historica res gestas poloniae illustrantia, vol. 15, Kraków (from Hoffmann 1994a).

Pintér, K. 1989. Magyarország halai. Biológiájuk és hasznosításuk. Akadémiai Kiadó, Budapest. 202 pp.

Plinius, G. S. 1958-1962. Pliny Natural History, with an English translation in ten volumes. Harvard University Press, Cambridge.

Ráb, P. 1994. Cytogenetické studie vybraných skupin holarktických sladkovodních ryb (Cytogenetic studies of selected groups of holarctic freshwater fishes). Doktorská disertační práce, obor 15-06-9 zoologie, Akademie věd České republiky, Ústav živočišné fyziologie a genetiky, Liběchov. 98 pp.

Raethel, S. 1972. Pheasants and hoatzins. pp. 49-81. *In*: B. Grzimek (ed.) Grzimek's Animal Life Encyclopedia, Volume 8, Van Nostrand Reinhold Company, New York.

Rajtár, J. 1990. Anfänge der römischen Bautätigkeit im Vorfeld von Brigetio. pp. 771-778. *In*: H. Vetters & M. Jandler (ed.) Akten des 14. Int. Limeskongresses 1986 in Carnuntum, Der Römische Limes in Österreich, Wien.

Rajtár, J. 1992. Das Holz-Erde-Lager aus der Zeit der Markomannenkriege in Iža. pp. 149-170. *In*: Probleme der relativen und absoluten Chronologie ab Laténezeit bis zum Frühmittelalter, Kraków.

Robinson, R. 1984. Rabbit. pp. 239-246. *In*: I.L. Mason (ed.) Evolution of Domesticated Animals, Longman, London.

Rudziński, E. 1961. Vergleichende Untersuchungen über den Wildkarpfen der Donau und den Teichkarpfen. Z. Fisch. 10: 105-135.

Ruetimeyer, L. 1860. Untersuchung der Thierreste aus den Pfahlbauten der Schweiz. Mittl. Antiquarische Gesellschaft, Zurich.

Sibbing, F.A. 1988. Specializations and limitations in the utilization of food resources by the carp, *Cyprinus carpio*: a study of oral food processing. Env. Biol. Fish. 22: 161-178.

Siebold, C. T. E. von, 1863. Die Süswasserfische von Mitteleuropa. Verlag von Wilhelm Engelmann, Leipzig. 430 pp.

Siebold, P.F. von, 1850. Fauna Japonica sive descriptio animalium, quae in itinere per Japaniam, jußsu et außpiciis superiorum, qui summum in India Batava imperium tenent suscepto, annis 1823-1830 collegit, notia, observationibus et adumbrationibus illustravit Ph. Fr. de Siebold conjuctis studiis Cr. J. Temminck et H. Schlegel pro vertebris atque W. de Haan pro invertebratis elaborata. Regis Auspiciis Edita, Lugnum Batavorum. 323 pp. (Pisces).

Sire, J.-Y. & I. Arnulf. 1990. The development of squamation in four teleostean fishes with a survey of the literature. Japan. J. Ichthyol. 37: 133-143.

Sitwell, N.H.H. 1981. Roman roads of Europe. St. Martin's Press, New York. 240 pp.

Steffens, W. 1964. Vergleichende anatomisch-physiologische Untersuchungen an Wild- und Teichkarpfen (*Cyprinus carpio* L.). Ein Beitrag zur Beurteilung der Zuchtleistungen beim Deutschen Teichkarpfen. Z. Fisch. 12: 725-800.

Steffens, W. 1967. Das Domestikationsproblem beim Karpfen (*Cyprinus carpio* L.). Verh. int. Verein. theor. angew. Limnol. 16: 1441-1448.

Steffens, W. 1980. Der Karpfen, *Cyprinus carpio*, 5th edition. A. Ziemsen Verlag, Wittenberg. 215 pp.

Strojnowski, S. 1609. Opisanie porządku stawowego y przestróg niektórych domowego gospodarstwa ... (Description of pond order and some guidelines on household ...). *In*: Z. Gawarecki & A. Kohn. 1860. Polskie Stawowe Gospodarstwo, Warszawa (in ancient Polish).

Strumienski, O. 1573. O sprawie, sypaniu, wymierzaniu i rybieniu stawów (On the repair, grading, measuring and stocking of ponds). F. Kucharzewski 1897, Cracow. 87 pp. (in ancient Polish).

Sumantadinata, K. 1995. Present state of common carp (*Cyprinus carpio* L.) stocks in Indonesia. Aquaculture 129: 205-209.

Svetovidov, A.N. 1933. Über den europäischen und ostasiatischen Karpfen (*Cyprinus*). Zool. Anzeiger 104: 269.

Szczygielski, W. 1969. Z dziejów gospodarki rybnej w Polsce w XVI - XVIII wieku (History of pond culture in Poland in 16 - 18 century). Studia z dziejów gospodarstwa wiejskiego 9 (2), Instytut Historii Kultury Materialnej Polskiej Akademii Nauk, Warszawa.

Tacon, A.G.J. 1994. Feed ingredients for carnivorous fish species. Alternatives to fishmeal and other fishery resources. FAO Fisheries Circular 881, FAO, Rome. 35 pp.

Talbot, L.M., W.J.A. Payne, H.P. Ledger, L.D. Verdcourt & M.H. Talbot. 1965. The meat production potential of wild animals in Africa: a review of biological knowledge. Commonwealth Bureau of Animal Breeding and Genetics Technical Communication, 16, Farnham Royal. 42 pp.

Tamadachi, M. 1990. The cult of the koi. T.F.H. Publications, Neptune City. 287 pp.

Tamura, T. 1961. Carp cultivation in Japan. pp.103-120. *In*: G. Borgström (ed.) Fish as Food, Vol. 1, Production, Biochemistry and Microbiology, Academic Press, New York.

Taylor, C.R. 1970. Dehydration and heat: effects on temperature regulations of East African ungulates. Amer. J. Physiol. 219: 1136-1139.

Taylor, C.R. 1972. Ranching arid lands: physiology of wild and domestic ungulates in the desert. pp. 167-192. *In*: Botswana Notes and Records 1, Proc. Conf. on Sustained Production from Semi-Arid Areas, Oct. 1971, Gaberone.

Thienemann, A. 1950. Verbreitungsgeschichte der Süsswassertierwelt Europas, Vol. 18, Die Binnengewässer. E. Schweizerbartsche., Stuttgart. 809 pp.

Valcanover, F. 1960. All the paintings of Titian, Part 2. Hawthorn Books, New York. Plate 127-128.

Valenta, M., A. Stratil, V. Šlechtová, L. Kálal & V. Šlechta. 1976. Polymorphism of transferrin in carp (*Cyprinus carpio* L.): genetic determination, isolation, and partial characterisation. Genetics 14: 27-45.

Varro, M.T. 1912. Varro on farming. M. Terenti Varronis Rerum Rusticarum libri tres. G. Bell, London. 375 pp.

Visy, Z. 1985. Der pannonische Limes in Ungarn. Corvina, Budapest. 150 pp.

Volf, J. 1965. Králík (The rabbit). *In*: J. Hanzák,, J. Volf & L.J. Dobroruka (ed.) Světem zvířat, Vol. 3, Domáci zvířata. SNDK, Praha.

Volf, J. 1975. Equines. pp. 539-579. *In*: B. Grzimek (ed.) Grzimek's Animal Life Encyclopedia, Volume 12, Van Nostrand Reinhold Company, New York.

Vooren, C.M. 1972. Ecological aspects of the introduction of fish species into natural habitats in Europe, with special reference to the Netherlands. J. Fish Biol. 4: 565-583.

Walton, I. 1676. The compleat angler or the contemplative man's recreation being a discourse of rivers, fishponds, fish and fishing not unworthy the perusal of most anglers, 5th edition (after the 1988 edition with modernized spelling by Bloomsbury Books, London. 224 pp.).

Wohlfarth, G.W. 1984. Common carp. pp. 375-380. *In*: I.L. Mason (ed.) Evolution of Domesticated Animals, Longman, London.

Wu, H.W. (ed.) 1977. Chinese cyprinid fishes. pp. 229-598. Scientific and Technical Publ., Shanghai. (in Chinese, e-mailed by J. Holčík).

Wünschmann, A. 1972. The wild and domestic oxen. pp. 331-398. *In*: B. Grzimek (ed.) Animal Life Encyclopedia, Van Nostrand Reinhold Company, New York.

Zaunick, R. 1925. Tritt der Karpfen schon im Diluvium Norddeutschlands auf? Mitteil. Fischereivereine Brandenburg-Pommern 17: 80-83.

Zeepvat, R.J. 1988. Fishponds in Roman Britain. pp. 17-26. *In*: M. Aston (ed.) Medieval Fish, Fisheries and Fishponds in England, BAR British Series 182(i).

Zeuner, F. E. 1963. A history of domesticated animals. Hutchinson, London. 560 pp.

ENVIRONMENTAL CHANGE AND THE CULTURE OF COMMON CARP IN MEDIEVAL EUROPE

RICHARD C. HOFFMANN

Department of History, York University, 4700 Keele St., North York, Ontario M3J 1P3, Canada

Synopis

Carp domestication and the culture of common carp in medieval Europe is approached as a problem in environmental and economic history. The development of aquaculture and the diffusion of *Cyprinus carpio* westward from a native range in the middle and lower Danube system were eventually intersecting results of economic development and environmental change. The expansion of human rural and urban economic activity characteristic of Europe during the three to four centuries after about 1000 CE had significant impacts on what had until then been relatively pristine aquatic environments. The effects notably damaged lotic habitats and anadromous fish populations, while favoring species more suited to lentic and flood plain habitats. Humans responded in various ways to rising consumption demand and shrinking supply of favored fish varieties. Among those responses was the formation in western Europe of a fish culture technology keyed to freshwater species preferring warm lentic conditions. Like fish eating, the fish-rearing technology was common to lay lords, monasteries, and other ecclesiastical landowners. An inventory of known material remains of common carp (archaeologically-recovered bones and scales) from post-glacial Europe is combined with critical examination of all relevant early verbal mentions. This evidence suggests that between the seventh and the eleventh centuries carp had spread slowly up the Danube basin and into nearby portions of the Rhine-Maas drainage, perhaps with some human assistance but without elaborate fish culture regimes. In the twelfth and thirteenth centuries, then, carp were taken up by western fish culturists and spread as both domesticated and feral organisms into the increasing amount of favor-able habitat on the western continent. Further expansion into the British Isles and elsewhere occurred later. An appendix delineates the earlier classical Greco-Roman evidence for a different kind of aquaculture based on coastal ponds and euryhaline marine fishes and not, in the known historical record, associated with the fish then called *cyprinus* or the one later called *carp*.

THE CRAFT OF HISTORY AND THE PROBLEM OF THE CARP

What can we learn of the European domestication of common carp? The event happened once or perhaps several times but certainly in complex circumstances that no longer exist and cannot now be replicated. If we cannot observe the event ourselves — because it took place before we were in a position to see it — we must reconstruct it from its surviving traces. Whether the traces which survive are words or objects they are the domain of the historical discipline (writ large). Historians *do history*, which is a shorthand way of saying that historians reconstruct the past from its surviving remains, objects we call "primary sources." Certainly a mid-twelfth-century[1] Rhineland abbess's remarks on the feeding and reproductive habits of a fish she called *carpo* (Hildegard) are a primary source potentially germane to the domestication question. So are rules governing the sale of *carpes* and *cuerpiaus* on the Parisian fish market about 1260 (Lespinasse & Bonnardot 1879) and bones authoritatively-identified as those of *Cyprinus carpio* which were professionally excavated from well-dated archeological contexts in a second through fourth century Roman frontier fort on the Danube near what is now Iža in Slovakia (Balon 1995b).

The past is not one but many. Its temporal pieces do not fold into a single simultaneity. An object from the past is a primary source or evidence only for the particular part of the past that produced it. The fundamental critical method of the historian is to locate or place surviving verbal or material remains in the correct past context. Where, when, by whom, and for what purpose was this object generated? How was the object's maker able to know what is there presented? A primary source so verified "speaks" with an authentic voice from a particular past. The historian can proceed to infer from that voice a probable reconstruction of that — not some other — past. Sometimes the evidence of the sources can sustain a single and convincing reconstruction of a past event or historical phenomenon. In many other cases few, ambiguous, or conflicting primary sources reveal contemporary disagreement on what happened, support different but equally probable reconstructions, or simply force acknowledgement that knowledge is limited in certain, sometimes even deeply interesting, areas. Should we wish to speculate on, for instance, the experience of ancient Romans with common carp (Balon 1974, 1995a, b), it is the more important to ascertain the precise bounds of the relevant evidence and the point where we go beyond it.

Historical research advances both by the discovery of new primary sources — e.g. findings of environmental archaeologists unimagined only two decades ago — and by people now conceiving and pursuing new kinds of questions about the past — e.g. the whole range of issues involving daily life, work, family relations, etc. covered by the rubric of social history. Both kinds of discoveries call upon historians to reconsider what had been thought true or important about the past, to explore its basis in evidence and its congruence with newer findings and understandings. Sometimes we can only point out that the received wisdom does not in fact accord with the full range of evidence; in other cases we can advance different views of the past which correspond to the critically evaluated relevant sources as well as or better than positions accepted until now. As in the natural sciences, que-

ries and testing drive the historical research enterprise. When historians "save the phenomena," the phenomena are not observations or experimental results, but the primary sources. In making assertions about the past, this paper will, to the maximum extent possible, include references to the sources or to works of scholarship based directly on precise identification and critical reading of them.

Environmental History

One lively area of current historical research is significantly inspired by present-day environmental awareness. At the most general level, people seek historical perspective on modern fears of environmental damage and hazards. Of course the problem is more complex than that, and runs much more deeply into the human past. The emerging historical subdiscipline which engages these questions of humans in the world about them is called environmental history.

The working assumption of environmental history (Fig. 1) acknowledges all encounters between nature and humankind as broad and complex *interactions* among three interdependent variables (McEvoy 1987, Worster 1988). Human culture (mentality, cognition) refers to the mental and conceptual framework for human life, a community's and individual's ways of seeing and thinking about itself and its surroundings. What is perceived, valued, and devalued? What are the goals and rules for social life? Human economy (production, action) is the process of meeting human wants and needs by manipulating the classic economic factors, labor, capital, and natural resources, in order to make, distribute, and consume desired goods and services. Ecological process (nature, environment organic and inorganic) is the "other," the stubborn pattern of order and chaos which humans did not and cannot create or, indeed, bring into as much obedience as some human groups may want to think. The environmental history paradigm knows no human action is without cultural meaning — whether explicit or not — and ecological consequence — whether visible or not. Equally, the autonomous operation of natural forces sets both conditions and responses to human aspirations and deeds. Hence understanding of the past demands we explore an interactive relationship.

The environmental history paradigm allows and supports everything from very large scale investigations of human civilization on the planet earth, as, for instance, the changing ecologies of parasitic disease or human energy use since the Pleistocene (McNeill 1976, Smil 1994), to what may seem the most closely-bounded case studies of, to take two sixteenth-century examples, herd animals in a Mexican valley or hydraulic engineering near Venice (Melville 1994, Cosgrove 1993). Work at an intermediate temporal and spatial scale is also possible. The workings and long-term changes of the preindustrial European economy have long been recognized as crucial to understanding the great transition of first the west, then the world, to modern industrial (and now post-industrial) conditions. From a concern with human use of natural resources in pre-industrial Europe (ca. 500-1750) to the wider frame of environmental history is no great leap. Recent studies of regional ecosystems (TeBrake 1985, McNeill 1992), urban water management (Guillerme 1988), or ideologies of human dominance (Cohen 1989) are illustrative examples. Each challenges older understandings.

For study of pre-industrial European fisheries the environmental history approach provides an obvious integrating mechanism. How did human use of fish for food fit into larger cultural, economic, and ecological relationships? Like most of everyday life in what we now call medieval (ca. 500-1500) and early modern (ca. 1350-1750) Europe, many of these activities were but rarely the object of purposeful written description. Literacy simply had other social purposes. Diligent and knowledgeable searching finds, however, that fisheries — and most of the concern here is with fresh water — did leave surprisingly numerous traces, verbal and material, in the historical record. The task is to decipher and assimilate this patchy but, I will argue, reasonably consistent body of evidence. Among other topics, the process of testing received wisdom directs attention to the myth of an East Asian origin for European common carp and carp culture and to the basis in evidence for both a claimed Roman origin of carp domestication and the proverbial assertion that "the medieval monks did it," When we recover, assess, describe, and interpret real medieval primary sources, the results are at least mildly revisionist.

This paper sets the culture of common carp into the larger context of medieval European economic growth and environmental change. It reconstructs two phenomena of the tenth through fourteenth centuries which may have

Fig.1. Schematic representation of the interaction among culture, economy, and ecology in environmental history (after Worster 1988 and McEvoy 1987).

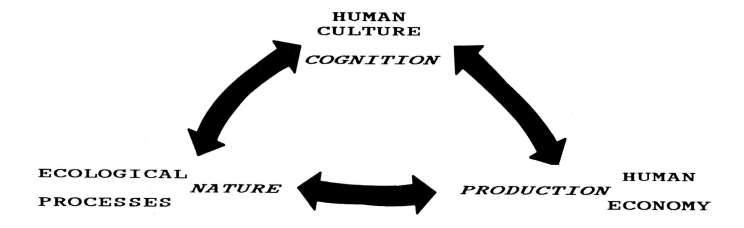

A PARADIGM FOR

ENVIRONMENTAL HISTORY

HUMAN CULTURE

COGNITION

ECOLOGICAL PROCESSES

NATURE

PRODUCTION

HUMAN ECONOMY

special resonance for fisheries scientists today. Critical analysis of authentic historical evidence now lets us determine that:

(1) Characteristic agricultural and urban developments in medieval Europe had especially damaging effects on lotic habitats and anadromous fish populations, while favoring species more suited to lentic and flood plain habitats.

(2) Humans responded in various ways to rising consumption demand and shrinking supply of favored fish varieties. Among those responses was the development and spread, especially in interior Europe, of a fish culture technology keyed to warm water, lentic species, especially *Cyprinus carpio*.

In other words, the *documented* process of carp's spread and rearing in Europe is associated historically with congruent changes to the economy and the environment during the Middle Ages.

Environment and Economy in Early Medieval Europe

My last prefatory task is to provide a most cursory introduction to relevant environmental and economic features of early medieval Europe, the conditions of the fifth through tenth centuries which preceded the story told below. Very briefly, before around 1000, the Po basin of northern Italy and Europe north of the Alps and Pyrenees had experienced little human modification of aquatic environments. These had evolved naturally since the retreat of the Pleistocene glaciers. Apart from montane zones near the Alps and a morainic belt inland from the Baltic, western Europe is naturally dominated by riverine drainage systems and contains rather few still waters with lentic habitats. It also possesses a limited freshwater fish fauna. The west and north of the European peninsula was by the early Middle Ages (and is still today) incompletely (re-)colonized by warmwater freshwater fishes, which had during the Pleistocene been confined to a southeastern (lower Danube and Balkans) refugium. The natural range of common carp provides an apt and notable illustration. We will discuss below the strong combination of verbal and archeological evidence indicating both (a) the presence of this fish south and east of the piedmont reaches of the Danube and (b) the absence of such evidence north and west of those reaches

up to the Middle Ages.

Early medieval Europe was certainly not, however, a wilderness devoid of human settlement and interaction with the environment. Already for a millennium and more, even long before Romans came north from Italy, iron age communities had exploited the resources of soils, woodlands, and wild and domestic plants and animals. In the post-Roman centuries scattered human agricultural populations were largely sustained by local subsistence economies producing both bread and meat with fairly extensive forms of agro-pastoralism. They plowed mainly the lighter soils, some naturally unwooded, in gently sloping and easily drained locations. Over most of Europe this meant natural woodland ecosystems had been modified but little disrupted by human activity. It was especially the case on hillsides and in riparian zones. Decline of Roman civilization where it had once prevailed also caused notable shrinking of urban centers and populations. Big local concentrations of human beings (towns) had little ecological importance in early medieval Christian Europe. Though some pockets of rising human numbers, expanding farmland, and the exchange of at least luxury commodities are certainly detectable in the eighth, ninth, and tenth centuries, by and large in Europe of about 1000 a small and stable population inhabited thinly humanized landscapes. Even where some people fished to feed themselves or their masters, Europe's waters were even less affected.

The next section sketches how the medieval economy changed and the impact of these changes on aquatic environments and fish populations.

SOME ENVIRONMENTAL EFFECTS OF MEDIEVAL ECONOMIC DEVELOPMENT

Twentieth-century historians have achieved reasonable consensus on characteristic patterns of medieval economic expansion (Lopez 1971, Pounds 1974, Cipolla 1994). Put simply, some time in the tenth century human numbers began to increase, and with them land under the plow for production of cereal grains. The medieval agricultural sector improved its equipment and farming methods. Higher productivity and more available surpluses permitted exponential growth of a hitherto tiny and luxury-dependent exchange sector, and this transformed Europe's minuscule groupings of non-agricultural administrators and consumers into new and dynamic cities, the nodes of a market economy. Even when the demographic and agrarian upsurge petered out into stagnation and decline in the fourteenth century, commercial specialization and trading networks continued to thicken and to infiltrate formerly subsistence activities.

What had this increase in economic activity to do with aquatic life? Substituting intensively used plowland for woodland changed basic hydrological conditions both directly and by proliferation of water-powered grain mills. Growing numbers of humans and their concentration into towns added nutrients and contaminants to water courses, while the demand for fish as food soared. As these impacts accumulated in each region, freshwater fisheries visibly came under stress. The process resembles but does not replicate the model of developmental damage to aquatic ecosystems advanced by Regier et al. (1989) from late twentieth-century observations. Some particulars follow.

Habitat Changes

One basic change in the medieval economy was growing reliance on cereal food. This meant permanent plowed fields replaced woodland from central Spain to Sweden and Wales to Poland (e.g. Darby 1956, Maas 1944, Rackham 1990, Rösener 1992). Clearance of forests, which slow runoff and maintain steady streamflow, inescapably alters the pattern of stream discharge to greater irregularity. Rain and meltwaters run more quickly off farmland. Larger and faster runoff exerts greater erosive force on stream beds and channels, and then falling water levels leave a contracted stream and deposits of eroded materials. One astute observer in late thirteenth-century Alsace noted how clearance of the Vosges in his own lifetime had caused much more rapid and dangerous runoff (Jaffé 1861). We can detect the same sequence of medieval deforestation and flooding in the Po basin and in central Poland (Fumagalli

1994, Dunin-Wąsowicz 1990). Unstable flow regimes create difficult habitats for fishes. Those living in running water must expend more energy during floods. They lose eggs and young to winter spates and suffer high mortalities when small streams dry up in summer. Species which spawn in flooded margins are adapted to consistent seasonal patterns of rising and falling water, so instability disrupts their reproductive behavior (Hynes 1970, Regier et al. 1989).

Soil erosion and alluvial deposition is a now often-recognized result of medieval agricultural expansion. After loss of natural vegetative cover, characteristic medieval practices of bare fallow, large open fields, and plowing with the slope, let topsoil flow to the watercourses, especially during heavy winter rains and snowmelt (Vogt 1990, Bell 1992). Siltation and sedimentation are well-dated to this period in places like the Leine valley of Saxony, the upper Thames basin, and the Lys and Scarpe Rivers in Artois and Hainault (Nitz 1983, Lambrick 1992, Derville 1990). Increased lake-bottom deposition in the Lac d'Annecy of Savoy precisely followed creation about 1300 of grain farms on its once-wooded shores (Oldfield & Clark 1990). Further downstream at this time, silt filled the Oude Rhin mouth of the Rhine in Holland and also what had been a large bay between Gdańsk and Elbląg where the Wisła River entered the Baltic (TeBrake 1985, Filuk 1968). An increased silt load makes water more often turbid, reduces light penetration, and can smother organisms living in weed or gravel beds. Like the more dramatic alternation of floods and low water, these effects favor certain species relative to others.

To process the new grain supplies a little-used late antique invention, the watermill, exploded across the medieval landscape. From perhaps a couple hundred in King Alfred's England of the 880s, they multiplied to 5,624 in the Domesday Book of 1085. In Poitou, Berry, Burgundy, and Lorraine mills proliferated from the tenth century through the twelfth. On the Aube River, where 14 mills are recorded in the eleventh century, 62 may be counted in the twelfth century, and almost 200 in the early thirteenth (Reynolds 1983 summarizes many local studies). As one modern student summed it up, "By the close of the Middle Ages watermills were in use on streams of every type. They dammed up the rivers of medieval man; they were on the banks of his brooks and creeks, in the middle of his rivers, under his bridges, and along his coastlines. They impeded navigation and created streams (in the form of mill races and power canals) and lakes (in the form of storage reservoirs behind waterpower dams) where none had existed before" (Reynolds 1983, p. 69).

In fact, the streams had existed in most of Europe, but not the ponds. Medieval watermills powered their overshot wheels by using a weir or dam to concentrate the falling water and pond a reserve supply of it. Medieval millwrights learned to do this on ever larger rivers. Dams blocked running water and created still water. As moving water slows, it drops the solids it has carried in suspension. On the Derwent in the English Midlands 2 meters of gravel and silt alluvium eventually covered a 1-meter timber mill dam, gate, and race dated by dendrochronology to the mid-twelfth century (Clay 1992). Polish archeologists report similar finds (Bagniewski & Kubów 1977). The broad surfaces of standing waters absorb more solar energy. This both warms the water and further improves conditions for growth of rooted plants. In the twelfth century Picard records slower, deeper, and weedier waters backed up behind mill dams and weirs all along the Scarpe, Oise, and Somme rivers (Fossier 1968). Ubiquitous watermills formed and multiplied a new kind of aquatic habitat into which we shall probe more deeply below.

On existing watercourses and their native fish populations, mills had an immediate effect, for they blocked movement of migrants. Like the concentrations at natural barriers, those at dams and weirs offered fishers profitable access to migratory species. Even deep in central Saxony, a mill dam at Lauenheim on the River Zschopau became the site of a salmon trap (Beyer 1855). Possession of mills was associated with the right to take eel on large rivers like the Duero in Castile, the Garonne near Toulouse, the Meuse around Liege, and small streams of Lincolnshire (Wamba 1986, Mousnier 1982, Sicard 1953, Van Derveeghe 1955, Luttrell Psalter 1932).

But impassable barrier dams kept migratory species from vital spawning habitat. Blocked runs of fish — were they trout or shad? — ascending the Sarca River from Lake Garda in 1210 caused the Bishop of Trento, who held sovereign fishing rights in that county, to require removal of mill dams at Arco (Stolz 1936). For the sake of the salmon a Scottish statute of 1214 required all dams to be fitted with an opening and all barrier nets to be lifted every Saturday (Noël de la Morinière 1815). About 1470 a Rhineland abbot was complaining that a three-year-old dam on the Dhünn (a Rhine tributary) meant "neither salmon nor [other] fish can go up...." (Mosler 1955). Dikes built in the Rhine delta during the eleventh and twelfth centuries to drain marshes for agricultural settlement arguably caused major declines in the sturgeon population (Boddeke 1971). These losses were especially important because the spawning environment in fresh water determines the productivity of anadromous fishes (Schalk 1977).

Turning from rural development to other aspects of the medieval economy, human population growth and urbanization affected both water chemistry and hydrological conditions for aquatic life.

Waste from more and larger human concentrations, from rural monasteries to towns of 20,000 or even 50,000, necessarily increased the nutrient load in watercourses. Under what were still largely preindustrial conditions, nineteenth-century engineers calculated an annual per capita output of 34 kg of feces and 428 kg of urine, totalling 462 kg of nitrogen-rich excrement (Grewe 1991). The several hundred monks and lay brethren at early thirteenth-century Clairvaux were served by a diversion of the Aube River, which ran through gardens, mills, brewery, fulling mill, tannery, laundry, and latrines before rejoining the main stream. Long rows of latrines over channels running back into the local stream were since at latest the eleventh century the norm among all monastic orders and, where location permitted, secular palaces (Lillich 1982). In one famous incident in 1184, the hall floor in the palace of the Archbishop of Mainz at Erfurt collapsed and pitched members of the imperial court into underlying cesspits through which the River Gera flowed. Local streams likewise received the human (and animal) waste of towns, whether by runoff from street disposal, by purposely emptying cesspits into flowing water below town, or by direct siting of latrines over water-courses (Grewe 1991, Guillerme 1988). Robert Guillerme has argued that organic acid- and alkaline-based processes used by early medieval textile and leather crafts caused "the precipitation of solid organic materials in water which river currents carried beyond city limits" (Guillerme 1988, p. 98).

And what was downstream? During the thirteenth-sixteenth centuries, a lagoon-like shoreline on the Bodensee at Konstanz was filled with town wastes. Archeological study of plant remains there shows disappearance of species native to clean waters, and massive appearance of a filamentous algae closely associated with strongly eutrophic conditions (Küster 1989). By the early 1400s Parisian effluent was making the River Seine below town "infectée et corrumpue" every summer (Mieck 1981). These are signs of aquatic ecosystems under stress.

Activities in the urban and commercial sector further impeded naturally free-flowing waters. Since the eleventh century castles and towns had diverted rivers to fill defensive moats (Guillerme 1988). Markets for fuel drove extensive peat-digging which created the Norfolk Broads and smaller but more numerous *plassen* in the Netherlands (Lambert 1961, Borger 1992). And between the eleventh and fourteenth centuries still more weirs, dams, and ponds were built to power new industrial operations like malting, fulling, metal-working, sawmills, and paper-making (Reynolds 1983).

The type and scale of physical and chemical changes which medieval economic development brought to European inland waters most directly and heavily affected small- and medium-sized watercourses. Brooks, streams, and small rivers are by their very size, high ratio of surface area to volume, and abundance in the landscape more closely tied than large rivers to their immediate terrestrial environments. Removal of bankside vegetation; local ditching, diversion, or embankment; small mill ponds and dams; and effluents from concentrations of livestock or humans have profound local impact, removing the whole waterway from its natural form and

sources of energy. Large rivers, in contrast, are linked to their surroundings through their multiple channels and extensive floodplains, so simple and local changes in riparian conditions have less effect on them (Regier et al. 1989). Hence the impact of preindustrial economic development differed in degree and kind from that of industrial development. Yet the finding should not be oversimplified. The much-studied Rhine River and its major tributaries, for instance, are said to have suffered little from human activity before channelizing and embanking in the early nineteenth century began a total degradation (Lelek 1989). But most studies of major European rivers start from a present and retrospective standpoint with little deeper historical knowledge or awareness. The evidence of medieval landscape change is overwhelming. Watersheds are systemic continua; what enters at the top flows all the way down. Besides dams cutting off what had once been the highest spawning sites, we must recognize medieval deforestation and erosion as a principal cause of more erratic flow regimes and contributor of material to the many mainstream sandbars and islands known from early modern records.

Fishing Pressure

Left for last is the most obvious human impact on freshwater ecosystems, the demand for fish as food. In part for cultural reasons, medieval Europeans consumed significant quantities of fish (Zug Tucci 1985, Bérard 1988). Especially before about 1200, both written and archaeological records of fishes in human diets show a preponderance of anadromous and freshwater species (Delatouche 1966, 1969, Hitzbleck 1971, Dyer 1988). For instance, the list of fishes eaten at late eleventh-century Cluny, then the most prestigious monastery in western Christendom, named six taxa from fresh water (salmon, sturgeon, trout, pike, eel, and lamprey) and but one purely marine organism (cuttlefish) (Ulrich). Actual remains of medieval fish dinners corroborate such verbal impressions: in food waste from eleventh-through fourteenth-century Schleswig locally-caught perch, pike, and cyprinids first equal, then outnumber imported cod and other marine varieties (Heinrich 1983, 1987); before about 1500 well-off Parisians on Rue Fromentau and their monastic contemporaries at La Charité-sur-Loire threw away almost exclusively the bones of fish from fresh water (Desse & Desse-Berset 1992, Audoin-Rouzeau 1986).

Continued predation by rising numbers of humans caused thirteenth-century legislators to complain about "overfishing." For example, the first full-scale royal fisheries ordinance issued by a king of France, Philip IV in 1289, grumbled that the fishers took too many fish before they had reached full size (Duplés-Agier 1852). Italian and south German authorities echoed this complaint, sometimes with concrete details (Trexler 1974, Stromeyer 1910, Freudlsperger 1936). When Jäger (1994) asserts no evidence before the 1500s for falling numbers of aquatic organisms he makes the unrealistic assumption that only governmental records of catches constitute "scientific" data. The issue, however, is historical.

Indeed, evidence less subjective than political rhetoric reveals shifts in catches and human consumption patterns during the high medieval period. These plainly identify fish populations under stress. To put one point briefly, from the tenth through the twelfth century, there is a decline in average body size of sturgeon, *Acipenser sturio*, salmonids (*S. salar*, likely also *S. trutta trutta*) and pike perch, *Stizostedion lucioperca*, in large collections of fish remains from central European sites (Susłowska & Urbanowicz 1967, Kozikowska 1974, Paul 1980, Driesch 1982).

Changes of species composition occur in some well-studied and unusually rich time series. Sturgeon had been a common dietary item in the early Middle Ages. Between the eighth and the twelfth/thirteenth centuries that species fell from 70% to 10% of fish consumed at 17 south Baltic sites (Benecke 1986). It declined to nil in Dutch records from the eleventh to the fourteenth century (Boddeke 1971). In thirteenth-century France and England sturgeon were legally reserved for the king (Fleta 1955). By the fourteenth century there circulated in England a recipe for cooks to "make sturgeon" from veal (Hieatt & Butler 1985), which seems a convincing sign of the prestige and favor still attached to an almost extinct food fish. As for salmon, catch records and price series from the several small coastal rivers of lower Normandy indicate loss of abundance between 1100 and 1300, when the best-documented river yielded 300-350 fish a year, and then a further drop by 1400 to less than 100 fish (Halard 1983). Even in wealthy Parisian households and prosperous Flemish monasteries consumption of once-favored sturgeon, salmon, trout, and whitefish shrank to nothing by around 1500 (Desse & Desse-Berset 1992, Sternberg 1992, Ervynck & Van Neer 1992, Clason et al. 1979).

In contrast, the same and comparable evidence reveals other fishes gaining dietary importance. Especially large increases are noted for eel and for common carp. Eel reached two-thirds of remains from twelfth-century Deventer, but thereafter fell back to only one third in favor of undifferentiated small cyprinids (IJzereef & Laarman 1986). After about 1450, eel comprised 20% and carp 40% of all fish (and together 90% of the local fish) consumed at Sint-Salvators abbey near Oudenaard (Ervynck & Van Neer 1992). Of the fish bones identified in twelfth through sixteenth century deposits at Gaiselberg castle in Lower Austria, common carp provided 60%, and most of those came after 1400 (Spitzenberger 1983). By that time the species also dominated tables in Paris and La Charité-sur-Loire (Desse & Desse-Berset 1992, Sternberg 1992, Audoin-Rouzeau 1986).

The well-evidenced remains of eel and common carp, both taxa easily recognized by an experienced ichthyo-archaeologist, lead and stand for general increases in relatively more lentic and heat-tolerant fish varieties. Financial records from the papal court at Avignon (1338-1375) trace large shipments down the Rhône and Saône rivers from Burgundy of carp, eel, bream, tench, barbel, and pike (Richard 1987). Accounts kept between 1349 and 1413 by managers of waters belonging to the church of St. Etienne at Troyes, Champagne,[2] record large catches of carp, eel, bream, and pike.

Characteristic differences between the fishes that rose in importance and those that fell argue for human impacts on medieval aquatic ecosystems more complex than can be ascribed to fishing pressure alone. The taxa that increased in dietary importance and appar-

---

[1] Except as otherwise specified, all dates in this paper are CE, that is, *Anno Domini*.

[2] "Comtes des pescheries de l'eglise de Troyes, 1349-1413", London, British Library Additional Manuscript 22496.

ent natural success may be characterized by greater tolerance, even preference, for warmer, more turbid, and quieter waters. Most cyprinids and pike spawn in weedy shallows, and eel leave fresh water when ready to breed. Reproductive success for the fishes displaying stress (e.g. salmonids, sturgeon), on the other hand, requires clean and cool running or estuarine waters, preferably with a gravel substrate (see Balon 1975, 1990). Precisely those aquatic habitats were being blocked or diminished by medieval agricultural, urban, and industrial developments, which were, quite without human intention, raising the amounts of silt and nutrients in Europe's watercourses and the proportion of standing water. Some responses by medieval Europeans to a perceived decline and shortage of the fishes they had long like to eat would, it is argued below, further accentuate precisely these alterations to aquatic environments and their biota.

FORMS OF HUMAN RESPONSE

Medieval Europeans became aware of shifts in the availability and usefulness of traditional inland fisheries resources. Several of the ways they responded to these changes can receive only brief mention here.

The Control and Exploitation of Wild Fisheries

Historians of medieval law recognize privatization of previously common or public fishing rights as a general trend (Cahn 1956, Górzyński 1964, McDonnell 1981, Materné 1991). By about 1200 grants from kings or simple seizure had put landowners in possession of all but the largest inland river fisheries. Peasant communities struggled with diminishing success to maintain some right of access to waters under elite control. Surviving rights were ordinarily limited to small gear used to take fish for family subsistence use (Heimpel 1963, 1964, Verriest 1956, Mákkai 1985).

Along with privatization came the important development of markets in both usufruct rights and the product. One-time lordly servants evolved into full-time fishers who paid annual money dues or, rarely, a share of the catch for the right to exploit the lord's waters. By 1300 such arrangements are fully visible in record sources from Austria, Warwickshire, León, and Picardy (Zeibig 1868, Hilton 1960,

Wamba 1986, Fossier 1968). In the different economic climate after the Black Death of 1347-1351 such leaseholds became the norm, and the local professional supplying fish to nearby markets a familiar figure. Operators of what were now commercial fisheries, in some places fishers and in others fishmongers, often tried to form producers' cartels. Fish-selling guilds were claiming special control over markets at Rome by the eleventh century (Vendittelli 1992), Worms in 1106 (Epstein 1991), Paris before 1260 (Lespinasse & Bonnardot 1879), and Kraków a century after that (Brzozowski & Tobiasz 1964). Prices for local wild fish rose almost everywhere, and fresh fish tended to become an elite consumption good. In fifteenth-century central European towns, for instance, fish cost three to five times more than beef (Hitzbleck 1971, Dirlmeier 1978, Dyer 1988).

Public authorities undertook regulation of fisheries for both consumption and conservation motives. Urban governments, especially, maintained strict supervision over the sale of fresh fish, legislating uniform inspection and requiring immediate retail sale at designated locations (Lespinasse & Bonnardot 1879, Pini 1975, Nicholas 1987). Territorial lords like the Count of St. Pol, the King of France, and city states like Perugia or Florence — all issuers of fishing ordinances before 1350 — aimed to preserve fish populations by controlling human use of them. Their laws set minimum size limits, forbade fishing during spawning time, and prohibited methods thought to kill too many small fish (Fossier 1968, Noël de la Morinière 1815, Duplés-Angier 1852, Jeulin 1962-1964, Trexler 1974, Mira 1937).

Medieval Europeans also undertook the significant long-run development of substitute sources of supply. Sometime around or after 1200 what had been local coastal marine fisheries in several western European regions began to extend operations further offshore. Records of fishing communities and middens of fish consumers mark when this happened (Aubenas 1953, Cutting 1962, Steane 1985, Durrenberger & Palsson 1985, Lepiksaar 1985, Jones 1985, Mollat 1987, O'Connor 1989, Coy 1989, Nedkvitne 1993, Ebel 1994). Under preindustrial conditions of inland transport and no refrigeration, a fresh marine catch could be moved inland about 150 kilometers

(Fig. 2). By the mid-thirteenth century Paris, just about that distance from the Norman coast, was served by elaborate relays of coaches and a strict inspection system for saltwater fish (Bérard 1988, Lespinasse & Bonnardot 1879). Further inland fresh sea fishes could not penetrate. The main output of the late medieval and early modern marine fisheries was therefore marketed as preserved fish (Michell 1977). Salt herring and dried cod (*stockfish*) were shipped to consumers far inland, but elites despised preserved fish: a later bishop of Speyer refused to be served herring because they could not be made edible (Fouquet 1988). All who could afford to pay for fresh fish did so. Especially across those large areas of medieval Europe where expanded marine supplies were inaccessible, intensified manipulation of freshwater ecosystems was a potential alternative. That route results in fish culture.

Medieval European Fish Culture

To serve human demand for fresh fish medieval Europeans established new freshwater habitats, modified the mix of fish species, and created new ecosystems, both domestic and wild. These activities both exploited and multiplied what have already been identified as unintended environmental consequences of medieval economic growth.

Artificial constructions for long-term retention and eventual rearing of live fish are plainly a response to inadequacy, whether conceived in nutritional or cultural terms, of natural supply. Fishponds can equilibrate seasonal irregularities, supplement insufficient wild catches, or even entirely replace wild varieties with preferred domesticates. In some circles the ponds and freshly-reared fish could also make a social statement. The intensity and sophistication of medieval fish culture varied along a spectrum jointly determined by growing technical expertise, priorities, and resources available for investment. Simple

Fig.2. Map depicting the zone of 150 km for successful shipment of fresh marine fish in preindustrial Europe.

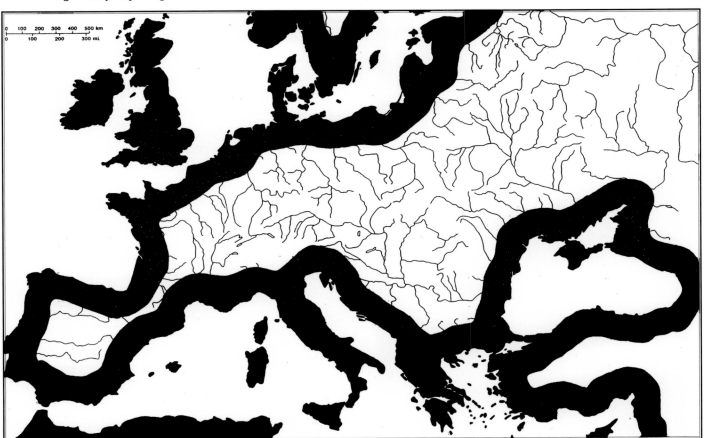

storage tanks for seasonally surplus catches were likely always to be found. Heavily capitalized and elaborately managed fish-rearing enterprises were relatively late phenomena. What follows touches mainly on ecologically significant aspects of their evolution.

Even on monastic estates, where rules against eating meat meant proportionally greater fish consumption, hard evidence for fish culture is simply not present in the early Middle Ages (compare Fichtenau 1991). On ascetic grounds the Rule of St. Benedict, since the early ninth century the dominant constitution for monastic life, prohibited eating the flesh of quadrupeds but did allow fish. Monastic dietary regimes generally both reflected and reacted against local consumption practices. No meat did call for more eggs, cheese, and fish than in lay diets (Zimmermann 1973). Fish was thought superior food, however,

Fig.3. Detail from a map drawn by French military engineers in 1744-1760 (Carte Cassini, feuillet 115) still shows three ponds, one above the other, in a side valley of the River Saône at Laperrière-sur-Saône in Burgundy. The ponds were constructed before 1300, probably for the Duke of Burgundy. In the early fourteenth century the duke's estate officials managed these and other ponds in the neighbourhood for intensive fish production (Hoffmann forthcoming).

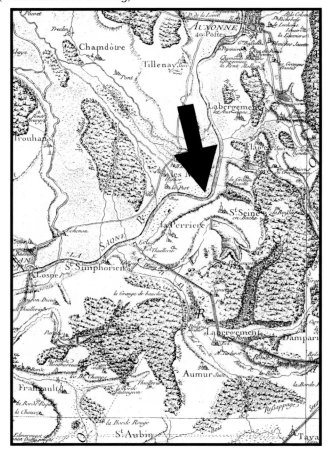

and not eaten daily by the monks. By the eleventh century fish appeared on the table at well-run Benedictine communities two or three days a week and on special holidays, including during the 40-day Lenten fast when monks ate no eggs or cheese. Austere new orders, the Cistercians and Carthusians, avoided even fish during their early decades, and but slowly capitulated to occasional "pittances," special endowments of a fish meal (Zimmermann 1973, Hoffmann 1994a).

All needs of monks and nuns for fish could often and long be satisfied from local wild resources. Of the six freshwater taxa named in Cluny's late eleventh-century customal, five (pike, trout, lamprey, eel, and sturgeon[3]) could be expected from the extensive river fisheries in the Saône and its tributaries which that house owned two generations later. The rich records of Cluny at its height of wealth and prestige up to the mid-twelfth century refer to the capture and temporary storage of fish but give no sign of their rearing in fishponds (Ulrich, Bernard & Bruel, 1876-1903, Duby 1952, 1956). The same may be said of Cistercians well into the twelfth century (Benoit & Wabont 1991, Hoffmann 1994a).

To build a fishpond — and not just a holding tank — is to create a new aquatic habitat. Active construction of ponds for this purpose got under way in the eleventh century and increased rapidly in the twelfth and thirteenth. People built fishponds in regions where human populations and economies were also growing. Disputes over Picard fishponds thus enter the written record around 1100, and major projects in hydraulic engineering there date between the 1170s and 1250s, coincident with such investments in Burgundy (Fig. 3) and Berry (Gislain 1984, Fossier 1968, Richard 1983, Richard 1986, Devailly 1973). Across the channel, from Wiltshire to Yorkshire and the late eleventh century to the late thirteenth, fishponds were made on estates belonging to bishops, major monasteries (Fig. 4), and the English crown (McDonnell 1981, Steane 1988, Bond 1988, Roberts 1986, Currie 1989).

It is important to recognize that, despite the ecclesiastical bias of a high medieval record written largely by and for churchmen, both lay and clerical landowners built, owned, and operated fishponds in the twelfth and thirteenth-century west. About 1160, while the count of Sancerre was flooding lands near Bourges to make himself a fishpond, Emperor Frederick Barbarossa was ordering construction of another large one at Kaiserslautern (Devailly 1973, Otto 1953). In 1216 Simon de Joinville, Seneschal of Champagne and lord of estates on the upper Meuse River, made sure he exempted his fishponds when he allowed the monks of Clairvaux to fish in his river (Evergates 1993). This should in no way surprise. Medieval religious and lay elites were everywhere interrelated and interdependent (compare Bouchard 1987). Church institutions were more durable and kept more records, and by the thirteenth century the Cistercians (latecomers who often received valley-bottom sites) were becoming unusually systematic in their management of water (Fig. 5), but recent scholarship is no longer convinced they were any more innovative than their lay neighbors and kin (Berman 1986, Bouchard 1991, Benoit & Wabont 1991, Hoffmann 1994a).

Active building of fishponds spread later to east central Europe. The Cistercian house founded in 1133 at Waldsassen in the German-Czech frontier zone of the Egerland did not make its first pond until about 1220 (Muggenthaler 1924). A few ponds may be recorded from eleventh or twelfth century Bohemia, but the first datable construction there was in 1263 and rapid increase came a century after that, when 87 new building projects are recorded between 1347 and 1418. Large and complex hydraulic works were especially undertaken by Czech lords between 1450 and 1550, resulting by the latter year in an estimated 26,000 artificial ponds covering thousands of hectares (Fig. 6) and some of them fed by rivers which had been diverted as much as 35 kilometers (Andreška 1984, Graus 1953-1957). Pond building in southern Poland lagged a generation or so behind that in Bohemia (Szczygielski 1965, 1969, Hoffmann 1989).

Whether fed by surface runoff, a spring, stream, or diverted river water, fishponds are still, not moving, waters. Medieval Europeans managed their purpose-built fishponds and other appropriate artificial or enhanced ponds (former river channels, millponds, moats) for production of fish varieties well-adapted to lentic habitats with high nutrient levels and warmed water. Probably in the twelfth century and certainly by the thirteenth careful management included close control over the in- and outflow of water and a regular (3-5 year) cycle from stocking with breeders or small fish to drainage of the pond for harvest, followed by a dry season and cultivation of the bottom to raise fertility when the pond was refilled. The elaborate hydraulic system built at thirteenth-century Vauclair put the fishpond where it received nutrient-laden outflow from abbey latrines (Courtois 1982). A like arrangement fertilized five of Maulbronn's eight nearby ponds (Seidenspinner 1989). Coordinated management of several ponds serving different functions or at different phases of the production cycle was essential for year- to-year operation of the enterprise. The entire technical system is visible in sources from the western continent and England by about 1200 and seems later further to the east (Grand & Delatouche 1950, Devailly 1973, Roberts 1986, Verriest 1950, Brouwers 1910-1926).

Anadromous or cold-water fishes had no place in the pond environment. Royal and monastic ponds in thirteenth-century Yorkshire yielded bream, tench, roach, dace, and pike (McDonnell 1981). In the 1384 catch from the millpond at Cryfield, Warwickshire, came bream, tench, roach, perch, and pike (Hilton 1960). Most of the fish species recorded in medieval ponds were these western European natives with preferences for still and weedy waters. They now received much increased habitat and even purposeful human help as a consequence of medieval economic development. So during the 1460s the Duke of Norfolk stocked his half-dozen fishponds with small pike, perch, roach, tench, and bream. He also put in common carp. Norfolk's financial account offers the first documented presence of carp in a specific water on the British Isles (Turner 1841, Currie 1991). The analogous record from France came earlier, so far seemingly as the hundreds of carp Count Thibaut V of

a

b

Fig.4. Long-dry traces still remain of Oldstead Grange Pond, Yorkshire, which covered some 18 hectares after it was built about 1240 by Cistercian monks from Byland abbey, located 2 km away: a–Former pond bottom and view of the earthen dam which blocked drainage from a natural hollow. b–Detail view down the pond-side face of the dam (photographs by R. Hoffmann, 1987).

Fig.5. This artificial fishpond at Horbach, in Franconia west of Nürnberg, was possessed by lay landowners before Heilsbronn abbey obtained it in the late 1200s. The abbey then managed it in concert with at least five more fishponds it owned there along the spring-fed valley of the River Zenn (photograph by R. Hoffmann, 1991).

Fig.6. A large Bohemian fishpond of late medieval origin is drained down and ready for harvest by traditional methods still being used in the late twentieth century (photograph courtesy of A. Lelek).

Fig.7. This map displays the evidence for the distribution of common carp in Europe up to 1100 (revised from Hoffmann 1994b).

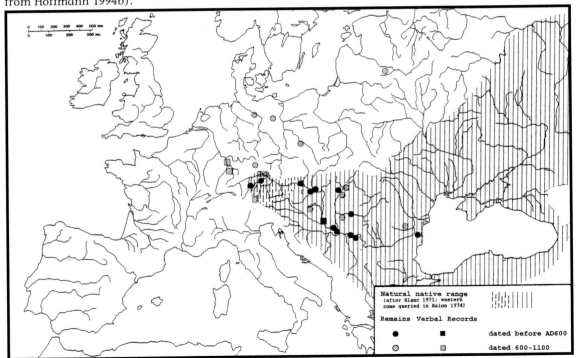

Champagne had set into his ponds at Igny-le-Jard on the Marne in 1258 (Bourquelot 1863, Grand & Delatouche 1950).

Common carp were not native to western and central Europe. Arrival of this exotic species necessarily meant interaction with the ecosystems now receiving it. "Successful establishment of an exotic species must necessarily precipitate changes in the physical and biological characteristics of the aquatic ecosystem receiving the introduction.... That no effects should result from such perturbations strains one's confidence in ecological principles" (Taylor et al. 1984, pp. 323 and 352).

In common carp medieval fish culturists introduced a new species remarkably well-suited to colonize the very type of freshwater habitats which economic development was multiplying in the west. Carp are omnivores, feeding principally on bottom- or plant-dwelling small animals. They prefer warm, turbid, slow and still waters with much vegetation for food and where they will broadcast their own eggs in early summer. Carp tolerate low oxygen levels in water and if kept cool and damp can survive some days out of the water. They grow faster than do bream, the native western European cyprinid most like carp in habits and habitat requirements (Balon 1995b). Medieval western ecosystems offered little competition.

Now it is possible to explore and begin to make sense of the evidence for the medieval spread of the carp from the middle Danube to the western European continent and beyond.

THE SPREAD OF CARP IN MEDIEVAL EUROPE

At least since the Pleistocene common carp in Europe had long been limited to the refugium area of the lower and middle Danube and other Balkan drainages into the Black Sea. From there natural (re-)colonization of the west required movement upstream and into the colder headwaters of the Danubian system. In order to learn what evidence bore

on various propositions about the timing and agency of that movement, I gathered and published (Hoffmann 1994b) a provisional inventory of sub-fossil remains (bones and scales) and of the earliest verbal records of *Cyprinus carpio* from post-glacial Europe. The hope was to encourage further discovery and publication of this evidence. To the 56 dated finds from 47 sites there reported can now be added the bones from the second to fourth century Roman fort at Iža (Balon 1995a, b). The 36 verbal references (all those known from before 1300 and thereafter the earliest in each major watershed or region) can now also be increased by two, namely a reference from the middle Rhineland at about 1100 and a northern Italian reference dating about 1450 (for details, see Appendix B below). With those additions, dates and locations of both osteological and verbal evidence are here again compiled and displayed on three successive maps, which together provide graphic proof of carp's diffusion process and vehicles for interpretive discussion. Of course any inferences continue to rest on evidence recovered to date, and new reports of credibly-dated and -identified remains or verbal records are always welcome.

The Evidence

The first map (Fig. 7) displays evidence of carp in Europe before the Middle Ages and the first signs of its spread. Until the early Middle Ages all written and archaeological records delineate a natural native range in the Danube system east of Bavaria and no further west. In the oldest known verbal reference to this organism (on the question of ancient Greek *kyprianos* and classical Latin *cyprinus*, see Appendix A below), Cassiodorus, the learned Roman minister for the Gothic kings who ruled early sixth-century Italy, listed "*carpam Danubius*" ("carp from the Danube") among the several exotic fishes the king would serve visiting ambassadors (Cassiodorus 1973). From Cassiodorus' northern Italian standpoint, the pertinent Danube lay to the east in Pannonia (including the river reach from modern Vienna down to Belgrade), whence the Goths had entered Italy a generation before, where they then still ruled, and where common carp were not only native but, as the map further indicates, already long

---

[3] The sixth taxon is *salmo*: Atlantic salmon (*Salmo salar*) do not run the Rhone or other Mediterranean watersheds, but they did run the Loire, whose upper tributaries reach within 20 km of Cluny. The word "salmon" itself could in the Middle Ages apply to any migratory salmonid, notably lake-dwelling, stream-spawning brown trout (*Salmo trutta lacustris*).

eaten by humans. No more than for the salmon Cassiodorus would have from the Rhine and other delicacies from Sicily and Abruzzi, however, does he imply the carp were other than culinary treats imported for the festive occasion. All carp remains from post-neolithic sites older than Cassiodorus were recovered from a middle and lower Danubian native range.

From the early medieval period, after Cassiodorus and before about 1100, finds of carp remains continue to confirm its natural distribution, and for the first time indicate its spread further west and north into the upper Danube, Rhine, Elbe, and Odra systems. No verbal sources corroborate the northward expansion, if only because literate culture first penetrated east of the Elbe only around 1000 and, of course, initially produced none of the records of economic or everyday activity where such mention might be anticipated. But no literacy also meant no Latin Christianity and no monasteries to deserve any later assignment of responsibility for those carp.

Carp's early medieval westward push across Bavaria, northern Swabia, and southern Franconia did result in three little-remarked written references from the late eleventh century. A secular fairy tale composed at Tegernsee abbey — a house with rich subalpine lake fisheries and no artificial fishponds before the 1450s — listed carp with other familiar fishes of upper Bavaria (Ruodlieb). The other two notices carry the fish — or at least literate human awareness of it — from the Danube into the Rhine watershed. William of Hirsau (d.1091), reared at Regensburg on the Danube, a student of Cluny's monastic reform, and abbot of a house in the northern Black Forest, expanded the Cluniac vocabulary of signs monks used during compulsory silence. Among several central European fish taxa he included "the fish which is popularly called carp" (William). Very shortly after William's death the fish was also named in the *Summarium Heinrici*, a Latin-German lexicon assembled near Worms (Hildebrandt 1974-1982).

No remains or verbal mentions of carp from before the twelfth century suggest carp culture or artificial fishponds. The fish were eaten but not, on the evidence, reared as domesticates. The verbal references, like most written records from eleventh-century Germany, have monastic origins, but the bones come from kitchen refuse at Nürnberg castle, a secular fort (Boessneck & von den Driesch-Karpf 1968).

Plausible outer limits may also be set to the range of common carp before about 1100. These are indicated by verbal and archaeological records giving considerable lists of local fishes from which carp is conspicuously absent. No carp appear in: Ausonius's fourth century description of eleven fish taxa in the Moselle (Ausonius 1972); the ten native fishes which a Greek-trained physician evaluated as dietary items for a sixth-century Frankish king (Anthimus 1963); the large catalog of fish remains from ninth-eleventh century Haithabu (Lepiksaar & Heinrich 1977, Heinrich 1983, compare Heinrich 1987); or extensive eleventh-century treatments of fish compiled at St. Gallen near the Bodensee (Ekkehard) and, as earlier remarked, at Cluny in Burgundy (Ulrich). Taken together with the positive occurrences, this all suggests carp were by about 1100 just beginning to enter the principal hotbed of medieval monastic culture, which extended from the western edges of the Alps down the Rhine valley and west into the basins of the Seine, Loire, and Rhone.

Without going into excessive detail, Figure 8 now delineates for the twelfth and thirteenth centuries the multiplication of records from the upper Danube and Rhine watersheds and further major extension westward into those of the Maas/Meuse, Seine, and Saône. In northern France two twelfth-century writers plainly familiar with local fishes in Champagne and around Paris, Gui of Bazoches (1969) and Alexander Neckham (1863), suggest by their silence a continued ignorance of carp. Then much evidence seems suddenly to emerge in and after the mid-1200s. Besides fisheries legislation, descriptions by learned encyclopedists, and records of stocking ponds with young carp, a recipe for preparing carp occurs before 1300 in the first French-language cookbook (Scully 1988). Elite secular sites such as castles, palaces, and towns predominate among the high medieval remains, and monasteries are curiously lacking. Among monastic sites well- and carefully investigated and yielding otherwise extensive fish remains, neither St. Albans in England (D. Serjeantson, personal communication) nor, from this period, La Charité-sur-Loire (Audoin-Rouzeau 1986), show carp. On the other hand, twelfth-century Rhenish abbess Hildegard of Bingen certainly expected her convent to eat them. Future excavators of high medieval monastic sites should be especially alert for remains of *Cyprinus carpio* (Hoffmann 1994a).

The final map (Fig. 9) illustrates the further spread of common carp, most likely after the Black Death, northeast to central Bohemia and southern Poland and west into the Loire watershed and southern England. In the current state of knowledge, Italian records come late as well. Fourteenth-century English and Italian cookbooks contain extensive lists of fishes, but not carp (Faccioli 1966, Boström 1985, Hieatt & Butler 1986). Nor did the Bolognese lawyer and landowner Pietro di Crescenzi mention them when covering fishponds and fishing extensively in the famous agricultural manual he wrote about 1304/5 (Crescenzi 1471). In the current state of knowledge, the oldest explicit Italian reference is a recipe for *carpani* given in the mid-fifteenth century *Libro de arte coquinaria* by Maestro Martino, a chef of Lombard origin then working in Rome (Faccioli 1966). This puts it just about contemporary with the earliest Polish and English records. Late medieval carp remains largely come from elite dietary contexts, both noble and ecclesiastical. Economic mechanisms serving this demand are documented by references to carp culture and to carp as an article of commerce.

Verbal and archeological evidence thus together corroborate three phases in the medieval diffusion of common carp west and north from an epicenter at the northwest margin of its native range in Pannonia (the piedmont section of the Danube, Balon 1967). The first phase between perhaps the seventh century and the eleventh principally carried the fish up the Danube and into at least some west-flowing tributaries of the middle Rhine. Some remains also indicate carp in waters north of the Danube. In a second phase (twelfth through early fourteenth century) carp radiated across most of the economic and cultural heartland of medieval northwestern Europe, from the lower Rhine/Maas region south to the Paris basin and Burgundy. A final stage, probably occurring after the mid-fourteenth-century shift of economic trends, extended common carp into the outer

periphery of the west, an arc from southwestern France through England and southern Scandinavia into east central Europe. Though carp are recorded in Italy at the end of the Middle Ages, the diffusion pattern at no time accords with radiation from there.

Working backwards from the latest and best data affirms an important role of fish culture in the third phase of the carp's expansion, and as early as its thirteenth-century appearance in the Paris basin. Periods before that are more dubious. We have already noted the extensive eleventh-twelfth century western documentation of elaborate fishpond enterprises without signs of carp. The common carp then found east of the Rhine occur without detectable connection to a fish culture still scarcely developed there. When was the association established between the fish and a technology of fish farming? Certainly Leonhardt's (1906) vision of monks in particular formulating methods to rear a well-known local fish has no basis in known medieval records, nor does Leonhardt assert one. On the much later analogy of the English experience, we might think rather of a useful food item being drawn when available into a technology already in the process of adoption by monks and lay lords alike. For now, at least, the limits to historical reconstruction may lie somewhere between Lorraine and Upper Austria.

Medieval Carp in Wild and Artificial Habitats

Certainly much of the carp's movement north and west from its Danubian native range did at some point benefit from human help. Captive common carp can survive stagnant store ponds and periods of overland transport; their fecundity, rapid growth, and large size attract an estate manager's attention. If medieval fishkeepers thus moved carp, even without much conscious identification or husbandry, and this put carp into a new, more westerly watershed, the fish were ready to do the rest. These creatures were never confined to modern isolation units.

Experimental results and observations of the nineteenth-century introduction of *Cyprinus carpio* into North America and other places formerly without it establish the unusual ability of this species to colonize explosively in "regions with either simple or relatively fragile fish communities or which are under pressure for other reasons such as excessive fishing or environmen-

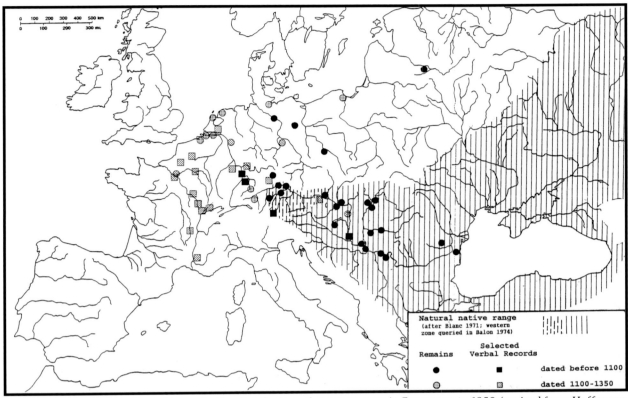

Fig.8. This map displays the evidence for the distribution of common carp in Europe up to 1350 (revised from Hoffmann 1994b).

Fig.9. This map displays the evidence for the distribution of common carp in Europe by about 1600 (revised from Hoffmann 1994b).

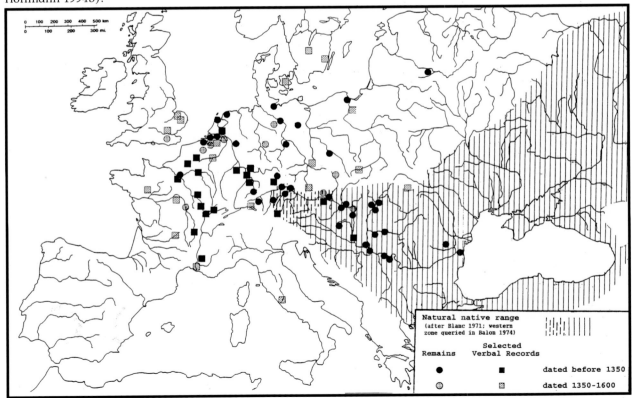

tal modification" (Welcomme 1984, p. 36, cf. Taylor et al. 1984). The simple fish communities of medieval western Europe were being stressed by environmental changes and by human predation. A shift toward lentic habitats suited common carp and the carp's own habits speeded up those changes. Carp's foraging behavior uproots vegetation and consumes substrate organisms, thus releasing nitrates and phosphates into the water. Turbidity increases, and is further raised by planktonic algae using the dissolved nutrients. The eutrophication process accelerates, altering the environment to the disadvantage of native clear-water species. Competition for food and carp predation on eggs further reduces population densities and species diversity in the native fauna. But common carp itself was an addition to the species list in western Europe and, like its several still-water relatives already present, could effectively exploit now more abundant habitat there.

By the early fourteenth century, if not before, the best fish culturists on the continent were emphasizing carp with a "side-crop" of pike. Standard managerial practices are then well-documented in many financial accounts kept by estate administrators (exemplary studies include Gresser & Hintzy 1978, Guerin 1960, Richard 1986, Hoffmann forthcoming. Other primary sources: Bourquelot 1863,

Fossier 1968, Brouwers 1910-1926, Neumann 1926). The main stock were put in as young fish, whether caught from the wild or produced by specially-selected brood stock, and reared together until ready for harvest as a single age class. Pike of suitable size went into the finishing pond to consume offspring of sexually precocious carp before the young competed for food with their parents. Two hundred years later the entire technical system would be described in the famous fish culture manuals of Jan Dubravius (1547 publication, composed in the late 1530s) and Olbrycht Strumieński (1573), who knew it from Czech and Polish practice (Inglot & Nyrek 1960, Hurt 1960, Szczygielski 1965, 1969), but every element was present in western record sources much earlier.

In well-managed fishponds, therefore, humans had created a complex domesticated stillwater ecosystem new to western Europe, while feral offspring of the pond carp joined in the reshaping of wild aquatic ecosystems as well. French records of the mid-thirteenth century knew carp as both a domestic pond fish and as wild river fish (Bourquelot 1863, Lespinasse & Bonnardot 1879), and so did the first writer to describe carp in the Polish vernacular, the early sixteenth-century Kraków scholar Stefan Falimirz (Rostafiński 1900).

Fig.10. This map indicates major European regions of fish culture about 1500.

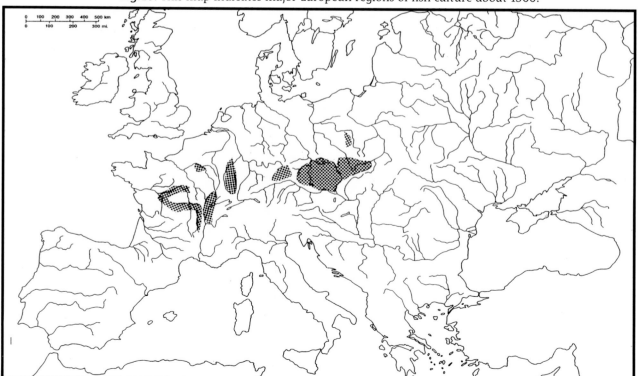

A NEW EUROPEAN GEOGRAPHY OF FISH CONSUMPTION

The collective pattern of European response to medieval damages to wild freshwater fisheries constructed a new regional geography, with some regions consuming fresh marine fish and others reliant on fish culture, principally of common carp. This configuration took some time to shake down and still needs research, notably into the origins and species of fresh fish supplied to important late medieval and early modern city markets. Paris, an important center of carp eating on the very edge of the sea fish zone (Bérard 1988, Desse & Desse-Berset 1992, Sternberg 1992), may be thought an exception to prove the rule.

All of the British Isles were fully accessible to fresh marine fishes (review Fig. 2 above). Most fishpond enterprises in England reached their peak importance and technical development by about 1300, while still using the native *Abramis brama* (McDonnell 1981, Roberts 1986, Steane 1988, Currie 1989, 1991). *Cyprinus carpio* arrived a century or so later and never achieved a major economic role there. Nor did fish culture, which in England always kept a strong tinge of aristocratic ostentation or dilettantism (Hickling 1971, Dyer 1988, Steane 1988, Currie 1989, Taverner 1600). By that time the English were eating the marine species they found abundant in previously unexploited offshore waters.

Likely the same was true of Italy, where marine access, entrapment of estuarine fishes, and the resources of the large subalpine lakes made inland fish culture an afterthought throughout and past the Middle Ages. Neither estate manuals nor inventories nor even Italian books on fisheries pay attention to carp (Crescenzi 1471, Tanara 1651, Taccola 1984, Mira 1937).

Contrast the regions of interior Europe famous for their carp culture (Fig. 10), all of them certainly in operation by the early sixteenth century. From Sologne and Berry all the way to Oświęcim-Zator, wherever not inhibited by permeable soils, abrupt relief, or large and still-productive inland lake fisheries, a carp belt extended right up the middle of that Europe which lay far outside the reach of fresh marine fish. Here would evolve the carp-centered folklore, the holiday customs, and the domestic forms of the fish. Yet common carp were not native to most of the areas then and now famous for their culture. They became carp country during the Middle Ages.

Had all this anything to do with an east Asian population of *Cyprinus carpio* and ways Chinese people had learned to rear carp? It seems improbable and implausible. Common carp are well-evidenced since the neolithic in southeastern Europe. Common carp were known and used in the fish culture of western Europe well before any direct European contact with China. The fish culture methods used in the west since at latest around 1200 were, with their emphasis on special ponds kept permanently filled for several years growth of a single age class and then let dry for a time after harvest, quite the reverse of a fish culture integrated with paddy rice cultivation. And finally, given the known locations of common carp in Europe and of the earliest European fish culture enterprises, we can rule out the indirect route from China via the Middle East and Islam which indisputable Chinese innovations, such as silk culture and goldfish, *Carassius auratus* (Balon 1969, 1995b), did take to the west.

ACKNOWLEDGEMENTS

Research reported here has been supported over the years by the Faculty of Arts, York University, by grants for travel from the International Research and Exchanges Board and the American Philosophical Society, and by a research grant from the Social Sciences and Humanities Research Council of Canada. I am also grateful for the help and advice of Elinor Melville, Jacob Imhof, Peter Stanisic, Carol Randall, Carolyn King, Paolo Squatriti, Jean Richard, Norbert Benecke, Hans-Hermann Müller, Anton Ervynck, Thomas Cohen, and colleagues in York's Historical Research Group Of course none of them bear responsibility for remaining errors of fact and reasoning. Special thanks are due Eugene Balon for encouraging this particular formulation of my findings, and to David Noakes for sponsoring my first public attempt to bridge the cultural divide between the life sciences and humanistic studies. *Carpe diem!*

APPENDIX A. ANCIENT GRECO-ROMAN EVIDENCE ON CARP AND FISH CULTURE

This appendix summarizes the state of the evidence from written sources and archeology bearing on (a) ancient Greek and Latin knowledge of the fish now called common carp and (b) the operation of fishponds and practice of fish culture by Romans during the late Republican and Imperial periods up to the generation after the late fifth-century disappearance of imperial government and authority in the west. It is important to recognize that only one ancient writer, the elder Pliny, actually mentions both fishponds and a fish, *cyprinus*, which could possibly (but not probably?) have been common carp. In all other cases, the evidence of carp and the evidence of fish culture in the ancient world occur in entirely different places and contexts.

A.1. On Identifying Carp as *Cyprinus*

No ancient Greek or Roman text refers to a *carp*. A fish which ancient Greeks called *kyprianos* and subsequent classical Latin authors *cyprinus* is reasonably well documented in writings of Aristotle (384-322 B.C.E.) and others who knew his work (Thompson 1947). This fish was never then discussed in the context of artificial fishponds or fish culture. In fact, classical writers in Greek and Latin treat it as frequenting both fresh and salt waters, and allude to Asia Minor and the Balkans. None gives this fish a comprehensive description, but rather passing mention.

In passages of the *History of Animals* Aristotle described *kyprianos* as a river fish with four gills on each side, a fleshy palate, and eggs the size of a grain of millet. It spawns five or six times a year, scattering its eggs in the shallows, but guarding the slowly-developing egg masses if it finds them again. Individuals without reproductive organs become very fat. With less harm than the catfish suffers, *kyprianos* can be paralyzed by a clap of thunder (Aristotle 1965).

Writing a *Natural History* in Latin some four centuries after Aristotle, Pliny the Elder (23-79), a Roman civil servant, noted only that, like the catfish in a river,

"in the sea the *cyprinus*" ("in mare ... cyprino") is made drowsy by lightning (Pliny 1942-1984), a fact he had, of course, from the ancient Greek writer. Another hundred years after Pliny, an author from southern Asia Minor, Oppian, dedicated his *Halieutica* ("On Fishing") to the Caesar Commodus, son of the reigning Emperor Marcus Aurelius. Writing in Greek, Oppian once refers to *kyprianos* as a fish of the gently sloping seashore and elsewhere repeats Aristotle on its breeding several times a year (Oppian 1928). A younger contemporary, Aelian, also speaks obscurely of what he calls "black *kyprianos*," caught in winter through the ice in the Danube (Aelian 1958-1959). In perhaps the last ancient reference, a learned Gallo-Roman administrator, Polemius Silvius, included the word *ciprinus* among marine fishes in a list of 147 names of aquatic creatures he put into his *Laterculus*, a compendium of geographical and other knowledge done in 449 (Polemius 1892).

It is important to note that ancient writers and texts nowhere equate the classical *cyprinus* with a creature called *carp*. This seems to happen very much later. Cassiodorus, whose sixth-century reference to *carpa* (Cassiodorus 1973), is acknowledged the oldest extant verbal record in any language, certainly did not gloss this barbaric word with *cyprinus*, despite his famous cultivation of classical literary knowledge. Nor was this done by any of the major scholastic encyclopedists, Vincent of Beauvais, Thomas of Cantimpre, and Albert the Great (Albertus Magnus), whose works were all compiled, revised, and known to each other between 1244 and 1260. In treating "*carpera*" (Vincent 1624), "*carpo vel carpera*" (Thomas 1973), and "*carperen*" (Albert 1916-1920) not one mentions *cyprinus* or any ancient Greco-Roman authority.

It looks rather like the ancient term was put on the familiar common carp only by sixteenth-century humanist-trained authors, always eager to link up their world with that of the classics. For the time being at least, the earliest equation I can find is that by Jan Dubravius. Writing in the late 1530s, the learned cleric found in no more than the passages from Aristotle, Oppian, and Pliny remarked above, just enough similarity between his carp and Aristotle's description to resolve his doubts. "Et quoniam uox Carponis barbara habetur, merito ob eam rem uidetur esse explodenda et in locum eius Cyprini substituenda, quae tum a Graecis, tum a Latinis promiscue usurpatur." (Dubravius 1547, fol. 9v). (And because the sound of 'carpo' is barbarous, it seems proper on that account to be rejected [literally: hissed off the stage] and in its place 'cyprinus' substituted, which is used widely by the Greeks and the Latins.) Plainly the "barbarity" of a non-classical term much bothered Dubravius and he was only too happy to find a more acceptable one. Carp is then *cyprinus* in all the path-breaking ichthyologies published in Latin by Pierre Belon, Guillaume Rondelet, and Conrad Gessner during the 1550s.

A.2 The Evidence of Roman Fish Culture

Fish culture facilities and practices among the ancient Romans have recently been reviewed in the Ph.D. thesis of James A. Higginbotham (1991). He thoroughly catalogues the fishpond structures of late Republican and early Imperial date now visible and archaeologically attested in Italy. This is followed by essays on pond construction and operation, and on the fishes Romans then reared. What here follows will summarize the most important discursive sources and Higginbotham's findings and add only a short discussion of the later Roman period, which Higginbotham does not treat.

The most important information on Roman fish culture is in the Roman writers on agronomy, the management and operation of rural estates. Fishponds (*piscinae*) are not mentioned in the oldest text (Cato ca. 175-150 B.C.E.), but do receive at least cursory treatment thereafter. Note that each successive writer was aware of and often used the works of his predecessors.

Most of what modern readers (e.g. Balon 1995a, b) think they know of Roman fish culture comes directly or indirectly

from Varro's *De Re Rustica* (37 B.C.E.) and Columella's *De Re Rustica* (about 50 C.E.). The two authors wrote while artificial fishponds were at the height of Roman elite fashion between the early years of the first century B.C.E. and the end of the first century C.E. Columella used Varro, and Columella's younger contemporary, Pliny the Elder, cribbed from both.

Writing from the viewpoint of the agri-cultural manager, Varro treated fishponds as social curiosities, emphasizing with many literary allusions their role in luxury display and consumption, especially at the estates of wealthy Romans around the Bay of Naples. Once, he says (Varro 1935), Romans kept small freshwater pools near their villae and stocked them with *squali* or *mugili* ("chubs" and grey mullet, both euryhaline marine varieties), but now such are sneered at in favor of saltwater ponds and fishes, notably *murenae*. He continues with several lurid tales of ex-travagance in rearing what were likely eels of several sorts, but chiefly *Anguilla anguilla* (Higginbotham 1991). Varro returns in a second passage to the two types of fishponds, fresh and salt water. Commoners, says he, have the former, where natural sources furnish the water for "our own domestic fish" (*piscibus nostris villaticis*). The elite, however, main-tain very costly artificial saltwater ponds and fishes, especially mullets and *murenae*, as much for recreational viewing as for consumption. All he describes are tidal and marine.

About two generations after Varro, Columella took a more serious view of fishponds on a Roman estate farm (Col-umella 1941-1968). Fish culture was once, says this expert, a fad, using saltwater fish in fresh water, and stocking eggs and young brought from the sea. In his own time there was less extravagance, and fish culture offered a good profit to a land-owner with marine access. He details the fishes appropriate to various coastal habi-tats. The most recommended ponds are open to tidal flow, with the water kept as cold and well-circulated as possible. The stock should be chosen in accord with the habitat — again all varieties mentioned are marine — and given small fish or other items to eat. Stock not kept fat would get a poor price on the fish market.

Writing about 70 C.E. Pliny (1942-1984) contributed nothing really new to the record of Roman fish culture. He used mainly Varro, but also Columella, to describe a luxury activity using coastal salt-water facilities to rear shellfish, *murenae*, and snails for elite consumption and the sheer pleasure of watching the fish.

In summarizing this period of intense Roman interest in artificial fishponds, Higginbotham (1991) emphasizes the overwhelming importance of coastal brackish-water ponds for rearing inshore marine species. At the peak of fishpond construction they served as elaborate symbols of aristocratic wealth and "demonstrated a control over nature." Fashionable interest waned as first century emperors moved against such ostentation, but smaller, often inland, ponds may have gained favor as a less extravagant way to control nature, please the eye, and perhaps supply some food. Fishponds in the Roman suburbs and at villa sites inland of the Bay of Naples, were built of concrete and used to house eel and bass (*lupus*), still euryhaline fishes. Facilities like these have also been recovered from Roman villas in Roman Britain (Zeepvat 1988).

Roman writers of the later Empire had less apparent interest in fishponds. In Oppian's *Halieutica* (Oppian 1928) the only fish preserve (Greek *bibarion*) is a marine area kept for imperial use. The next important agronomist, Palladius (1975), who wrote his *Opus agriculturae* about 380, having advised building a cistern of stone and cement, pointed out that the owner could stock "eels and river fish" (*anguillas sane pisces que fluviales*) so that their swimming would make the water surface ripple as if it were moving. His chapter called *De piscinis* (On fishponds) advises choosing a site near the farmstead which is easy to feed from a spring or surface runoff and useful for livestock and waterfowl. It mentions no fish, and neither do any of Palladius' other passing references to *piscinae* as sources of water

for irrigation, livestock. or household purposes. The word seems disconnected from its original root.

The unravelling thread of Roman agricultural expertise was pulled together about 600 into a compilation called *Geoponika* (1895), perhaps attributable to a writer named Cassianus Bassus, but now surviving only in a redaction made about 950 under the auspices of learned Byzantine Emperor Constantine VIII Porphyrogenitus. Book 20 contains 40 chapters on fishes and fishing, which are almost entirely marine, but it begins with one on fishponds. These occur in inland situations, where they are filled with fish from nearby rivers or lakes, or along the coast, where sea fish are used. The stock should come from a habitat like that in the pond, and can be fed herbage, small aquatic creatures, or bits of fig, cheese, or bread.

Perhaps it is fitting that a final echo of those classic Roman coastal rock-cut fishponds come in the writings of Cassiodorus, not the letters written in his middle years for the Gothic kings, where he once introduced *carpam Danubius*, but in the *Institutiones*, a guide for reading and study done in his old age at the Vivarium monastery established on his hereditary estate at Squillace in the Brutti, the ball of the Italian foot.

The place even took its name from the fishponds (*vivaria*), which Cassiodorus described as follows: "Maria quoque vobis ita subiacent, ut piscationibus variis pateant; et captus piscis, cum libuerit, vivariis includi. Fecimus enim illic (iuvante Domino) grata receptacula, ubi sub claustro fideli vagetur piscium multitudo; ita consentanea montium speluncis, ut nullatenus se sentiat captum, cui libertas est escas sumere, et per solitas se cavernas abscondere. .... Ita fit ut monasterium vestrum potius quaeratur ab aliis, quam vos extranea loca iuste desiderare possitis." (Cassiodorus, Inst., col. 1143) ("The site of the monastery of Vivarium conduces to making provision for travelers and the poor, since you have irrigated gardens and the nearby river Pellena full of fish — its waves threaten no

poisson au 16ème siècle: que disent les sources bibliographiques? Que peut on espérer des données ichtyofauniques des Jardins du Carrousel? Anthropozoologica 16:127-130.

Stolz, O. 1936. Geschichtskunde der Gewässer Tirols. Schlern-Schriften 32, Innsbruck.

Stromeyer, H. 1910. Zur Geschichte der Badischen Fischerzünfte. Heidelberger volkswirtschaftliche Abhandlungen 1:3, Karlsruhe.

Strumieński, O. 1573. O sprawie, sypaniu, wymierzaniu i rybnieniu stawów [On the construction, filling, measuring, and stocking of ponds], Kraków. [2d. ed., Kraków, 1897].

Susłowska, W. & K. Urbanowicz. 1967. Szczątki kostne ryb z wczesnośredniowiecznego Gdańska (X-XIII w.) [Bone remains of fishes from early medieval Gdańsk (10th-13th century)]. Gdańsk wczesnośredniowieczny 6: 53-65.

Szczygielski, W. 1965. Gospodarka stawowa na ziemach połodniowo-zachodniej Rzeczypospolitej w XVI-XVIII w.: Studium z dziejów postępu w dawnym gospodarstwie wiejskim [Fishpond enterprises in the southwestern territories of the Commonwealth in the 16th-18th centuries: A study on the history of progress in the old rural economy]. Prace Instytutu Historycznego Uniwersytetu Łódzkiego 11, Łódź.

Szczygielski, W. 1969. Z dziejów gospodarki rybnej w Polsce w XVI-XVIII wieku [On the history of fishpond enterprises in Poland in the 16th-18th centuries]. Instytut Historii Kultury Materialnej Polskiej Akademii Nauk, Studia z Dziejów Gospodarstwa Wiejskiego 9(2), Warszawa.

Szymczyk, W. 1987. Szczątki kostne ryb z odcinka II w Novae [Bone remains of fishes from sector II at Nova]. Studia i Materiały Archeologiczne 6:113-129.

Taccola, M. 1984. Mariano Taccola De ingeneis. Liber primus leonis, liber secundus draconus, addenda. Books I and II, On Engines, and Addenda ... Facsimile of Codex Latinus Monachensis 197, Part II ... with additional reproductions.... G. Scaglia, F. Proger, & U. Montag (ed.) 2 volumes. Wiesbaden.

Tanara, V. 1651. L'economia del cittadino in villa. Eredi del Dozza: Bologna. [Also rev. & augmented edition, Bertani: Venice, 1661.]

Taverner, J. 1600. Certain experiments concerning fish and frvite. William Ponsonby, London. [Facsimile reprint: The English Experience, 75. Amsterdam, 1968.]

Taylor, J., W. Courtenay & J. McCann. 1984. Known impacts of exotic fishes in the continental United States. pp. 322-373. *In*: W. R. Courtenay, Jr. & J.R. Stauffer, Jr. (ed.) Distribution, Biology, and Management of Exotic Fishes, Baltimore.

TeBrake, W. 1985. Medieval frontier: culture and ecology in Rijnland. College Station.

Thomas of Cantimpré. 1973. Liber de natura rerum. Editio princeps secundum codices manuscriptos. Teil I: Text, H. Boese (ed.), Berlin.

Thompson, D. 1947. A glossary of Greek fishes. London.

Tischler, J. 1994. Fische: Sprachliches. pp. 120-126. *In*: H. Beck et al. (ed.) Reallexikon der Germanischen Altertumskunde 9, Berlin.

Trexler, R. 1974. Measures against water pollution in fif-

teenth century Florence. Viator 5: 455-467.

Turner, T. H. (ed.) 1841. Manners and household expenses of England in the thirteenth and fifteenth centuries illustrated by Original Records. Roxburghe Club, London.

Ulrich of Cluny. Udalrici Consuetudines Cluniacenses. cols. 633-778. *In*: J. P. Migne (ed.) Patrologiae cursus completus. Series latina, 149. Paris. [also in B. Albers (ed.) 1945. Consuetudines Monasticae, vol. II. Montecassino.]

Van Derveeghe, D. 1955. Le Domaine du Val Saint-Lambert de 1202 à 1387, Paris.

Varro, M. 1935. On agriculture, W. D. Hooper & H. B. Ash (ed. and transl.) Loeb Classical Library, Cambridge.

Vendittelli, M. 1992. Diritti ed impianti di pesca degli enti ecclesiastici Romani tra X e XIII secolo, Melanges de l'ecole francaise de Rome: Moyen Age 104:387-430.

Verriest, L. (ed.) 1950. Le polyptyque illustré dit Veil Rentier de messire Jehan de Pamele-Audenarde (vers 1275). Bruxelles.

Verriest, L. 1956. Le Régime seigneurial dans le Comté de Hainaut du XIe siècle a la Révolution, 2d ed. Louvain.

Vincent of Beauvais. 1624. Speculum naturale. Speculum quadruplex sive speculum maius, 1, Baltazaris Belleri: Duaci. [reprinted Graz, 1964-1965].

Vogt, J. 1990. Aspects of historical soil erosion in western Europe. pp. 83-91. *In*: P. Brimblecombe & C. Pfister (ed.) The Silent Countdown, Essays in European Environmental History, Berlin.

Wagner, N. 1975. Zur Datierung des 'Summarium Heinrici'. Zeitschrift für deutsches Altertum und deutsche Literatur 104:118-126.

Wamba, J. 1986. El Cister en Castilla y Leon: Monacato y dominios rurales (Siglos XII-XV). Junta de Castilla y Leon, Consejería de Educación y Cultura, n.p. [Salamanca?].

Welcomme, R. 1984. International transfers of inland fish species. pp. 22-40. *In*: W. Courtenay & J. Stauffer (ed.) Distribution, Biology, and Management of Exotic Fishes, Baltimore.

William of Hirsau. S. Willhelmi constitutiones Hirsaugienses seu Gegenbacenses. cols. 923-1146. *In*: J. P. Migne (ed.) Patrologiae cursus completus, Series latina 150, Paris.

Worster, D. 1988. The ends of the earth: perspectives on modern environmental history. Cambridge.

Zeibig, H. (ed.) 1867-1868. Urkundenbuch des Stiftes Klosterneuburg bis zum Ende des vierzehnten Jahrhunderts, 2 volumes. Fontes rerum Austriacarum, 2. Abt. Diplomatario et acta 27-28, Wien.

Zeepvat, R. 1988. Fishponds in Roman Britain. pp. 17-26. *In*: M. Aston (ed.) Medieval Fish, Fisheries and Fishponds in England, BAR British Series 182, Oxford.

Zimmermann, G. 1973. Ordensleben und Lebensstandard. Die Cura Corporis in den Ordensvorschriften des abendländischen Hochmittelalters. Beiträge zur Geschichte des alten Mönchtums und des Benediktinerordens 32, Münster.

Zug Tucci, H. 1985. Il mondo medievale dei pesci tra realta' e immaginazione. pp. 291-372. *In*: L'uomo di fronte al mondo animale nell'alto Medio Evo, XXXI Settimane di studio sull'alto Medio Evo, Spoleto.

GLOSSARY

In the following glossary all basic koi varieties are listed, together with their sub-varieties. The other words included represent both those in very popular use and those which are infrequently seen but have been applied to unique koi so ar likely to reappear in the future, or may possibly be seen on dealer lists.

In koi certain terms are used for given varieties so that while Aka, Hi and Beni all mean red, one would not say Aka Utsuri but Hi Utsuri; likewise, one would say Aka Bekko not Beni Bekko. Such usage is learned only by familiarity with Japanese use of the terms.

Ai Indigo blue.

—goromo Sub-variety of the Koromo with blue edging to scales.

Aka Red. It often precedes other terms.

—Bekko Sub-variety of the Bekko which has a red body carrying black patches.

—hajiro Sub-variety of the Kohaku which has red pectoral fins tipped with white.

—matsuba Sub-variety of the Kawarimono in which the Matsuba pattern is seen on an all red koi.

—muji Sub-variety of the Kohaku in which the whole body is red.

—Sanke Sub-variety of the Taisho in which the Hi color extends from head to tail without a break.

Akabo Red.

Akami Eye with red iris.

Akebi Light blue.

Aragoi Jumbled scales -applied to Doitsu mirror scales, an alternative to **Yoroi**.

Asagi A basic variety in which the scales are blue in an all-over reticulated manner; the edges are light blue or white.

—Sanke A sub-variety of the Asagi with red on the head and upper abdomen.

Ato-sumi Late black. It refers to black areas that develop as the koi matures and which did not show in the young koi.

Bekko A basic variety in which red, white, or yellow bodies are patched with black (Sumi). Doitsu scales may also be seen as a sub-variety.

Beni A dark red -darker than Aka, of which it is a shade.

Beta-gin A scale type of the Kinginrin in which the whole scale surface glitters.

Boke A blurred or faded effect to the color or pattern.

—Showa A sub-variety of the Showa Sanke.

Bongiri Applied to a koi which has no red in the tail region -a fault in the Kohaku, which should have red in the peduncle (though not in the tail itself).

Bozu A priest -applied to a Kohaku that has no Hi (red) on it head. A fault.

Budo Grape. A cluster of scales that are likened to bunches of grapes.

—Sanke A sub-variety of the Koromo.

Bunka A Sanke (Sanshoku) in which the pectoral fins are metallic or shiny.

Chagoi A sub-variety of the Kawarimono. **Cha** means brown or yellow-brown (saffron).

Dagara A stepped pattern as seen in Kohaku in which the areas of red are likened to stepping stones.

Daiya Diamond Ginrin. A scale type of the Kinginrin which was developed in Hiroshima and is often referred to under this latter name.

Danmoyo This means stepped pattern and is applied to the Kohaku and is likened to stepping stones in a pond -it is the alternative word to **Dagara**.

Doitsu A variety derived from the German mirror carp. It may be mirror scaled or leather or combine both types. Mirror scales scattered at random on the body are a decided fault.

—Aka Sanke A sub-variety of the Taisho in which mirror scales are found on the Taisho, with a Hi that extends from head to tail.

—Kohaku A sub-variety of the Kohaku with Doitsu scale.

—Ogon A sub-variety of the Ogon.

—Sanke A sub-variety of the Taisho.

—Showa A sub-variety of the **Showa** Sanke.

Dorogoi This means mud black koi and refers to the various forms of the Magoi or wild carp of Japan, of which this is one.

Echigo This is a collective name sometimes applied to the three scale types, other than Daiya, which are found in the Kinginrin variety.

Enyu Doitsu scales with a platinum color. It is a cross between the Shusui and the Midori (green) varieties. A variable koi in its colors which tend to fade with maturity.

Era-Aka An early form of Kohaku in which the gill covers were red.

Etsu No Hisoku A variety of the Midorigoi of the Kawarimono. It was first bred in 1965 and the name combines an old Chinese state and a green chinaware.

Fuji When a koi has a beautiful sparkling silver patch on its head or, more rarely, on its pectoral fins, it is likened to snow on the top of Mount Fujiyama. It is extremely striking but at present is not a stable condition and disappears after 2—3 years.

—Kohaku A sub-variety of the Kohaku with Fuji markings.

—Sanke A sub-variety of the Taisho with Fuji markings.

Gin Metallic silver. It is seen in many varieties.

—bo A sub-variety of the Ogon that has no value; they exhibit silver in parts of their scales against a black base color.

—Matsuba A sub-variety of Ogon in which the reticulate pattern lies over a platinum body color.

—Kabuto A sub-variety of the Ogon in which the head has silver scales that are likened to a helmet or cap. The body is variable speckled with silver scales; base color is black. They ar not values.

—Shiro A sub-variety of the Hikari Utsuri in which the white form (Shiro Utsuri) carries metallic silver scales.

—Showa A sub-variety of the Hikari Utsuri in which the Showa Sanke carries a platinum or silvery metallic sheen to its scales.

—sui A sub-variety of the Hikarimoyo in which the Shusui has a less golden appearance to the Hi marking than in the **Kinsui**. It is thus not a platinum or silver shade as such.

—rin Platinum or silvery sheen to the scales.

Goior Wild carp -an old name for koi.

Goke A scale of a fish.

Goshiki This is five colored koi. They are very variable, some being extremely dark in color, others being visually lighter and invariably better looking as the colors are more apparent. It is a sub-variety of the Kawarimono.

—Shusui This is a sub-variety of the Kawarimono.

Gotensakura Castle cherry blossom. It is a sub-variety of the Kohaku which has a dappled pattern in clusters evenly spread on both sides of the body.

Hachibi Red Head.

Hageshiro A sub-variety of the Kawarimono in which the koi is black, but with white tips to the pectoral fins and a white patch on the head.

Hagoromo Ha is angel's wings and in this variation it refers to the pectoral fins of a Koromo of the Aigoromo type.

Hajiro This is a sub-variety of the Kawarimono in which the black koi has white tips to its pectoral fins.

Hakushu Green lateral scale son a platinum body. A hybrid of Midorigoi and platinum Ogon.

Hana Flower -round red markings between the dorsal and lateral lines.

—ko Flower maiden -a pet name for koi in Japan.

—Shusui A sub-variety of the Shusui in which there is red between the dorsal blue color and the lateral line.

Hanatsuki A sub-variety of the Kohaku in which the head Hi patch extends to the tip of the mouth.

Haramaki A color which forms a band rather like a belt over the dorsal surface -used as descriptive term in unique koi.

Hariwake A two colored koi with metallic sheen and where one of the colors is platinum. A member of the Hikarimoyo group.

—Doitsu A sub-variety of the Hikarimoyo with mirror scales.

—Matsuba A sub-variety of the Hikarimoyo with the reticulated Matsuba pattern spread over the dorsal area of the body.

Hatsuhi The first rising sun of the New Year -a pinkish white; descriptive term used in unique koi.

Hi Red. The term precedes a number of sub-varieties and unique koi.

—aka A dark form of Akamuji which is the all-red koi of the Kohaku. It means the same as **Beni**.

—Botan Scarlet Peony. A term used on unique koi which have a large Sumi patch on a red body.

—goi An all-red koi same as Akamuji and used as general term.

—Ogon A sub-variety of the Ogon which is rarely seen –it is the same as the Orange Ogon.

—Showa A sub-variety of the Showa Sanke in which the red runs from the head to the tail without a break. It is the Showa equivalent to the Aka Sanke of the Taisho or the Straight Hi of the Kohaku.

—Shusui A sub-variety of the Shusui in which the red should cover the whole dorsal surface.

—Utsuri A sub-variety of the Utsuri in which the body is black and it carries numerous red (Hi) patches.

Hikarimoyo A basic variety which features metallic scales and a scale patten. Hybrids of the Ogon.

Hikari Utsuri A basic variety which are hybrids of the Ogon and Utsuri lines.

Hinomaru A red disc -as in the national flag of Japan and as featured in the Tancho variety.

Hiroshima Gin A scale type of the Kinginrin which sparkles like a diamond. Also called **Daiya**.

Hisoku A yellow-green color of the Midorigoi of the Kawarimono.

Hoo-Aka Red Cheeks. This was the term used to describe very early forms of basically white koi with just small red patches. An alternative term was **Era-Aka** meaning red gills.

Hoo-Kazuki Red Cheeks. this term was used on the very first mutational wild carp that carried red on their body, i.e., on their cheeks. Those which had red abdomens were called **Hara-Aka**.

Hotsujiro Four white areas on a koi.

Inazuma Lightning or a zig-zag pattern. Especially in relation to the sub-variety of Kohaku which displays this pattern variation of the Straight Hi.

Ippon-Hi A continuous pattern from head to tail. In Kohaku this has little value.

Iro Color.

—age Bringing out the color. Often used in respect of feeding but correctly refers to all aspects of husbandry.

—goi Former name for colored carp or koi that is rarely used.

Ishigaki Stonewall effect as seen in Doitsu varieties where the scales are scattered on the bodyin a random manner -a fault. See also **Aragoi** and **Yoroi**.

Ishugrudel This refers to the body shape of the koi and here it is of the old German carp type -deep. It has regained some popularity in recent years but is still not greatly favored.

Jiro White.

Juji A cross-like marking on the head of a koi and made by one of the colors, normally Sumi.

Kabuto A cap or helmet; seen on inferior koi. See Ogon.

Kado Gin A scale variety of the Kinginrin where the highly reflective surface is restricted to the edge of the scale.

Kagamigoi Mirror scales of the Doitsu family.

Kage A shadow or phantom -a hazy pattern.

—Utsuri A sub-variety of the Kawarimono in which the Utsuri koi have a hazy pattern.

—Showa A sub-variety of the Kawarimono in which the Showa has a hazy pattern.

Kagami Mirror scales to the dorsal and lateral surfaces of a koi of the Doitsu type.

Kanoku A dappled effect of red spots on a white background; likened to the spotting of your deer.

—Kohaku A sub-variety of the Kawarimono.

—Sanke A sub-variety of the Kawarimono -the Taisho.

—Showa A sub-variety of the Kawarimono.

Karasu Black.

—goi A sub-variety of the Kawarimono developed from he original wild carp or from Asagi lineage.

Kasane A Sumi (black) marking or patch on a red (Hi) background; the term is used in relation to Taisho Sanke.

Kasu Gin Sake-dregs, silver metallic. Used to describe the **Sudare** scales of the Kinginrin. Another, but derisive, term for the worst of the Kado type scales.

Kata Moyo One-sided pattern. Seen in Kohaku where the Hi markings run down one side of the dorsal line, or mostly so.

Katasumi One large shoulder patch of black. Well-liked in Taisho.

Kawagoi The scaleless or leather koi of the Doitsu type, but which retains mirror scales near the dorsal fin.

Kawarimono A basic variety or group of koi from various other lines but which are not placed in their group for various reasons. A miscellaneous group of koi and also the group in which unique koi are exhibited.

Ki Yellow.

—goi A yellow koi.

—Bekko A sub-variety of the Bekko which has a yellow body patched with black.

—Shusui A sub-variety of the Shusui in which the base color is yellow instead of red. The back is usually blue.

—Utsuri A sub-variety of the Utsuri. Yellow patches on a black basic color.

Kikusui A sub-variety of the Hikarimoyo. It is a Hariwake Doitsu with either yellow or orange patterns on a platinum base. It is of the leather type.

Kimon Three yellow patches.

Kin Golden metallic sheen.

—bo A black koi which has random golden scales scattered about its body. Considered worthless. See **Ginbo**.

—dai A sub-variety of the Showa Sanke which has a large amount of white on its body.

—Ginrin A basic variety of koi which can include any koi which features a golden-silvery high metallic sheen to its scales. Even Ogons and Hikaromoyo can be Kingirin.

—Kabuto Golden helmet. A sub-variety of the Ogon. It is not highly valued. See **Gin Kabuto**.

—Ki Utsuri A sub-variety of the Hikari Utsuri basic variety with a golden sheen to the yellow and black scales.

—Matsuba A sub-variety of the Ogon in which the Ogon is covered by the Matsuba pattern. See also Gin Matsuba.

—porai A brownish gold Matsuba Ogon.

—Shiro Is applied to the **Gin Shiro** of the Hikari Utsuri -a metallic silvery sheen on the white areas.

—Showa A sub-variety of the Hikari Utsuri in which the Showa Sanke has a golden hue to it.

—shu An orange koi with a green-blue dorsal area -a unique koi of the midori type in the Kawarimono variety.

—sui A sub-variety of the Hikarimoyo in which the Shusui has a golden metallic shine to it. It tends to fade with age.

—tobi Means the same as Bunka -shining pectoral fins.

—zakura Golden cherry blossom. A sub-variety of the Kohaku in which dappled (Kanako) scales have a golden edge.

Kobesuki A thin covering of a color, such as the red in Kohaku, which allows the outline pattern of the scale to show through. In the Kohaku this is a fault.

Kohaku The oldest basic variety of koi. A red and white koi.

Koi Carp.

Komoyo Small red markings or patches.

Konjo A dark blue as seen in the Asagi basic variety.

Koromo Means robed and is applied to a basic variety which comprises hybrid of the Asagi and other basic varieties.

—Sanke A sub-variety of the Koromo which is a hybrid of the Aigoromo and the Taisho Sanke.

—Showa A sub-variety of the Koromo which is a hybrid of the Aigoromo which is a hybrid of the Aigoromo and the Showa Sanke.

Koshiki Also **Koshinishiki**. A hybrid of Taisho Sanke and Ogon.

Kuchibeni Red lips. A sub-variety of the Kohaku and also of the Taisho Sanke. Any koi with the Hi (red) extending onto the lips.

Kujaku A hybrid of the Goshiki and the Ogon.

—Ogon A sub-variety of the Hikarimoyo.

—Doitsu A sub-variety of the Hikarimoyo.

Kumonryu Like a rising dragon. A sub-variety of the Kawarimono in which a Karasu (black) koi has a white pattern.

Kuro A black (Sumi) patch on the head rather like that of the Tancho. Rarely, it may appear on the back.

Ma Wild as in Magoi -wild type koi.

Madoaki A few scales appear in relief -a fault.

Makibara Red wrapped around the stomach; applied to Kohaku.

Maki-ga-fukai Deep wrapping. Same as **Makibara**.

—ga-okii Large wrapping of red around abdomen. Formerly disliked but now popular.

Maru Round.

Maruten A red spot on the head which is divided into two by a Sumi mark. Seen in unique koi of the Kawarimono.

Matsuba A reticulated pattern in which the center of the scale is darker than the edges thus forming a pattern. A sub-variety of the Kawarimono and a pattern featured in many koi.

Matsukawabake A sub-variety of the Kawarimono in which the colors change place –black and white.

Meija The period 1868-1912 that preceded the Taisho era.

Menkaburi Red mask. A sub-variety of the Kohaku in which much of the head is covered in red. If it extends to the pectoral fins then it is additionally called **Aka-te** -dishwashers' hands. Neither are desirable in good Kohaku.

Menware A black mark roughly in the shape of a Y that appears in a Showa Sanke.

Midorigoi Yellowish green or green. A sub-variety of the Kawarimono.

Mizhu Ogon An orange Ogon with black Doitsu scales. A sub-variety of Ogon.

Mizu Light blue.

—Asaki The lightest color blue of Asagi. A sub-variety of Asagi; it means the same as ebi.

Momiji Ogon Autumn leaves: red, purple, and white colors seen on unique koi.

Mono One. Not the number but as in metallic ones or Utsuri ones or Utsuri ones (Utsurimono) types.

Monyo Figured or shaped.

Motogura Having a black color to the base of the fins as opposed to striped effect, e.g., Utsuri, Showa Sanke, Hajiro.

Moyo Pattern, as in Hikarimoyo -metallic pattern.

Muji Plain or of one color only; a self color.

Muraski Purple, a term used in unique koi and in Goshiki (five-colored koi).

Napoleon A sub-variety of the Kohaku.

Narumi A mid blue color named for the town in Japan where a cloth of this color pattern is produced. a sub-variety of the Asagi.

Nezu Gray or mouse color. Nezumi means mouse or gray. A sub-variety of the Ogon.

Niban Subsidiary. Applied to a Hi spot or mark on the abdomen of a Kohaku.

Nidan Hi A two-step pattern in red.

—Kohaku A sub-variety of the Kohaku with two-step pattern.

—Moyo Two-step pattern.

Nishikigoi A colored cloth or silk exported from India to China and Japan. The term is used in Japan for the colored carp.

Ochiba-shigure This is a member of the Chagoi line of the Kawarimono and is a greenish and gray koi.

Odome Tail stop. The last color line before the tail.

Ogon Also **Ohgon**; golden metallic. a basic variety.

Ohaku A white and yellow koi of the Kigoi group, Kawarimono.

Ojime The last Hi patch on a Kohaku.

Omoyo A large Hi patch on a Kohaku. Well like in this variety.

Orange Ogon A sub-variety of the Ogon. Same as Hi Ogon. Quite rare.

—Doitsu A sub-variety of the Ogon which has Doitsu mirror scales.

—Hariwake A sub-variety of the Hikarimoyo which is orange and platinum.

Ohaku A white and yellow koi of the Kigoi group, Kawarimono.

Orenji Orange.

Pearl Shusui A sub-variety of the Shusui which has pearly scales of the Gin Rin on its dorsal surface.

Platinum Metallic white.

—Doitsu A sub-variety of the Ogon which has Doitsu mirror scales.

—Ogon A sub-variety of the Hikarimoyo in which the scales have a silvery sheen to them.

Purachina The whitest of the platinum color seen in Ogons.

Raigo Sunrise viewed from a mountain top. The term is applied to a Shusui hybrid of the Midorigoi. Such koi are very rare and variable in their colors.

Rin A scale, as in Kinrin -golden scales.

Sakurakana Cherry blossom pattern.

San Three.

Sandan A three-step pattern, likened to stepping stones.